TREATING
THE ELDERLY

THE JOSSEY-BASS LIBRARY OF CURRENT CLINICAL TECHNIQUE

IRVIN D. YALOM, GENERAL EDITOR

NOW AVAILABLE

Treating Alcoholism
Stephanie Brown, Editor

Treating Schizophrenia
Sophia Vinogradov, Editor

Treating Women Molested in Childhood
Catherine Classen, Editor

Treating Depression
Ira D. Glick, Editor

Treating Eating Disorders
Joellen Werne, Editor

Treating Dissociative Identity Disorder
James L. Spira, Editor

Treating Couples
Hilda Kessler, Editor

Treating Adolescents
Hans Steiner, Editor

Treating the Elderly
Javaid I. Sheikh, Editor

FORTHCOMING

Treating Posttraumatic Stress Disorder
Charles R. Marmar, Editor

Treating Anxiety Disorders
Walton T. Roth, Editor

Treating Difficult Personality Disorders
Michael Rosenbluth, Editor

Treating Sexual Disorders
Randolph S. Charlton, Editor

Treating Psychological Aspects of HIV
Michael F. O'Connor, Editor

TREATING THE ELDERLY

**A VOLUME IN THE JOSSEY-BASS
LIBRARY OF CURRENT CLINICAL TECHNIQUE**

Javaid I. Sheikh, EDITOR

Irvin D. Yalom, GENERAL EDITOR

Jossey-Bass Publishers • San Francisco

Substantial discounts on bulk quantities of Jossey-Bass books are available to corporations, professional associations, and other organizations. For details and discount information, contact the special sales department at Jossey-Bass Inc., Publishers. (415) 433-1740; Fax (800) 605-2665.

For sales outside the United States, please contact your local Simon & Schuster International Office.

 Manufactured in the United States of America on Lyons Falls Pathfinder Tradebook. This paper is acid-free and 100 percent totally chlorine-free.

Library of Congress Cataloging-in-Publication Data

Treating the elderly/Javaid I. Sheikh, editor; Irvin D. Yalom, general editor.
    p.   cm.—(A volume in the Jossey-Bass library of current clinical technique)
    Includes bibliographical references and index.
    ISBN 0-7879-0219-5 (alk. paper)
    1. Geriatric psychiatry. I. Sheikh, Javaid I. II. Yalom, Irvin D., date. III. Series: Jossey-Bass library of current clinical technique.
RC451.4.A5T68 1996
618.97'689—dc20   95-26782
                                        CIP

FIRST EDITION
PB Printing 10 9 8 7 6 5 4 3 2 1

CONTENTS

FOREWORD ix
Irvin D. Yalom, General Editor

INTRODUCTION xiii
Javaid I. Sheikh

CHAPTER 1
DEPRESSION 1
Dolores Gallagher-Thompson and David W. Coon

CHAPTER 2
BEREAVEMENT 45
Robert D. Hill, Dale Lund, and Ted Packard

CHAPTER 3
ANXIETY DISORDERS 75
Javaid I. Sheikh

CHAPTER 4
INSOMNIA 105
Leah Friedman

CHAPTER 5
SEXUAL PROBLEMS 131
Diane Morrissette, Antonette M. Zeiss, and Robert A. Zeiss

CHAPTER 6
COGNITIVE IMPAIRMENT 163
Greer M. Murphy, Jr.

CHAPTER 7
PSYCHIATRIC PROBLEMS IN
NURSING HOMES 195
Joel E. Streim

CHAPTER 8
THE IMPACT OF MEDICAL ILLNESS ON PSYCHOLOGICAL WELL-BEING 223
Barbara R. Sommer

ABOUT THE AUTHORS 243

INDEX 249

FOREWORD

At a recent meeting of clinical practitioners, a senior practitioner declared that more change had occurred in his practice of psychotherapy in the past year than in the twenty preceding years. Nodding assent, the others all agreed.

And was that a good thing for their practice? A resounding "No!" Again, unanimous concurrence—too much interference from managed care; too much bureaucracy; too much paper work; too many limits set on fees, length, and format of therapy; too much competition from new psychotherapy professions.

Were these changes a good or a bad thing for the general public? Less unanimity on this question. Some pointed to recent positive developments. Psychotherapy was becoming more mainstream, more available, and more acceptable to larger segments of the American public. It was being subjected to closer scrutiny and accountability—uncomfortable for the practitioner but, if done properly, of potential benefit to the quality and efficiency of behavioral health care delivery.

But without dissent this discussion group agreed—and every aggregate of therapists would concur—that astounding changes are looming for our profession: changes in the reasons that clients request therapy; changes in the perception and practice of mental health care; changes in therapeutic theory and technique; and changes in the training, certification, and supervision of professional therapists.

From the perspective of the clientele, several important currents are apparent. A major development is the de-stigmatization of psychotherapy. No longer is psychotherapy invariably a hush-hush affair, laced with shame and conducted in offices with separate entrance and exit doors to prevent the uncomfortable possibility of clients meeting one another.

Today such shame and secrecy have been exploded. Television talk shows—Oprah, Geraldo, Donahue—have normalized psychopathology and psychotherapy by presenting a continuous public parade of dysfunctional human situations: hardly a day passes without television fare of confessions and audience inter-actions with deadbeat fathers, sex addicts, adult children of alco-holics, battering husbands and abused wives, drug dealers and substance abusers, food bingers and purgers, thieving children, abusing parents, victimized children suing parents.

The implications of such de-stigmatization have not been lost on professionals who no longer concentrate their efforts on the increasingly elusive analytically suitable neurotic patient. Clin-ics everywhere are dealing with a far broader spectrum of prob-lem areas and must be prepared to offer help to substance abusers and their families, to patients with a wide variety of eat-ing disorders, adult survivors of incest, victims and perpetrators of domestic abuse. No longer do trauma victims or substance abusers furtively seek counseling. Public awareness of the nox-ious long-term effects of trauma has been so sensitized that there is an increasing call for public counseling facilities and a grow-ing demand, as well, for adequate counseling provisions in health care plans.

The mental health profession is changing as well. No longer is there such automatic adoration of lengthy "depth" psy-chotherapy where "deep" or "profound" is equated with a focus on the earliest years of the patient's life. The contemporary field is more pluralistic: many diverse approaches have proven thera-peutically effective and the therapist of today is more apt to tai-lor the therapy to fit the particular clinical needs of each patient.

In past years there was an unproductive emphasis on territo-riality and on the maintaining of hierarchy and status—with the more prestigious professions like psychiatry and doctoral-level psychology expending considerable energy toward excluding master's level therapists. But those battles belong more to the psychotherapists of yesterday; today there is a significant shift toward a more collaborative interdisciplinary climate.

Managed care and cost containment is driving some of these changes. The role of the psychiatrist has been particularly affected as cost efficiency has decreed that psychiatrists will less frequently deliver psychotherapy personally but, instead, limit their activities to supervision and to psychopharmacological treatment.

In its efforts to contain costs, managed care has asked therapists to deliver a briefer, focused therapy. But gradually managed care is realizing that the bulk of mental health treatment cost is consumed by inpatient care and that outpatient treatment, even long-term therapy, is not only salubrious for the patient but far less costly. Another looming change is that the field is turning more frequently toward the group therapies. How much longer can we ignore the many comparative research studies demonstrating that the group therapy format is equally or more effective than higher cost individual therapies?

Some of these cost-driven edicts may prove to be good for the patients; but many of the changes that issue from medical model mimicry—for example, efforts at extreme brevity and overly precise treatment plans and goals that are inappropriate to the therapy endeavor and provide only the illusion of efficiency—can hamper the therapeutic work. Consequently, it is of paramount importance that therapists gain control of their field and that managed care administrators not be permitted to dictate how psychotherapy or, for that matter, any other form of health care be conducted. That is one of the goals of this series of texts: to provide mental health professionals with such a deep grounding in theory and such a clear vision of effective therapeutic technique that they will be empowered to fight confidently for the highest standards of patient care.

The Jossey-Bass Library of Current Clinical Technique is directed and dedicated to the frontline therapist—to master's and doctoral-level clinicians who personally provide the great bulk of mental health care. The purpose of this entire series is to offer state-of-the-art instruction in treatment techniques for the most commonly encountered clinical conditions. Each volume offers a focused theoretical background as a foundation for practice and then dedicates itself to the practical task of what to do for the patient—how to assess, diagnose, and treat.

I have selected volume editors who are either nationally recognized experts or are rising young stars. In either case, they possess a comprehensive view of their specialty field and have selected leading therapists of a variety of persuasions to describe their therapeutic approaches.

Although all the contributors have incorporated the most recent and relevant clinical research in their chapters, the emphasis in these volumes is the practical technique of therapy. We shall offer specific therapeutic guidelines, and augment concrete suggestions with the liberal use of clinical vignettes and detailed case histories. Our intention is not to impress or to awe the reader, and not to add footnotes to arcane academic debates. Instead, each chapter is designed to communicate guidelines of immediate pragmatic value to the practicing clinician. In fact, the general editor, the volume editors, and the chapter contributors have all accepted our assignments for that very reason: a rare opportunity to make a significant, immediate, and concrete contribution to the lives of our patients.

Irvin D. Yalom, M.D.
Professor Emeritus of Psychiatry
Stanford University School of Medicine

INTRODUCTION

Javaid I. Sheikh

Intelligence, and reflection, and judgement,
reside in old men,
and if there had been none of them,
no states could exist at all

CICERO, 44 B.C.,

IN HIS ESSAY "DE SENECTUTE"

A huge demographic revolution is taking place in the United States. There is unprecedented growth in the proportion of older people, a "graying" of the population. The 1990 census estimated the number of people age sixty-five and older at 31.3 million, ten times larger than in 1900. This number is expected to reach 70 million by 2030 as "baby boomers," a large cohort born between 1946 and 1964, reach age sixty-five beginning in 2011. For a better perspective, consider this: in 1900, the elderly represented only 4 percent of the population; they represent 12 percent of the population today, and will constitute 20 percent of the population by 2030. Moreover, individuals over the age of eighty-five years are the fastest growing age group in the United States.

Despite these demographic shifts, mental health professionals in general seem woefully unprepared to tackle the problems of such a large group of patients. Historically, most therapists, whether psychiatrists, psychologists, marriage and family therapists, social workers, or nurses, have had little exposure to mental health problems of the elderly during their formal training. During the last decade, however, we have witnessed encouraging signs that mental health professionals increasingly are recognizing such problems in the older age group. Training programs in geriatric psychiatry, gerontology, geriatric social work, and geriatric nursing have multiplied in the past several years. Even so, the demand for mental health services will definitely outstrip the supply of practitioners with specific geriatric training.

I anticipate that most older patients with mental health problems will be seen by therapists who have not had formal training in dealing with these disorders. These more "generalist" therapists are those for whom this volume is designed. The seasoned gerotherapist will also, however, find much useful information in these pages.

Old age can be a time of multiple losses, such as those of loved ones and of one's own physical health. Death of a spouse can be the single most important stressful event in old age. In addition, caring for a disabled spouse, retirement, and a change in financial status are other common stressors. Adaptive tasks for old age thus include adjusting to a decline in physical abilities and changes in health status, adjusting to deaths of one's spouse and close friends, and adjusting to retirement and a possible declining financial status. Establishing close affiliations with those of one's own age group, joining formal or informal social networks, and finding satisfaction in activities other than one's job or homemaking seem to be the keys to successful adaptation. Adaptation to such losses occurs successfully in many cases over a period of time. In other cases, a successful outcome may require additional social support and professional help.

Mental disorders of late life are quite common and usually lead to serious dysfunction in those afflicted. Those individuals who are close to such patients or those who assume caregiver roles are also affected. The more common mental health problems include anxiety, depression, and cognitive impairment. In most cases, these problems do not have a simple causal mechanism but seem to occur as a result of a complex interplay of biopsychosocial factors. Similarly, therapeutic approaches to these problems also need to be multifaceted, targeting various contributory or causal factors and stressors.

Because this book is about understanding and managing the mental health problems of the elderly, it addresses several unique issues related to the elderly that can make our tasks as providers of mental health care quite difficult. Essential points to consider include ageist attitudes of providers, the high likelihood of multiple medical problems in elderly patients, and recognition that older patients may not be very open about their feelings and probably view mental health problems as a stigma.

Ageism as a negative stereotype is probably as old as society itself. For example, in 44 B.C. when Cicero was sixty-two years of age, he wrote an essay, "De Senectute," on the problems of old age, describing ageism in Roman society. Certainly ageism is one of the most prevalent negative stereotypes in our society. We professionals are thus not immune to these stereotyped beliefs ourselves. Beginning with Freud's pessimism about the value of psychoanalytic techniques in old age, a long-standing and widely held belief among psychotherapists is that older patients are not good candidates for psychotherapy as they cannot change. This is analagous to the assumption held by society at large that "you can't teach an old dog new tricks." Historically, such attitudes have not served older patients well as they led to therapeutic nihilism even before the treatment began.

The information presented in these pages belies this most damaging cliche of old age. Those of us working with older adults have seen a radical shift in our own preconceived notions, notions that were developed from attitudes we were exposed to during our training as psychotherapists. We have found that indeed, older adults do change, can change, and will change if the therapist is understanding, open, flexible, and patient. Our original ideas about our patients' capacity to change have thus been completely transformed by our experiences. With psychotherapeutic techniques becoming more focused and patients living much longer, therapeutic optimism abounds among professionals working with the elderly.

Throughout the text are attempts to counter other misperceptions and myths about old age with facts, data, and clinical anecdotes. Thus, a conscious attempt has been made to give readers a clear idea about the differences between normal aging processes and disorders. For example, clinically significant cognitive impairment needs to be distinguished from normal age-associated memory decline, with the former needing clinical intervention.

Therapists do need to be fully aware of one special dimension of working with the elderly: a much higher likelihood, compared with younger people, of having coexistent mental and physical ailments. More often than not, older patients will be referred to the therapist by their primary care physician who has tried unsuccessfully to deal with their myriad and somewhat intractable physical complaints resulting from underlying depression or anxiety. To serve these patients better, it is imperative that the therapists work in close collaboration with their medical colleagues as in many cases a patient's care will be shared, with the therapist providing psychological treatments complementing medications prescribed by the physician.

The present generation of older patients grew up during a time when admitting to any kind of emotional problem brought a major stigma. Such attitudes on the part of patients can contribute to a failure to get adequate help for mental health problems. Even when referred to us by their primary care physicians, these patients may not be fully cooperative at first with an evaluation of their emotional problems. Many times they are quite upset initially at being referred to us, letting us know right away that they are not "psychos." In these situations, careful attention needs to be directed to nonverbal communication and the general context of their symptoms. We need to take the advice of Gallagher-Thompson and Coon who state in Chapter One that "we, as health professionals, must listen carefully to the language of our older patients, and increase our awareness of both what's spoken and what is left unsaid."

Finally, another reality that the therapist needs to be aware of is that, along with adolescents, the elderly seem to be among the age groups with the highest rates of suicide. The ratio of completed to attempted suicides rises dramatically in old age from 1:200 in young adult women to 1:4 in elderly people, suggesting that any suicidal ideation or intent in this population should be taken very seriously. Another sad fact is that fully 75 percent of the elderly who commit suicide see their primary care physician in the last month of their life. I would hazard to guess that some of these suicides might be prevented if the patients were referred to mental health professionals in time. We must hope that better collaboration and coordination of care between primary care providers and mental health professionals can make a difference in this area.

Despite some of the difficulties mentioned above in providing mental health care to the elderly, the future looks promising. In the past decade an increasing amount of research effort has been directed at understanding the mental health problems of the elderly and studying various treatments. In the past several years we have thus witnessed the emergence of a broad array of pharmacologic, psychologic, and social interventions for disorders of late life. These strategies, when used appropriately in a wide variety of health care settings, can be safe and effective while considerably improving the patient's quality of life.

Although the scope of this volume is primarily to address the needs of frontline therapists, it does go deeper than that. Many of the contributors are well known nationally in their fields and thus cover the mental health disorders of the elderly in some depth without undermining the practicality and clinical usefulness of their contributions. All the contributors are clinicians who work primarily with older populations and have extensive experience in their particular areas of expertise. Throughout the book, authors have drawn on real-life examples for illustration. All the names and data in these case examples have been altered and any identifying information has been removed to preserve the anonymity of the individuals involved.

OVERVIEW
OF THE CONTENTS

The first chapter by Dolores Gallagher-Thompson and David Coon is a tour de force in the field of depression in the elderly. The authors explore various dimensions of depressive syndromes in old age, including the language and context of depression, the role of family, the relationship of physical illness and substance abuse to depression, and multiple psychosocial factors contributing to depression in old age. Using their considerable clinical acumen, the authors then provide practical techniques with which to assess and treat depression in old age.

Robert Hill, Dale Lund, and Ted Packard tackle the complicated issue of bereavement counseling in Chapter Two. Beginning by exploring the psychological impact of bereavement, including grief and mourning, they present some generalizations about the process of bereavement for the benefit of therapists. The authors then tap their wealth of clinical experience, recommending ways to help the bereaved elder cope and discussing counseling strategies for the therapist.

In the third chapter, I discuss various methods to assess anxiety in the elderly and alert the therapist to its co-morbidity with physical illness, depression, and insomnia. Then I describe various treatment methods the therapist can use to effectively treat anxiety in a variety of clinical situations.

Leah Friedman translates her clinical and research expertise into a picture of older patients with insomnia that even the most novice of therapists can understand and benefit from. In Chapter Four she outlines step by step the process of evaluation and the treatment strategies available to the therapist.

Sexuality is perhaps one of the least talked about and most misunderstood subjects of old age. Diane Morrissette, Antonette Zeiss, and Robert Zeiss debunk multiple myths about sexuality in old age. In Chapter Five, the authors first educate us about normal sexual changes with aging and then use clinical vignettes to describe sexual function problems in old age. They describe a practical approach to assessment and treatment of sexual problems in the elderly.

In Chapter Six, Greer Murphy addresses the key issue of cognitive impairment in the elderly. This is an area with which every therapist working with the elderly needs to be familiar. The author presents a systematic way of evaluating cognitive impairment and points out the common causes of this problem. He then presents ways to minimize disability commonly associated with cognitive impairment through working closely with family and caregivers. He also addresses important legal issues that can arise in these situations.

Joel Streim tackles the challenging subject of managing mental health problems in the nursing home setting. He begins Chapter Seven by pointing out the special problems inherent in nursing home settings, including a high frequency of physical and mental illness among the residents, the serious lack of resources, the misuse of psychotropic drugs and physical restraints, and the federal regulations governing assessment and treatment in these settings. He then presents various ways to deal with these issues emphasizing a collaborative, interdisciplinary approach.

Finally, Barbara Sommer presents an overview of the impact of medical illness on psychological well-being and how it can complicate the therapist's task. She raises awareness of the more common medical problems in old age and their psychological impact and prepares the therapist to work closely and effectively with the patient's physician.

ACKNOWLEDGMENTS

My deepest appreciation is due to a number of individuals who have helped me directly or indirectly in completing this volume. First and foremost, I want to thank the chapter authors. As you can see, these are individuals with widely different backgrounds who were willing and flexible enough to put up with several revisions of their work to bring about a cohesive volume. I appreciate very much their scholarship and their ability to translate their work into a practical format useful for even the most novice therapists.

I would like to thank Irvin Yalom for his invitation to put this book together. I appreciate all the help and support of Alan Rinzler, senior editor for Jossey-Bass Publishers. I thank Pamela Swales for reviewing my chapter on anxiety disorders and giving her valuable feedback and suggestions for improvement. I thank Vivian Söderholm-Difatte, my administrative assistant at Stanford, for her multifaceted help in all stages of this project. Over the years many have contributed to my growth as a therapist and a healer. These include teachers, colleagues, trainees, geriatric psychiatry treatment team staff members at Stanford Medical Center, and many collaborators on various projects. Though they are too numerous to mention individually, I would like to take this opportunity to mention two in particular. Jerome Yesavage and George Gulevich, both professors of psychiatry at Stanford, have played key roles in stirring my interest in working with older patients during my residency and fellowship years. I am grateful to them for that.

I would also like to thank my numerous older patients who over the years helped me learn from them firsthand both the positives and negatives about the aging process: the beauty of wisdom gained from life experiences, the healing power of reflection and reminiscence, and the pain and discomfort resulting from the ageist attitudes of a youth-centered society.

Last but most important, I am grateful to my lovely wife, Asma, for her unwavering love and understanding while I worked many a late night on this volume.

NOTES

P. xiii, *The 1990 census:* Taeuber, C. M. (1992). Sixty-five plus in America. In U.S. Bureau of the Census, *Current population reports, special studies.* Washington DC: U.S. Government Printing Office.

P. xiv, *Training programs in:* Lebowitz, B. D., & Niederehe, G. (1992). Concepts and issues in mental health and aging. In J. E. Birren, R. B. Sloane, & G. D. Cohen (Eds.), *Handbook of mental health and aging* (2nd ed.). San Diego, CA: Academic Press.

P. xiv, *The more common mental health problems:* Anthony, J. C., & Aboraya, A. (1992). The epidemiology of selected mental disorders in later life. In J. E. Birren, R. B. Sloane, & G. D. Cohen (Eds.), *Handbook of mental health and aging* (2nd ed.). San Diego, CA: Academic Press.

P. xv, *Beginning with Freud's pessimism:* Freud, S. (1948). Sexuality in the aetiology of the neuroses. In E. Jones (Ed.), *Freud collected papers*, Vol. 1. London: Hogarth Press.

P. xvii, *The ratio of completed to attempted suicides:* National Center for Health Statistics. (1991). *Suicide by age, race, and sex: United States—1988.* Hyattsville, MD: Centers for Disease Control.

To my father
for being so nurturing when I was young
and for aging so gracefully

TREATING
THE ELDERLY

I

DEPRESSION

Dolores Gallagher-Thompson and David W. Coon

MARY SMITH

Dr. Jones realized she hadn't seen Mary Smith since Mary's retirement from the courthouse well over a year ago. Mary had come to see Dr. Jones for a regular checkup, "just to see how her sixty-seven-year-old body was holding up." During the examination, she complained she had difficulty sleeping through the night, had lost weight due to a lack of interest in cooking, previously one of her favorite pastimes, and often felt fatigued and lethargic. However, her physical examination was normal as were all her lab results, findings that were puzzling at first to Dr. Jones. In addition, both Dr. Jones and her nurse noticed that Mary's typically well-kept appearance and outgoing disposition had changed. Mary just felt "blank" most of the time, except when she got teary-eyed watching those greeting card commercials on television. She couldn't understand why she didn't enjoy her retirement more and do all the activities she had once planned for so avidly.

Mary sent Dr. Jones, the nurse, and each of us a message. She was probably clinically depressed.

Although depression may be the best descriptor for health and mental health practitioners assigning a diagnosis, our elderly patients typically avoid using the word. For those of us on the front lines to assist in the effective diagnosis and treatment of this potentially life-threatening problem, we need a greater understanding of depression's signs and symptoms presented by the elderly.

Most public health research to date has found that depressive symptoms are no more likely to occur among the old than the young. Still, some groups of older adults, particularly the chronically ill, the bereaved, nursing home residents, and caregivers, do report a higher amount of depressive symptoms than others over age sixty who are not in these circumstances. We must also remind ourselves that if depression goes undetected and untreated, its repercussions are dangerous, including the neglect of health and hygiene, physical deterioration, increased substance abuse, failure to take prescribed medication, and even suicide. Thus, the assessment and treatment of depression among the community of elders and its various subgroups is an important and multifaceted health problem. Although it is beyond the scope of this chapter to address the various forms of depression in detail, the material presented here is applicable to most depressive disorders, including major depression, dysthymia, mood disorder due to a general medical condition, adjustment disorder with depressed mood, and bereavement. Less attention is paid to bipolar disorders and more specific varieties of depression like those that include seasonal fluctuations and psychotic features. Readers interested in the specifics of these disorders are referred to the *Diagnostic and Statistical Manual of Mental Disorders* (DSM-IV) of the American Psychiatric Association.

This chapter explores key factors necessary for a substantive understanding of effective assessment and management of depression in the elderly. These important factors include the language of depression among older adults; the careful consideration of the elder's personal context and shared social history; the potential avenues to identifying, assessing, and treating depressed older adults; and the variety of treatments appropriate for the different faces of depression among the elderly.

THE LANGUAGE OF DEPRESSION

Today's elderly were not heavily influenced by the pop psychology explosion of the 1970s and 1980s. They don't typically walk in our office, sit down in the chair, and say "I'm really depressed." Please realize that we aren't saying older adults never use the word *depressed* as a self-descriptor, but we do believe that revelations like "I'm a little blue," "I'm down," or "I've been feeling a bit sad since the Mrs. died" are used more frequently and hold more meaning for older patients compared with their younger counterparts. More important, we, as health care professionals, must listen carefully to the language of our older patients and increase our awareness of both what's spoken and what is left unsaid.

A depressed elder's initial complaint to us may be of a physical, interpersonal, or financial nature. However, we generally find that with some additional well-intentioned probing, depressed elders will begin to unmask many of their depressive symptoms. A previous history of depression may seem to be an obvious predictor of a current depressive episode; but without a quality history or persistent questioning, this predictor goes undetected and the subsequent diagnosis and treatment of current depression is not made.

Like Mary Smith, elderly patients will generally describe depression in terms of increasing social withdrawal and isolation, as characterized by a loss of interest in their life and its activities or hobbies. The world to them now appears bland, blank, or boring. Depressed elders typically express a sense of hopelessness and helplessness about their future and their ability to affect its outcome; such feelings frequently occur concurrently with a sense of nervousness and anxiety. In addition, many elders may describe instances of feeling useless and complain of difficulty concentrating.

Low self-esteem is not seen as frequently among depressed elders as it is in depressed youth and younger adults. A sense of emptiness, by contrast, is more often present in severely depressed elders. This emptiness should serve as one of our red warning flags as research has found it to be associated often with suicidal ideation and action. In sum, the sudden severity of even one of these symptoms or the mild manifestation of a cluster of such symptoms warrants further investigation for appropriate diagnosis and treatment.

Many older persons never present any of the symptoms discussed thus far; more often they experience and discuss depression through various physical complaints. As a result, these elders will first contact their primary care physicians and related health care teams. There are several common physical signs and symptoms of depression among elders. A noticeable disruption of the sleep-wake cycle, fatigue, and change in appetite are signs often associated with late-life depression. A sad or blank expression and crying spells as well as constipation and psychomotor agitation and retardation are also frequent signs. Observable indicators such as these can be particularly important clues when you are interviewing older patients who much of the time are reticent about or detached from depressive thoughts and emotions.

In our view, effective assessment and management of depression not only requires understanding of its signs and symptoms but also demands careful consideration of the influence of elders' personal and cohort experiences on our conceptualization and treatment of the problem. Health and mental health professionals need to be reminded that until the 1960s, few effective treatments for mental illness were available; and by the time better treatments emerged, today's senior citizens were thirty to forty years old. Many still carry distorted images of mental health care from the 1930s and 1940s and may fear the stigma and shame associated with depression and mental illness (for example, long hospitalizations and intensive medication/regimens). Furthermore, fear of genetic contributions to depression may prevent elders from identifying either their relatives or themselves as depressed. Last, today's societal structures very often require a mental illness diagnosis for managed care treatment and for third-party payments. These diagnoses can be frightening to anyone, but to elders on a fixed income facing rising insurance and medical costs, such diagnoses could encourage further masking of depressive signs and symptoms. All in all, we can see how the elderly might be afraid to discuss directly any symptoms that imply depression or other psychological difficulties.

Our society sends out a number of conflicting messages about depression and its treatment. Elders have lived through decades of these conflicting messages, and they bring these beliefs and concerns into the assessment and treatment process. On the one hand, many of the elderly believe in a traditional medical model of health care and go to their primary care physician with their depressive signs and symptoms. They want a pill to make them feel better, thus avoiding a fuss and the risk of exposure. Consequently, these older adults are typically resistant to other forms of treatment. On the other hand, elders with poor health care experiences may resist taking another drug or may quickly discontinue medical treatment if they experience drug side effects or interactions.

One final introductory point: most practitioners who work with the elderly recognize that the aging process carries with it many psychological and physical losses such as retirement, widowhood, and various chronic and acute illnesses. Given the sheer number and severity of such losses, some professionals and family members may view depression as a normal consequence of growing older. However, this is not the case: we should recognize that even substantial losses have necessary but reasonable periods of adjustment and do not automatically cause a clinical level of depression. Depression among the elderly is not a part of the normal aging process. Once it is recognized, it needs to be treated in a manner consistent with the client's needs and cultural background.

EXPLORING THE CONTEXT OF DEPRESSION

We view depression as a psychosocial phenomenon brought on and potentially exacerbated by changes in a client's environment. Although it is difficult in any given case to determine the exact cause of depression, we do encourage professionals to examine closely both the physical and psychosocial environments of their clients. These include not only their physical living and working situation but also the social context in which these activities occur.

Changes in the self and its various contexts (such as role changes, retirement, death of loved ones, or loss of physical functioning) can precipitate a variety of reactions at any age. Often people can adequately manage these changes in young and middle adulthood and, consequently, do not experience serious depression in relation to them. Professionals must remember, however, that losses in late life are typically plural in number; often elders have inadequate time to recuperate or adjust before the next set of losses enters their lives.

Each change potentially creates stress and strain between the impacted elder and an altered living, working, or social situation. Many times, people in the elders' environments are carelessly unresponsive or simply incapable of adequately responding to the elders' new needs or demands. Depression may thus be a by-product of a person's inability to manage these changes. Ineffective coping or change management strategies are often magnified when an individual has unhelpful thoughts and beliefs about the situation, and these, in turn, intensify negative feelings and less effective functioning.

Depression is by no means a reaction to recent or accumulated losses in every instance. Some individuals experience a temporary adjustment reaction or feelings of demoralization, which many view as subsyndromal depression. Often, their quality of life improves with relatively minor intervention, along with the passage of time. Others develop a full-blown depressive episode that requires treatment but is of relatively short duration. Still others suffer from depression across the life span; and no matter what setting they enter, their depression follows them. New losses and circumstances of old age can trigger more debilitating depressive episodes among this group. Dutiful professionals can learn to work effectively with these chronically depressed elders to help them better manage their current losses and perhaps ameliorate some of their lifelong depressive symptoms.

Furthermore, we should not dismiss the possibility of a biological substrate in late-life depression. However, our model emphasizes psychosocial components and rejects the perspective that depression is solely a disease to be managed most effectively by drug treatment. Ultimately, "getting better" in our model is not enough. Helping elders develop a set of cognitive and behavioral skills to help them *stay* better continues to be a primary goal of this approach.

Understanding the Sociocultural Context

Critically important to our model is the notion that depressed individuals, even when isolated, still experience their depression through multiple layers of social influence. These influences shape people's understanding and acceptance of what is happening to them and what action is appropriate for them to take in order to feel better.

Older adults enter our current health care system with an individualized set of beliefs, values, and stereotypes about depression and its treatment that are shaped and reshaped through years of family, peer, neighborhood, social class, and other cultural influences. Today's health care professionals are challenged to determine how and where to most effectively intervene—at the individual biological or psychological levels, within the family or particular social support system, or even throughout an entire community. In any case, we suggest that the needs of elderly patients be explored within the context of their particular sociocultural cohort.

These social influences can be thought of as a series of concentric circles affecting individuals and their experience of depression. It is beyond the scope of this brief chapter to describe each possible influence identified in Figure 1.1, but we would like to provide you with a few examples.

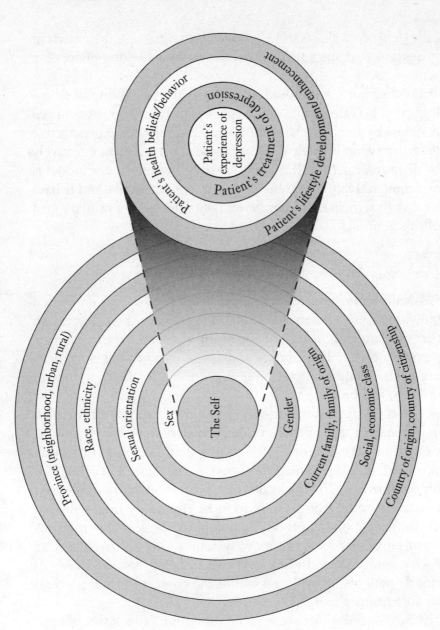

Figure 1.1
Social Influences on the Experience of Depression

Consider for example, the "gender" circle in this figure. On the one hand, women in this society are generally allowed, and even encouraged through their socialization process, to express their emotions openly, including feelings of sadness or depression. Right or wrong, this open display of emotion is often attributed to the "biological" circle and the influence of hormonal changes on females.

On the other hand, the social construction of gender in this society teaches most men at a very early age to internalize their emotions. The "big boys don't cry" message is everywhere, and the end result is a rampant myth that men aren't depressed simply because they do not show it in ways that are easy for others to recognize. How do we then explain that elderly white males have the highest rate of suicide in our society—a rate three to four times higher than the general population? It seems reasonable that they, in fact, may be suffering significant clinical depression, and because of socially defined gender roles, they have become unable to discuss it. This is one example of the powerful influences that can seriously affect people's beliefs and behavior about psychological distress and its treatment.

To various degrees, all the circles (and perhaps others we didn't think to include) do mold the older adult's beliefs and behavior regarding help-seeking and treatment for depression. Again, these influences include not only past messages that shape patients' health beliefs and behaviors but also present messages of what is acceptable.

The family of origin or the current group of significant others is yet another circle of influence that affects older people's experience of depression. Some families do not want to hear about depression, dissatisfaction, or related emotional difficulties. "What would Dad have to be depressed or worried about? Mom died over five years ago, and we have all adjusted. He sold the old house and moved to be near us. He's retired and without grandchildren, a big house, or any real commitments. All he has to do is lie around all day. That's what he worked to achieve." Is it really what Dad wanted or envisioned for his future? To many older and younger adults alike, this scenario sounds downright bleak and boring.

Similarly, an elder's current neighborhood or community living environment can sway the expression of sadness and grief. Think for a moment about the "active senior" movement in our society that markets a lifestyle that either purposely or inadvertently excludes elders who appear "physically or emotionally impaired." We would like to believe these communities have seniors' best interest at heart by expressing concern about what their community could provide for depressed elders. Unfortunately, it has been our experience that such communities actively dissuade the expression of "negative emotions" by elders and thwart efforts by social workers, psychologists, and residents to develop support groups, psychoeducational classes, or other interventions to assist with difficult life transitions and their accompanying feelings. Why is this so? Perhaps these communities fear that depression is a powerful contagion capable of dismantling active leisure communities and leaving only stereotypical old folks' homes in its path. The following case illustrates this fear.

SALLY

Two years after her husband Harry died, Sally sold their home and moved to a senior retirement community in another state near her eldest son. Sally felt isolated from her old friends and familiar church groups. However, she valued her regular discussions about politics and social issues with a local college student who participated in a twice-weekly friendly visitor program. Still, she felt unable to protest when the senior community director discontinued the program because "they will want me to leave if I say it gave me a boost each week. They don't want any sad Sallies at that place. It's like a sorority house for the aged!"

The not-so-hidden message from Sally's particular neighborhood influence is this: "Don't express your sadness, depression or emptiness in our active and vibrant senior community!" Not only is it possible that mental health could spread the other way, helping or enhancing more than it hurts, but several controlled research studies have demonstrated that depressed individuals actually reap therapeutic benefits from helping one another.

Powerful influences beyond those of the immediate family and community also help shape the health beliefs and practices of the patients we see. These include potent messages embedded in the elders' social standing and culture as reflected by their ethnicity, tribe, race, and national origin. Preliminary research has shown that the signs and symptoms of depression can be quite different across cultural groups within our own country as well as across nationalities. Among U.S. ethnic and racial minority elders in general, the subjective reporting of depression occurs much less frequently than the expression of somatic complaints. However, the frequency and nature of the symptoms described vary significantly across cultural and ethnic groups. The end result is an array of physical, mental, and spiritual problems associated with depressive feelings and physical symptoms that are attributed by the elder to a myriad of causes from guilt and atonement to "bad blood" and sorcery.

A wide variety of beliefs and customs exists within any particular minority group, just as within the dominant culture. How strongly elders identify with their cultural, regional, or national backgrounds is a complex interaction among the effect of all the influential forces mentioned in the model as well as the elders' level of acculturation into the dominant culture. Many minority elders are even less likely than their Euro-American counterparts to seek out and receive treatment for depression. Obstacles can include such factors as language barriers, divergent beliefs about the causes and treatments of depression, and unspoken expectations about how they should be treated by health care professionals. Yet, it is important not to automatically attribute particular cultural beliefs and customs to individual minority elders. We must increase our awareness that beliefs and customs held by an elder are not necessarily embraced by their children or grandchildren. For a better understanding of these issues, we refer the reader to our references for further reading at the end of the chapter.

The influences described in the concentric circles shown in Figure 1.1 are not necessarily static or fixed. The power each band exerts on the person can vary over time and across persons who share similar social contexts, as illustrated in the following case.

A first generation Japanese-American woman was raised in a family with traditional expectations of limited career aspirations and heavy child-rearing responsibilities. She felt happy and satisfied with life until her children left home. In response, she returned to college (against her husband's wishes) and now reports significant marital conflict and depressive feelings. In your discussion with her about these concerns, she states that these changes came about as a result of her growing friendships with other reentry women as well as through her course readings and discussions concerning the subjugation of women in society.

A key ingredient for effective assessment and treatment of all elders regardless of their cultural and ethnic heritage is respect. Much of older adults' lack of health care compliance and high dropout rate from intervention regimens can be attributed to practitioners' lack of respect for the individual, which typically stems from a real failure to understand the influence of current and previous social contexts on the particular patient's health beliefs and behavior. Without this understanding, little hope exists for an effective therapeutic relationship. Finally, age differences between the elderly patient and therapist can encourage a negative attitude toward change, involving beliefs such as "This patient is just too different from me." It can also foster questions like "How can I possibly understand their life experiences?" This age difference can be compounded by differences in gender or sexual orientation, and in ethnicity, race, or national heritage. Our effectiveness begins with an awareness of these various influences on elders' beliefs about the depression and its subsequent treatment. However, our efforts cannot stop there. Effective practitioners will also exhibit therapeutic competence by using the language of the older adults, by exploring their complaints within their social contexts, and by demonstrating respect for individual differences.

In summary, today's most effective clinicians will consider physical and psychological changes in their patients within several contexts of the individual including age, gender, sexual orientation, family constellation, socioeconomic status, race, and ethnicity. We must remain cognizant of these contexts as we ask ourselves relevant questions about how to best assess and treat mental health issues. For example, how will depression present differently in the rural elderly Mexican-American widow with breast cancer versus the urban older gay man caregiving for a partner with AIDS? And what treatment or combination of interventions will best help alleviate the depression faced by each individual given his or her familial, social, and cultural history?

Health care and mental health professionals cannot expect to find a one-size-fits-all assessment and treatment package that matches every member of our diverse group of elders. The rapidly growing fields of clinical gerontology and ethnogerontology will continue to provide us with new understanding regarding the reality of these influences on the mental and physical health of our pluralistic society of elders. This new information presents us with the continuous challenge of updating our skills and knowledge for more effective diagnosis and treatment of a variety of mental health problems.

EFFECTIVE SCREENING
AND ASSESSMENT

With increased awareness of the variety of social influences on the health beliefs and practices of elders, we must now be prepared to accept referrals and perform screens and assessments within the varied contexts in which elders live and function. As noted earlier, many elders are not accustomed to approaching mental health professionals about emotional problems like depression. Instead, they may discuss their feelings with their priest or minister first, holding beliefs that they are being punished or deserve to suffer. Others who survived our country's Great Depression believe that nothing will ever amount to the same feelings of hardship, and therefore they cannot bring themselves to discuss their emptiness or hopelessness. Still other older adults seek out self-help books that may or may not alleviate their symptoms.

In our experience, the majority of elders experiencing depressive symptoms will consult their physician first. Those with physical signs who do not have a primary care physician may even end up in an emergency room for treatment. Thus, it is likely that the first contact with a mental health practitioner will be made by any one of a variety of people (other than the elder) such as the primary care physician, family members, senior center staff, clergy, and friendly visitors. These individuals may have noticed changes in the elder's everyday function, or they may be responding to their own experience of the depressed elder as less involved, more withdrawn, and perhaps more difficult to engage in usual activities. Their input can be quite valuable in identifying and understanding the patient's distress. In addition to careful review of the information given by the referral source, practitioners may want to utilize more objective measures of depressive symptoms. These will elicit the patient's perspective in a very direct way.

Self-Report Screens and
Structured Interviews

Several brief screening questionnaires for depression are available that are easily completed at home or in an office. These help determine patients' own views of their symptoms as well as the degree to which their daily routine is being disrupted and the seriousness of any suicidal thoughts or feelings they may have. Most cognitively intact elders can complete these questionnaires in five to fifteen minutes, depending on the length and complexity of the measure and the reading and visual acuities of the individual. At times, elders will need to have the forms read to them—because of extreme anxiety, trouble concentrating, or difficulty understanding the questions.

Two of these self-report screens, the Beck Depression Inventory (BDI) and the Geriatric Depression Scale (GDS), appear to be particularly useful in assessing the severity or amount of depression experienced by elderly patients. The BDI is somewhat more complex in format than the GDS; as such it may be more appropriate for better educated and more cognitively intact patients. It is available from the Psychological Corporation. The GDS was developed specifically for the elderly and addresses many of the symptoms exhibited by depressed older adults. It uses a simple yes/no response format and limits the number of somatically oriented questions to minimize the chances of overreporting the level of depression. Some studies have reported its successful use in detecting depression in nursing home residents as well as general outpatient populations. It is available from its developer, Dr. Jerome Yesavage of Stanford University and the Veterans Affairs Palo Alto Health Care System. A short version of the GDS developed by Dr. Javaid Sheikh is available from its author; its brevity is appealing for use in busy primary care settings or when time is a key consideration.

Although the long version of the GDS has been translated into a number of languages including Spanish, Chinese, and

Japanese, there is still serious doubt about the validity and reliability of most self-report measures with minority elders. Research studies indicate that such screens frequently yield significant under- or overreporting of distress in this population. Even with adequate language translation for interview questions and screens, the cultural expression of affect and its related concepts and meaning need to be assessed and interpreted within the particular sociocultural context.

Various interview-administered or observer-rated instruments are also available to assess depression; these include the Diagnostic Interview Schedule (DIS), the Hamilton Rating Scale for Depression (HRSD), and the Structured Clinical Interview for Diagnosis (SCID). None of these structured interviews were designed with the elderly specifically in mind, though, and the instruments demand a good deal of time and training for proper administration and interpretation. Technical reviews of various screens and structured interviews for depression are listed at the end of the chapter in "For Further Reading."

Personal Interview

In our view, a screen or structured interview is not enough, even when a rational assumption of depression is made. Quality assessment and treatment warrants a complete psychosocial and medical history; these are best obtained through a personal interview with the patient, along with consultation with the primary care physician (always) and the patient's family or social support system (when appropriate) in order to have all relevant information needed for diagnosis and treatment. This comprehensive assessment begins with a genuine respect for the elderly and a sincere effort to maintain the older person's sense of dignity and privacy. Part of this respect comes from an exploration of our own beliefs and feelings about aging and the role of elders in our society, including our views about disability, illness, and death. When we find ourselves stereotyping all elders as disabled, isolated, senile, and maudlin without hope of better mental and physical health management, it is time for an extended vacation or a new profession!

Respect and dignity can be demonstrated early in the process by using the proper name of the elder; protecting privacy when certain questions are avoided; and being aware of body language, gestures, and eye contact. Personal respect can be shown indirectly as well, by remembering that an older adult may have difficulty hearing and may need you to speak louder and close the window to lower background noise, may have a visual impairment and need adequate lighting to communicate clearly, or may not respond immediately because of a word-finding problem, which will require extra time for the elder to think. Our questions often need to be broken down into simpler queries if we are to ascertain changes that affected the patients' depression in the past and present. In addition, many elders grew up with a family physician who spent time with them, discussing their problems. We must recognize that the rush of today's health care professionals is often viewed as disrespect by elders and directly leads to ineffective communication and medical noncompliance. The crucial goal of a comprehensive assessment is to gain an accurate and sincere understanding of the individual's view of the world and his or her concerns, along with current and past treatments that have been attempted and biopsychosocial elements that are contributing to the current distress.

Medical Evaluation

A critical component of the assessment and subsequent treatment of depression is a complete medical evaluation to identify and treat potential physical disorders, including pain syndromes, malnutrition, and drug interactions or toxicities that may contribute to or even cause the depression. Several physical illnesses such as cancer, hypothyroidism, and acquired immune deficiency syndrome (AIDS) often contribute to the myriad of somatic symptoms suggestive of depression. A thorough history and medical checkup include an assessment of the relative contribution of physical conditions to depression as well as an exhaustive inventory of current medications.

Older patients frequently consume a number of drugs whose side effects can mimic depressive symptoms. These drugs range from antihypertensives, analgesics, antiparkinsonisms, antimicrobials, cardiovascular preparations, hypoglycemic agents, and psychotropic drugs (sedatives, antipsychotics, hypnotics, steroids) to alcohol, over-the-counter medications, and recreational street drugs. Careful assessment of the types of medications used regularly, along with analysis of their common side effects and common drug-drug interaction effects, is essential. A clinical pharmacist's appraisal can be most helpful at this point. Then, this information should be reviewed along with the medical and psychosocial data already obtained in consultation with the primary care physician. This procedure will enable alternative hypotheses to be evaluated and will permit greater confidence in the diagnosis. It will also foster collaborative efforts among medicine, psychiatry, and psychology, a result that can only benefit the patient who too often is subjected to fragmented care from professionals who do not communicate with one another.

The Role of the Family

Family members and significant others can provide a clearer picture of the elder's current and previous behavior, coping strategies, and living situation. This is particularly critical if the cognitive functioning of the elder is impaired. Children or siblings who can address cultural beliefs and customs regarding the treatment of mental health problems can be particularly helpful. Keep in mind, however, that cultural mores may still preclude children's discussing their parents' emotional or physical health in depth. By questioning the patient and family, we can also develop a clear understanding of the amount of formal and informal support available to and used by the elder. In sum, a psychosocial history gathers information on current and past symptoms, the length and characteristics of depressive episodes, the available social support network, substance use patterns, and responses to any previous mental health treatment. What did the patient or family members see as helpful or effective and for whom? It is very beneficial to get a sense of both the patient's and the family's beliefs about the cause of depression and their views about appropriate treatment. Answers to these questions can give a treatment team ideas about how to proceed, what interventions to implement, and what social and physical obstacles need to be addressed to help maximize treatment compliance.

A screen or structured interview combined with a psychosocial history and medical evaluation helps identify the etiology, course, and variety of depression, its co-morbid conditions, and relevant interventions for treatment. Whenever there is doubt about the diagnosis of depression, we encourage practitioners to consult with experienced geriatricians and geropsychologists and to begin to treat the depression safely while other physical or situational stressors are ruled out. In short, we believe when in doubt, *treat;* not, when in doubt, *wait.*

Diagnostic Categories

For the sake of completeness, major pertinent categories are briefly reviewed here. Fuller descriptions are contained in the *Diagnostic and Statistical Manual of Mental Disorders* (DSM-IV). For discussion of the appropriateness and applicability of these categories to elders, see Dr. Dan Blazer's book, *Depression in Late Life. Major depression* or a clinical level of depression is described by the DSM-IV as a significant depressed mood or loss of interest or pleasure in regular activities, combined with at least four of the following symptoms: insomnia or increased sleep, physical agitation or retardation, fatigue, feelings of worthlessness or guilt, difficulty concentrating, significant weight change, or recurrent thoughts of death or suicide.

Dysthymia, a chronic, mild yet disruptive depression lasting two or more years occurs more frequently among older people than major depression. Dysthymia and major depression can occur together, and major depressive episodes often recur. Another variety of depression, *Adjustment Disorder with Depressed Mood*, is a time-limited reaction to a physical illness or an environmental stressor, such as retirement, relocation, or financial stress. In this case, depressive symptoms may remit when the stressor is removed or the elder adjusts or copes more effectively with the situational change.

Similarly, some symptoms of depression normally ensue after the death of a loved one through the process of *bereavement* (see Chapter Two). Although no specific time frame or symptoms are consistent across cultural groups, normal signs and symptoms of the process seem to be a general lack of interest in activities, sleep disturbances, crying spells, and difficulty concentrating. These symptoms seem to peak about six months after the loss and frequently reappear on significant calendar dates such as anniversaries and birthdays. Two years after the loss, many of the signs and symptoms have faded although grief itself may continue for many years, depending on a number of factors such as circumstances of the death and nature of the relationship. Elders can also suffer from *Mood Disorder Due to a General Medical Condition*, in which an illness or physical condition is the direct cause of the depression.

Most common among elders seems to be a condition for which there is no current DSM-IV code. This condition is referred to by many as subsyndromal depression in which the individual experiences several depressive symptoms that interfere with his or her quality of life, but the distress experienced is not at a level sufficient to meet diagnostic criteria. Individuals suffering with subsyndromal depression are least likely of all the types discussed to ask for help or to be recognized by others as needing help. In the future, this group is anticipated to increase in size and in its need for services, and as a result, it will need to be properly addressed. Finally, mental health professionals must remain mindful that late-life physical and psychosocial losses are many times experienced simultaneously or sequentially, and they can lead to any one or more of these varieties of depression.

KEY INTERACTIONS THAT OFTEN TRIGGER DEPRESSION

Depression among the elderly is not simply a reaction to a particular event, series of events, or a situation but is typically more complex, involving a multidimensional interaction that includes both patient and environment. Next, we discuss several of these situations that are particularly salient to older adults.

Physical Illness

The most common emotional response to physical illness is depression in some form, and the onset or worsening of one's physical condition can in turn exacerbate coexisting physical illness and increase the likelihood of a depressive episode. Today's older adults usually face more than one physical illness or problem at a time. A broad spectrum of illnesses found in the elderly—from diabetes, cancer, kidney or liver dysfunction, and heart disease to brain lesions, stroke, various infections, and chronic pain—can precipitate the full range of depressive reactions.

Although depression in the context of a physical illness may remit when the disease and its related consequences (such as pain or loss of function) are managed effectively, this is not always the case. Several variables have been identified that affect both the likelihood that depression will occur among the physically ill as well as the level of depression presented. Some of these key variables include the severity and duration of the physical illness; its potential for disability, pain, or death; and the degree of functional impairment that it causes. Most older patients do not experience depression associated with illness solely as a result of physiological changes like neurochemical and hormonal imbalances that disrupt sleep and produce fatigue or other signs of depression. Rather, physical illness can contribute directly to other physical problems like sexual dysfunction, immobility, and incontinence. Also, as a consequence of physical illness, psychosocial losses often ensue including job restructuring or actual loss, reduced capacity to exercise and engage in other pleasant activities, and diminished social interaction. A number of questions arise: Does the illness involve multiple organ systems that present a real threat to life? Will it require amputations or create sensory deprivation? Do patients have time to adjust or are there abrupt physical changes and losses? Will medical treatment and medication side effects foster social isolation and dependency?

Psychosocial characteristics of the patients themselves (including prior bouts with depression or serious physical illness, their ability to manage the situation at hand effectively, and their beliefs about illness and its treatment) obviously contribute to the experience and course of the current depression. Misinterpretations of illness and treatment as well as maladaptive coping mechanisms in response to illness often lead to negative thinking and behaviors. These negative thoughts and actions in turn fuel behavioral and emotional reactions that potentially exacerbate both the illness and depression. Effective management of physical illness and concurrent depressive symptoms requires enhancement of the patient's cognitive and behavioral coping strategies in order to improve quality of life.

In addition to patients' understanding and adaptation to physical illness, the attitudes of family and friends about the illness and its potential stigma can either provoke additional emotional stress or lend stress-buffering support. Family members or friends who avoid physical or emotional contact with ill elders contribute to a wall of social isolation around these patients that can seal in their depression. In contrast, active involvement by elders and their families in the management of illness and concomitant depression will support positive treatment adherence and outcome.

Psychosocial treatment of medically ill, depressed elders generally can proceed successfully along lines similar to those used in the treatment of physically healthy depressed elders. However, some modifications will be necessary to tailor the particular form of therapy to the main presenting problem of the patient (which may involve pain management, for example, as the top priority rather than treatment of the depression per se).

Dementia

Depression is found quite frequently among demented older adults. Over half of Alzheimer's patients experience depressive symptoms before the more obvious signs of the illness appear, and about a third are both significantly depressed and demented. Moreover, several symptoms of Alzheimer's disease or other dementing processes—including difficulty concentrating, memory lapses, and irritability—actually mimic depression. Because these same cognitive difficulties are frequent symptoms of depression among the elderly, considerable confusion in diagnosis and treatment can arise. In fact, the frequency of these dementialike symptoms is so high among depressed elders that it has come to be called *pseudodementia*.

However, cognitive deficits, emotional lability, or personality changes should not be accepted as conclusive evidence of either dementia or significant depression. Instead, a complete medical evaluation, along with relevant neuropsychological assessment, is warranted. Both federally and state funded specialized centers exist in most of the country where thorough multidimensional assessments are conducted to evaluate these particular co-morbid conditions in depth. Mental health practitioners should have knowledge of these referral sources and should routinely make referrals when there is a serious question about the presence or absence of a dementing disorder in addition to depression. Medical and neuropsychological evaluations need to be reviewed in tandem to determine appropriate treatment and follow-up for each identified problem. Patients' cognitive deficits should be monitored closely and assessed at regular intervals so that treatment goals and processes can be refined. In general, supportive therapy, life review, and behavioral forms of treatment have been found helpful with individuals who are both demented and depressed.

Bereavement

Bereavement is a normal reaction to the loss of a significant other that typically includes certain depressive symptoms but does not result in major depressive disorder for most people. The bereavement process is generally acknowledged to have three different phases beginning with an initial shock, numbness, and disbelief. During this time, severe anxiety and physical symptoms such as diminished appetite and sleep disruption occur. Approximately four to six weeks after the death, the numbness gives way to more notable depressive symptoms like crying, chronic sleep disruption, and lack of interest in routine activities. During this second phase, the bereaved individual commonly becomes preoccupied with searching for and yearning for the loved one. Typically, there is a strong sense of the "presence" of the deceased, and many report that they experience the person as being present—either by seeing or hearing him or her. Such phenomena, which have similarities to hallucinations, should not be a cause of concern unless they occur with such frequency and intensity that they generalize beyond the deceased to other persons or events in the bereaved's life.

Generally, this time period encompasses considerable grief work in which the relationship with the deceased is remembered and explored. A review of the relationship helps the survivor manage unresolved thoughts and feelings. Anniversaries, birthdays, and other significant dates usually lead to a recurrence of depressive symptoms and the experience of considerable pain and loss. The third phase ordinarily begins some time after the first anniversary of the death and involves resolution and acceptance of the loss, accompanied by a reintegration of the self into new social roles and activities. Note that the bereavement process varies widely across cultures and individuals. The time frame and the sequence of these phases are not universal. In general, however, the depression associated with bereavement is most severe during the first few months and tends to soften considerably over time without formal treatment, unless "complicated grief" has occurred. This situation is discussed below.

Gender differences in the social roles and the expression of emotion can give rise to bereavement complications. Women in our society are more likely to outlive their male partners. In addition to the loss of an intimate confidant and little hope of repartnering, they frequently face new financial concerns and constraints. It is also possible that women are well aware of their own greater life expectancy and may in some way prepare themselves psychologically over their life span for widowhood. In contrast, older men expect to die before their wives and may have more difficulty than women in adjusting to spousal death. Not only are men socialized to present a stiff upper lip, constrict their expression of emotion, and reject social support, but they often know little about cooking and other domestic activities necessary to sustain physical and mental health.

In some situations, an abnormal grief reaction or complicated bereavement can develop. This occurs when grief is suppressed, a condition our society may reinforce through comments like "Don't you look great; you're really handling this well!" and "We just need to get you back out and meeting people." Complicated bereavement can also occur when certain cognitive distortions are present, such as severe guilt and a sense of direct personal responsibility for the death combined with extremely negative views of oneself and the future. Other red flags can also alert us to potential bereavement complications. Personal characteristics of the widow or widower, details of the death itself, and qualities of the relationship with the deceased are the most important of these. For example, a widow who has struggled consistently with depression or an anxiety disorder over the years and is living in an unresponsive social environment will probably have a difficult time adjusting to the loss. Likewise, unexpected or particularly traumatic deaths such as suicide or homicide can lead to blocked affect and other trauma responses. If the relationship with the deceased regularly gave rise to domestic violence, then excessive anger and conflicted guilt can also impede the grief process.

Interventions for normal grief typically involve peer-led support groups, bibliotherapy, and recognition of the healing power of the passage of time. Treatment for more complicated grief reactions often involves direct treatment of the depression; when that has abated, the individual can be helped to resume the normal grief process.

Caregiving

Caregivers to frail elders are usually either adult middle-aged children or spouses, friends, or family members who are seniors themselves. Over time, caregiving appears to wear down caregivers' psychological and physical resources. This attenuation of resources leads to a greater proportion of these elders suffering from significant depression, anxiety, guilt, and anger compared to the general older adult population. Deficits in the caregivers' social support system (including a lack of intimate interaction, limited time for recreational and social activities, and insufficient physical assistance with domestic activities) contribute to caregiver stress, isolation, and depressive reactions. Depression is also magnified among caregivers because they are regularly confronted with stressful situations that can end in dissatisfying interactions with their care-receiving relative and other support network members.

Services that directly address caregivers' mental health and psychosocial functioning (such as respite programs, support groups, psychoeducational classes, and individual or group psychotherapy) have proven useful to a greater or lesser extent for reducing caregivers' depression and other negative emotions. In particular, easily accessible services that increase caregivers' sense of their ability to adequately handle the situation and that help them to maintain their social support system are especially useful. This generally means participation in programs that increase cognitive, behavioral, and problem-solving skills that improve the caregiver's sense of self-efficacy and in turn lead to more effective functioning in the caregiving role. Formal services that improve the care-receiver's situation, such as mobile meals, friendly visitor programs, and health care home visits that assist with bathing, exercise, or improving the safety of the home, can have an indirect effect on caregivers' mental health as well.

As contemporary health service providers, we must also let go of stereotypes and simplistic views of the family and social support systems of minority groups in our country. Outgroup marriage, social mobility, acculturation processes, and shifting immigration patterns are altering caregiving expectations, roles, and responsibilities. These changes, combined with differences across minority groups and variation among members of each individual group, make minority caregivers particularly challenging to treat effectively.

Stress and Conflict with Adult Children

Life events, from retirement and relocation to illness and death, can create role changes and conflict in both patients and their adult children. Cross-generational family conflicts can be heightened by unfulfilled expectations of family traditions, roles and responsibilities, and opposing value systems. Moreover, old conflicts may resurface in late life, particularly when there was a history of physical, sexual, or emotional abuse in the family system. Depression, guilt, and anger for past action or inaction subsequently emerges for the elder and other family members. The role of family therapy in treating these conflicts is just beginning to be explored and may hold promise for effective treatment.

Unfortunately, in some instances we see adult children who are now charged with the care of their formerly abusive parents. They may turn to elder financial abuse, physical abuse, or neglect in retaliation for their parents' past misdeeds. Elders trapped in this situation are caught in a cycle of dependency, depression, and physical danger. Once physical safety is assured, interventions that help the family to identify old communication and behavior patterns and to substitute more effective patterns that reduce stress and distress can be especially helpful in these instances. These are topics about which little is known, either empirically or clinically, but which need further investigation.

Substance Abuse

As we have seen, illness, multiple loss, caregiving, and family stress (singularly or in combination) can all precipitate depressive episodes. These same changes can simultaneously or sequentially encourage increased alcohol or inappropriate drug use among our patients. However, the coexistence of substance abuse and depression is difficult to assess because elders typically deny substance abuse in any form and are extremely reluctant to seek help for it once it is identified as a problem by others. Information about misuse of alcohol or drugs can sometimes be obtained by getting a thorough history covering not only the amount, frequency, and type of alcohol or drugs consumed but also the circumstances and reasons given for why the elder uses the substance. Then we can begin to understand the role depression plays in substance abuse. For instance, is the drug of choice "a pick-me-up to make me feel better," "a little something to take the edge off my family problems," or a "sleep aid"? This information is critical if we are to understand the problem and recommend appropriate treatment.

Of course, we cannot rely simply on self-reporting by elders to verify substance use or abuse. Falls, accidents, overexposure to hot or cold weather, malnutrition, bone thinning, cognitive confusion and memory loss, sexual dysfunction, incontinence, self-destructive behaviors, and violent outbursts can all be signs of serious substance abuse. Clinicians should ask significant others about these signs and symptoms and use these individuals to verify patient self-reported substance use.

We also need to be aware of the necessity of letting go of our own ageist views about substance abuse, as reflected in statements like, "Oh, it's the only little vice she has left." Just as important, we must give up our embarrassment over asking elders about their patterns of substance use and remember not to limit our substance considerations to alcohol. Elders may "doctor shop," getting a large supply of medications from a number of doctors, or they may borrow medications from friends and family. More important, older adults may use sleeping pills and tranquilizers, over-the-counter psychoactive substances, pain relievers, and prescribed drugs in a "fruit salad" combination that's potentially lethal. Elder substance use is exacerbated by age-related changes in the body. As the body ages, its capacity to metabolize and eliminate drugs and alcohol from the system is diminished. So much for what was once considered "her little vice."

In general, concurrent treatment of substance abuse and depression in our present health care system is problematic. Lack of adequate treatment models for the elderly and physical withdrawal symptoms including hallucinations and memory loss, particularly for lifelong users, are just two of the reasons concurrent treatment is difficult. Right or wrong, we find the substance abuse problem is generally addressed first, followed by treatment of the concomitant depressive disorder.

TREATMENT OF
LATE-LIFE DEPRESSION

Many treatment approaches appear to be successful, and often a combination of approaches is most helpful. The information we gather through the assessment process ultimately guides the approaches selected. Among the key factors to consider are (1) type and severity of the symptoms including potential for suicide along with the type of depression presented (as reflected in the diagnosis); (2) the context of depression such as physical illness, family conflict, situational stress, caregiving, or bereavement; (3) sociocultural influences on the patient's views of depression and the situation; and (4) availability, practicality, and utility of various treatment approaches.

Given our emphasis on depression as primarily a psychosocial phenomenon triggered and exacerbated by changes in the social and physical environment, we will emphasize psychosocial interventions for their effective treatment. Once again, we do acknowledge the biological substrate that seems to be present in some forms of depression, and so we also present information on both drug therapy and electroconvulsive therapy (ECT) for certain varieties of depression.

In an ideal world with adequate personal, social, and financial resources, the effective treatment of depression includes both brief and longer-term interventions not only for individuals but also for their social networks and environments. For example, a severely depressed widower experiencing suicidal ideation as well as suffering from malnutrition several months after his spouse's death would receive individual assessment and psychotherapeutic intervention; and potentially he would be considered for psychiatric hospitalization. The longer-term individual intervention might encompass strategies that explore and refute his negative thoughts about his future and incorporate pleasant activities for him to do daily. Immediate system interventions could include working with the man's family to increase their awareness of the grief process and explore options by which the family could provide emotional support, or locating social agencies to provide social support or nutritional support services. Longer-term system or environmental change may include family therapy to discuss the effect of the loss on the family unit and to develop rituals to help manage grief in the system. Another system change might include the widower's taking in a boarder or a younger family member as a roommate to decrease his isolation and address his nutritional deficiencies.

However, given the various constraints (such as finances, time, and energy) under which most of us work, it is unlikely that all these interventions will be made. A useful maxim in selecting possible interventions to offer a particular patient is to be as minimally intrusive as possible, yet to choose therapies likely to "get the job done" efficiently and effectively. For this, the reader needs to keep abreast of the ever-growing literature evaluating the efficacy of various interventions for late-life depression.

Drug Therapy

Each variety of depression discussed earlier may have a different precipitating factor that is centered within the psychological or biological makeup of patients or their social environments. All three parts of the biopsychosocial model may have some role to play in depression; however, elders suffering from severe depressive episodes whose family histories suggest a strong hereditary component or other indices of a biological substrate can often benefit from antidepressant drug therapy. Two other varieties of depression, *bipolar depression*, characterized by alternating manic highs and severely depressed lows, and *depressive episode with psychotic features* are frequently treated with drug therapy including antipsychotics. In the interest of space, these are not discussed in detail here.

In addition to heredity as a biological precipitator, important chemical messengers in the brain are thought to decrease with age. Antidepressants are believed to affect the reuptake of these chemical messengers between brain nerve cells. In particular, scientists assume these drugs increase the amount of two messengers, norepinephrine and serotonin, and as a result decrease the experience of depression.

Drug treatment is complex among the elderly and is best handled by referring your client to an experienced geropsychiatrist or geriatrician. For example, other medications taken by the elder must be reviewed first and eliminated or adjusted to avoid drug toxicity or inactivity. As we mentioned before, some drugs used to treat physical conditions like hypertension or hypoglycemia may actually create depressive signs and symptoms and demand review. Diet and exercise can alter the body's processing of medications and their effects, so they also need to be considered in the treatment equation. Just as important, drug half-life is prolonged in the elderly, and consequently, many older persons do not need as high a dose as young or middle-aged adults. With all these factors to consider, a professional knowledgeable of the older adult's overall health status can best determine appropriate dosage amount, frequency, and timing.

Tricyclic antidepressants (TCAs) and heterocyclic antidepressants (HCAs) have been the most frequently prescribed drugs for depression in the last three decades. However, most of these including the more popular amitriptyline (Elavil), nortriptyline (Pamelor), desipramine (Norpramin), imipramine (Tofranil), and doxepin (Sinequan) have undesirable side effects. Frequent TCA or HCA side effects are drowsiness, dry mouth, orthostatic hypotension, and constipation. In addition, some people suffer from memory problems, confusion, blurred vision, or cardiovascular difficulties while taking these drugs. Dividing dosages may help minimize these side effects, but dose division also increases the opportunity for the patient to forget or skip the medication.

Anxiety or nervousness is often associated with depression among elders. Effective drug therapy and management requires that the patient's most salient problems be identified and a treatment plan be developed. Drugs known as monoamine oxidase (MAO) inhibitors are usually prescribed to treat depression associated with anxiety. However, adherence to these drugs is difficult for patients because they cannot be taken with certain foods and thus they are rarely prescribed now. Drugs of a relatively new class of antidepressants called serotonin selective reuptake inhibitors (SSRIs) appear effective in the elderly with considerably fewer side effects than TCAs or HCAs. These drugs also seem to be quite effective in mixed anxiety-depression. Notable SSRIs currently prescribed for older patients include fluoxetine (Prozac), sertaline (Zoloft), and paroxetine (Paxil). The search continues for new drugs with fewer side effects and greater efficacy that minimize cost and dosage.

In sum, drug therapy can be impeded by several obstacles such as adverse side effects, a consistent need for medication evaluation and adjustment, and compliance problems. All these often lead to a person's skipping or missing medications, resulting in a diminished response or even drug therapy failure. We believe that even if the biological substrate is disrupted and warrants drug treatment, psychosocial and behavioral therapies should also be introduced for the most effective management of the episode. A review and discussion of the individual characteristics of patients and their context will help us make the best treatment plan for these elders.

Electroconvulsive Therapy (ECT)

Please put aside for the moment all your horror stories about "shock therapy." Electroconvulsive therapy (ECT) is the treatment of choice in select cases. What types of cases, you might ask? Severely depressed elders whose depression is intractable—that is, those patients who have had numerous drug and therapy attempts and have "failed" them—are good candidates for ECT. Acutely suicidal elders can respond very well to ECT, which has a quicker therapeutic action than either medication or psychotherapy. Also, depression with psychotic features, which results in poor psychosocial functioning including hallucinations or delusions, appears to respond well to ECT. In fact, given the problems with compliance, adequate dose determination, and adverse side effects, ECT may prove more beneficial than drug therapy or psychotherapy in these three select cases.

Today's ECT treatments are typically provided in a hospital on an outpatient basis, are carefully monitored, and are quite safe. Most individuals require six to ten treatments for substantial alleviation of their depressive symptoms. To help diminish the memory disturbances usually found with ECT, most current administrations of this treatment are unilateral rather than bilateral, and a mild muscle relaxant is given to the patient prior to treatment so that the seizure induced does not also cause thrashing and damage to the patient, as had been the case in the past. Typically, treatment is extended one or two more times after the patient shows marked improvement. The reason for ECT's effectiveness is still not clearly understood, but most researchers in the field speculate that ECT affects the same receptor areas that antidepressant medications do.

Finally, some precautions with regard to this treatment should be noted. Elders with hypertension or cardiac arrhythmia require a cardiology consultation when being considered for ECT. In addition, most people suffer some memory difficulties following ECT. Consequently, depressed elders already complaining about memory problems may not respond well to this treatment.

Psychotherapy and Other Psychosocial Interventions

The effectiveness of psychotherapy and related interventions in the treatment management of late-life depression is well documented. Before we describe psychotherapy, we would like to present several points critical to therapy with older adults.

Given the sociohistorical context in which today's elders developed beliefs and responses to depression, the chances that psychotherapy will be offered as a solution by elders themselves will be slim. To make psychotherapy more "user friendly" for elders, we encourage practitioners to allow them to tell their own story and describe how *they* view depression and its treatment. This personal story can aid in the potential integration of not only the various psychosocial and biological approaches presented in this chapter but also spiritual and culturally defined approaches not reviewed here. Once psychotherapy is seen as an acceptable treatment by the client, we believe that regardless of the specific approach, older clients will probably need to be socialized into therapy. This process involves a clear articulation of the roles and expectations of both the therapist and the patient.

In addition, sensory problems and cognitive changes may make it difficult for older adults to process information in therapy as quickly as younger clients, and therefore the pace of therapy often needs to be slower. Moreover, severe sensory and cognitive losses may ultimately preclude some clients from psychotherapeutic approaches. Furthermore, the length and frequency of sessions, as well as their location, need to be individualized for patients. We must bear in mind that these too may change over the course of physical illness, caregiving, situational stress, or bereavement. A number of different psychotherapeutic approaches can be used to reduce depression among various subgroups of depressed elders. We provide here a brief review of some of these successful approaches; additional sources of information are included in the list of references for further reading at the chapter's end.

Cognitive Behavioral Psychotherapeutic Interventions. Cognitive behavioral (CB) therapy is a time-limited approach, usually involving fifteen to twenty sessions, that encourages patients to explore the interrelationships among what they think about their current situation, what they do behaviorally to manage their lives, and as a result, how they feel. The basic premise of CB is that how we think and what we do daily ultimately affects how we feel. Therefore, CB posits that positive changes in thinking styles and daily activities will help diminish depression.

The cognitive component of CB uses various psychoeducational techniques including patient homework to help elders identify unhelpful thinking patterns and ultimately challenge and replace these negative thoughts with more adaptive thoughts. This step is particularly important for elders who have experienced multiple losses, as CB therapy will help them to develop a more adaptive view of themselves and the situation at hand.

The behavioral component of CB therapy concentrates on the interrelationship between behavior and feelings. Elders learn behavioral strategies such as relaxation techniques, assertion and problem-solving skills, and how to monitor changes in their mood relative to increases in daily pleasant activities. Successful cognitive and behavioral strategies are often collected and developed into a workbook for patients to use in the future to help themselves prevent relapses. The relative emphasis on cognitive versus behavioral techniques employed in therapy is determined by the individual needs of the elder.

CB's time-limited and active psychoeducational nature permits flexibility in the number, frequency, and length of sessions; it also allows the elders to collaborate with the therapist in developing individualized strategies that will work for the elders both inside and outside the therapeutic milieu. CB interventions are particularly good for caregivers, bereaved persons, and elders with chronic physical illness. Challenging the negative thinking patterns of older adults can lead to the development of new roles and responsibilities for them, the identification of choices still available to them, and their active participation in improving their quality of life. We have identified three CB-oriented books we find especially helpful for both professionals and their patients: *Feeling Good: The New Mood Therapy* (1980) and *The Feeling Good Handbook: Using the New Mood Therapy in Everyday Life* (1989) both by David Burns, M.D.; and *Reinventing Your Life* (1993) by Jeff Young, Ph.D., and Janet Klosko, Ph.D.

Behavior Therapy.   Behavior therapy alone has proven to be effective with depressed elders. In particular, depressed individuals suffering from some type of dementia who have difficulty tracking their thoughts can benefit from behavior therapy. The emphasis is on changing behavior that affects mood. The elders or their caregivers learn specific methods of behavior management, such as tracking daily pleasant events and subsequent fluctuations in patients' mood. Clear and specific reinforcers of positive mood are identified and frequently replicated to diminish depression. This approach appears to work with depressed elderly persons who have grown isolated over time, who have social skills deficits, or who have minimal pleasurable activities in their lives.

Psychodynamic Therapies.   Depressed elders who want more insight into their own personal development and who present unresolved issues from earlier in their lives may be good candidates for psychodynamic therapies. Developmental oriented psychodynamic psychotherapy focuses on the psychological challenges elders face as their family and social roles shift. Self-psychology interventions stress the impact of the negative experiences of aging, such as physical decline and social support shrinkage on the self system. Traditional psychoanalysis emphasizes the importance of internal psychological processes in coping with late-life problems. Successful outcomes in old age are dependent on the resolution of life's early developmental issues. Effective treatment in all three variants is facilitated by the older patient's ability to form a good therapeutic alliance, to retain cognitive flexibility, and to develop some psychological mindedness.

In general, the focus with depressed elders is in helping patients reinstate more positive self-perceptions and provide replacements for their losses. Therapists need to remain mindful of several potential differences between their older and younger depressed clients:

1. Issues of transference in therapy will typically be related to the older patients' spouse or children as opposed to their parents.
2. The elderly person's financial constraints may dictate fewer therapy sessions than the therapist wishes.
3. Termination needs to be considered and discussed in treatment within the older adult's world of cumulative losses.

Family Therapy and Interventions. People are part of a social context, and for family therapists, the depression of the elderly family member is defined as a problem of the entire social unit. In the treatment of depression, families help elders meet social needs, define lineage, and maintain continuity across the life span; they mark family rituals and provide reciprocal financial and caregiving support. With increased life expectancy, rising financial constraints on elders and their adult children, rising divorce rates, and declining fertility rates, the functioning of the multigenerational family becomes quite complex. We must prepare ourselves to be flexible with whatever persons the patients define as part of their family unit and accept the reality that these definitions vary across the generations within the family.

Family therapists may differ in how they view and ultimately treat the elder's depression. Some may emphasize cognitive distortions, behavioral deficits, psychodynamic processes, or family structural changes (including family roles and rules) in order to understand and treat depression. Still, the thrust of family interventions is similar. The therapist considers the family structure and how it operates, along with the needs of each individual as well as the unit. The focus lies in the interaction between family members and the factors that influence these communication patterns.

After family interactional patterns are identified, the therapist helps determine how the family has defined and managed depression in the past. What have they done to try to solve this before? Who was involved? What were the various members' perceptions of success or failure? How does this experience relate to the current situation?

Family therapists recognize that changes in the depressed elder will affect all unit members. The therapist models open communication with the entire family including the depressed elder, expressing optimism that change is possible. Family treatment aims to improve the stability and coping resources of the entire system and avoids treatment of the depression in isolation. Family allies can assist the therapist in treating the depressed elder through everything from increasing behavioral or social activities, challenging negative thinking, and improving nutrition, to facilitating medication compliance, providing transportation to therapy appointments, and helping complete homework assignments. When the elder is suicidal or delusional, family therapy is of critical importance in providing control of self-destructive devices and materials, ensuring medication compliance, and supervising the elder as needed.

Within the process of family interventions, professionals must attend to issues of power and nurturance. A fine line exists between family assistance that is supportive and empowering and that which is intrusive and detrimental. One key to this distinction appears to be mutual respect for all family members and an ability to focus on the issue at hand rather than dredging up all past issues and conflicts. However, shifts in power over late-life transitions; differences in caregiving expectations and realities; and unspoken rules and beliefs about family, culture, gender, aging, and illness do uncover different levels of needs. For example, the autonomy needs of the caregiving adult daughter may conflict with the nurturance needs of the frail depressed mother. The professional is left with a delicate balancing act that alleviates the elder's depression while maintaining her dignity and at the same time decreases dependency on the family caregiver.

Group Interventions. Up to this point we have concentrated on individual or family psychosocial interventions. However, depressed older adults can benefit from the input of peers who share many of the same depressive symptoms and psychosocial stressors that they currently experience. In addition, a substantial amount of research literature suggests that the process of helping others with their problems and life transitions can be therapeutic and may actually help some people manage their own depression more effectively.

An array of group interventions are available in most communities to help depressed elders. These interventions run the gamut from psychoeducational skill development classes (such as an eight-week program, "Coping with Depression," that emphasizes the acquisition of cognitive and behavioral skills to facilitate lifestyle changes) to support groups and insight-oriented, self-help groups that emphasize intraindividual development, interpersonal understanding, or spiritual development.

The benefits derived from a group depend on the personal characteristics of patients and leaders as well as the amount of congruence between patient goals and group goals and purpose. We as professionals can facilitate cost-effective treatment and management of late-life depression through more extensive use of group interventions. Included in this category should be referrals to various self-help and support groups when appropriate. To use referrals beneficially, the therapist must carefully review groups in the area and integrate these groups effectively into the overall treatment plan (for example, to help the elder maintain gains once formal therapy is completed).

One effective group process that may have relevance for more mildly depressed elders is the *life review* approach in which group members are encouraged to consider who they are now and how they lived their lives. They create an autobiography that emphasizes the positive aspects of their lives in an effort to overcome negative thinking about their current and past situations. Within this framework, clients are encouraged to be as creative and active in the process as feasible. Some groups and individuals within groups use video- or audiotapes, photos, artwork, music, and other media to fashion their reviews and tell their stories. Generally, individuals are encouraged to deal with unresolved conflicts from their past and concerns about their future. The process also seems to provide the opportunity for forgiveness of self and others and a sense of letting go. Life review may also be helpful for individuals with quite severe physical health problems and for those in hospice situations who may be too vulnerable to participate in more demanding types of treatment.

FINAL REMARKS AND
RECOMMENDATIONS FOR THE FUTURE

Before closing, we would like to reinforce the critical importance of context in the effective assessment, treatment, and management of late-life depression. As professionals, we can encourage elders to tell their own story, to express their own views about how they interpret their situation, and to consider how they think they can manage it better. This story, in turn, should be seen in light of the sociocultural context of the elder and the powerful influences this context has on the elder's health beliefs and practices.

A thorough assessment process, combined with continued exploration and ongoing evaluation of treatment, increases both our respect for individual differences and our chance of treatment success. We need to allow for flexibility within our traditional ways of managing depression and begin to think more broadly. There are opportunities to treat patients individually, through classes and groups, and within family meetings. The pluralistic nature of our growing multicultural society creates opportunities to interweave traditional Western psychology and medicine with culturally specific folk remedies and spiritual practices. The elder's personal story can point the way to problem definition and management.

In addition, the boundaries between various professional roles are not as clean as they once were—and perhaps rightly so. From one case to the next, we will see our roles shift when we work with depressed older adults. One case will require crisis intervention and a directive, problem-solving style. Another case will involve the active facilitation of an elder's role changes through individual therapy that examines cognitive distortions. Yet another situation will include a family intervention that mobilizes family support and skill development to improve communication with a dying parent.

As mental health professionals, we cannot expect to sit in our offices and wait for elders to schedule today's "traditional" fifty-minute session. Older adults need to be seen in a variety of settings that offer the opportunity to provide more comprehensive treatment with potentially more satisfying and successful results, such as at home, in the nursing home or other extended care setting, or in the acute care hospital. The length and frequency of sessions will vary by individual context. Visits may need to be multipurpose or of longer or shorter duration than the typical session. Visits may change locations across the course of therapy; and spouses, family members, or significant others may need to participate sometimes but not all the time. Whereas we typically develop therapeutic interventions to foster patient independence, we may need to do more for some patients and assist others in doing more in vivo work away from the therapy room. These departures from the norm may raise eyebrows from some colleagues, but when used appropriately they can do much to enhance the therapeutic endeavor.

All these considerations point to a professional who becomes more, not less, active when working with the elderly. Finally, in our opinion, there is a great deal more to be learned about effective assessment and treatment of depression. We encourage professionals to think creatively, develop and try out new treatment models, and share their successes and their failures openly with one another. In particular, we would like to see the field over the next five to ten years develop more of a scientific database, grounded in research, that addresses the issue of *which type* of intervention is most appropriate for a client or patient with a given set of problems, presenting characteristics, and sociocultural background.

This information will be invaluable for practitioners—particularly as we move into an era of health care reform, including increased use of managed care companies that will serve as the gatekeepers of mental health service delivery. Although there are many potential problems with managed care (for example, compromises to confidentiality and the sometimes arbitrary determination of total number of sessions a client or patient may receive), one of the basic concepts underlying this approach to health care may well be beneficial: the need for time-limited, effective treatments to be identified and used. Whenever possible, these should be therapies based on clinical research findings and not just on hunches or clinical lore. To the extent that the managed care movement is fostering the performance of carefully controlled intervention research, it will have made a significant contribution to the field of geropsychology in particular as well as to the field of mental health service provision at large.

FOR FURTHER READING

American Psychiatric Association. (1994). *Diagnostic and statistical manual of mental disorders* (4th ed.). Washington, DC: Author.

Blazer, D. G. (1993). *Depression in late life* (2nd ed.). St. Louis, MO: Mosby.

Burns, D. D. (1980). *Feeling good: The new mood therapy.* New York: Signet.

Burns, D. D. (1989). *The feeling good handbook: Using the new mood therapy in everyday life.* New York: Morrow.

Gallagher-Thompson, D., Futterman, A., Farberow, N., Thompson, L. W., & Peterson, J. (1993). The impact of spousal bereavement on older widows and widowers. In M. Stroebe, W. Stroebe, & R. Hansson (Eds.), *Handbook of bereavement: Theory, research, and intervention* (pp. 227–239). Cambridge, England: Cambridge University Press.

Gallagher-Thompson, D., & Thompson, L. W. (1995). Psychotherapy with older adults in theory and in practice. In B. Bongar & L. Beutler (Eds.), *Comprehensive textbook of psychotherapy: Theory and practice* (pp. 359–379). New York: Oxford University Press.

Gaw, A. C. (Ed.). (1993). *Culture, ethnicity and mental illness.* Washington, DC: American Psychiatric Press.

Knight, B. G. (1992). *Older adults in psychotherapy: Case histories.* Newbury Park, CA: Sage.

National Institutes of Health Consensus Development Panel on Depression in Late Life. (1992). Diagnosis and treatment of depression in late life. *Journal of the American Medical Association, 268,* 1018–1024.

Pachana, N., Thompson, L. W., & Gallagher-Thompson, D. (1994). Measurement of depression. In M. P. Lawton & J. Teresi (Eds.), *Annual review of gerontology and geriatrics* (Vol. 14, pp. 234–256). New York: Springer Press.

Qualls, S. H. (1988). Problems in families of older adults. In N. Epstein, S. Schlesinger, & W. Dryden (Eds.), *Cognitive-behavioral therapy with families* (pp. 215–253). New York: Brunner/Mazel.

Salzman, C. (Ed.). (1992). *Clinical geriatric psychopharmacology* (2nd ed.). Baltimore: Williams & Wilkins.

Sue, D. W., & Sue, D. (1990). *Counseling the culturally different: Theory and practice* (2nd ed.). New York: Wiley.

Thompson, L., Gantz, F., Florsheim, M., DelMaestro, S., Rodman, J., Gallagher-Thompson, D., & Bryan, H. (1991). Cognitive-behavioral therapy for affective disorders in the elderly. In W. A. Myers (Ed.), *New techniques in the psychotherapy of older patients* (pp. 3–19). Washington, DC: American Psychiatric Press.

Worden, J. W. (1991). *Grief counseling and grief therapy: A handbook for the mental health practitioner* (2nd ed.). New York: Springer.

Young, J. E., & Klosko, J. S. (1993). *Reinventing your life: How to break free from negative life patterns.* New York: Dutton.

2

BEREAVEMENT

Robert D. Hill, Dale Lund, and Ted Packard

One of the most difficult yet common adjustment issues faced by older adults is the loss of a loved one through death. Coping with the death of a central member of one's intimate social or family system is a major part of a long-term process called bereavement. We have found that professional intervention is often useful in helping older individuals deal with bereavement issues, and this is particularly true when bereavement is complicated by psychological or social factors that interfere with the person's ability to adapt to the loss. Recent research findings support our experience. In some instances, professional help may be important as, for example, with complicated bereavement, now often classed as a major psychological disorder.

Collectively, the three of us have had extensive experience doing clinical work with grieving individuals and families and in conducting research on the bereavement coping process of older adults. In this chapter we share our knowledge of bereavement counseling with the goal of facilitating your clinical work with older clients. Our chapter contains a number of vignettes that illustrate how older people might struggle with the death of loved ones. In some instances, the vignettes represent direct quotations from research participants. In others, brief statements have been reconstructed from clinical records and recollections. In all instances, care has been taken to disguise confidential information so that real persons are not individually identifiable to others. When relevant, we also draw upon what we have learned from the professional literature.

BEREAVEMENT LOSSES

Loss by death of a spouse or close family member is an inevitable part of the aging process. This reality is highlighted by examining the general increase in widowhood across the life span. The 1990 census revealed that only 1 percent of the population between the ages of eighteen and fifty-four were widowed. The prevalence rates increased to 34 percent of those sixty-five and older and to 67 percent of those eighty-five and older.

Increasing numbers of females and males are living into their eighties and beyond. Individuals over eighty-five years of age have been identified as one of the fastest growing age groups in the United States. In fact, the increasing number of very old adults is a worldwide trend expected to continue for at least fifty years. Many individuals over age eighty-five have already experienced the death of their parents, parents-in-law, spouse, siblings, and even children. These cumulative experiences are often overwhelming and generate the problematic feelings and assumptions associated with bereavement overload, particularly when they occur close together in time or when the bereaved individual lacks coping resources.

Conversely, bereavement losses can provide a framework for dealing with life challenges and transitions and may be construed as opportunities for personal growth. We believe that mental health care providers can benefit from an enriched understanding of the diverse ways, both adaptive and maladaptive, that people manage and adjust to bereavement losses. For example, a sixty-five-year-old widow in a research project described herself in the following way four weeks after her husband's death.

> I'm a very lonely person. Lousy, all washed out, despondent, feel deserted, angry, hurt, hopeless, alone, mixed-up, cannot

concentrate, very emotional, very tired, cry a lot, hateful, very bitter, misfit, nobody, very miserable, very much of a loner.

This same woman described herself in much the same troubled way two years later. She added that she was concerned about herself and really hurt inside, but she also noted that she was sick of living alone and didn't care about life. In contrast, another sixty-nine-year-old widow described herself six months after her husband's death as being "independent, excited about keeping busy, enjoying the company of others, and working in my yard and doing handiwork."

These contrasting examples illustrate the critical role beliefs and behaviors play in enabling older adults to deal constructively with bereavement issues. In the remainder of the chapter we explore why some people are better able to manage bereavement issues than others and how mental health professionals can intervene effectively with those who are troubled.

THE PSYCHOLOGICAL IMPACT OF BEREAVEMENT

Although the death of a loved one is a common experience in later life, many people are not prepared when the event occurs. The following is indicative of how an individual might react to the death of a loved one, even when there is a clear understanding that death is imminent:

My husband had been in a nursing home for several months. We all expected him to die at any moment and some of us even talked about the relief we would experience when he did die. It was surprising, however, when the call came from the nursing home that he had passed away in his sleep. Although I knew he had been mentally "gone" for a long time, his death seemed so permanent and shocking to me. It was only when I went to the funeral that I fully realized that my husband was gone and that I must get on with my life.

Losing someone to death results in grief and mourning, two related but distinct processes. Grief refers to the intense sense of loss usually associated with the death of a loved one and includes the strong feelings and emotions experienced by the bereaved individual. The concept of mourning, on the other hand, represents the person's behavioral responses to the loss and is defined primarily by the cultural and social groups with which the individual identifies.

Grief

The experience of grief is an expected transitional reaction that occurs following personal loss. Grief is the most central reaction in bereavement and generally involves strong feelings and emotions such as fear, sadness, anger, or guilt. Grief may also be expressed through physical signs and symptoms including previously unexperienced illness. The example that follows highlights how grief might also be expressed through physical signs and symptoms including previously unexperienced illness.

> When my mother died of cancer, I became quite ill. My husband remarked that I seemed to be experiencing the same physical symptoms that my mother had reported. These symptoms were so intense that I even went to the doctor believing I also had cancer. After extensive testing, the doctor concluded that I was in excellent health. It was only then that I realized these symptoms were my way of grieving the loss of my mother.

Grief diminishes over time as the individual progresses through the bereavement process. Although the expression of grief is highly individualized, we have often found it helpful to think of the grieving process as including at least three partially overlapping phases: (1) an initial period of shock and dismay; (2) a sometimes lengthy period of acute physical and emotional discomfort often associated with social withdrawal; and (3) a time of restitution or reintegration during which the person comes to terms with the grief reaction and reinvolves with others. In some instances, the grieving process may sustain itself over long periods of time and may become linked to previously existing dysfunctional states or tendencies, such as major depression. The example that follows highlights the difficulty individuals may have communicating their grief reactions with family and close friends, particularly when the loss is unexpected.

> At first I kept trying but found that I just didn't have anything to say to anyone. I couldn't stand to be around other people. They kept wanting to support me or to hug me and make me feel better. I didn't want to be touched. I certainly couldn't make the pain go away, and I really didn't want to feel better either. I was so overwhelmed with my own grief and sadness that I had nothing left for others. I had to drop out. Even though I felt really depressed for a long time, it didn't seem like there was any other alternative. Finally, after a long time, I started feeling like I was ready to reconnect with others, and that's when I was willing to see a counselor.

This example suggests that it may be important, as mental health providers, for us to recognize and expect grieving to occur as part of the bereavement process. In fact, the absence of a grief response may be an important diagnostic sign of a more serious and complicated bereavement condition, unless the person's lifelong pattern of coping has been characterized by little or no expression of emotion. We recommend that therapists and helping professionals consider the guidelines summarized in Table 2.1.

It's also very important that clinicians distinguish between individuals who experience common and typical grief responses and those who show pathological grief reactions for which a more intensive intervention may be warranted. Critical signs of pathological grief taken from the American Psychiatric Association's recently published *Diagnostic and Statistical Manual of*

Table 2.1
Some Guidelines for Dealing with Grief

1. Acknowledge that grieving takes time and is always hard work.
2. Encourage, accept, and acknowledge the expression of emotion.
3. Try to understand and then support the client's unique process for dealing with his or her grief.
4. Allow the client to talk about his or her grief without attempting prematurely to solve problems or resolve issues.
5. Encourage sharing of memories and special moments associated with the deceased.
6. Avoid premature expressions of optimism and hope. Encouragement is effective only when the counselor's words and the client's hopes are congruent.
7. Be aware of issues potentially related to pathological grief responses (such as suicide threats) and be prepared to intervene directly in such circumstances.
8. Be dependable and predictable in meeting with the client on a regular basis, especially during the acute stage of grieving.

Mental Disorders (DSM–IV) include (1) pronounced guilt about things other than issues surrounding the deceased person, (2) preoccupation with death beyond the typical feeling that the individual should have died with the loved one, (3) recurring and intense beliefs about the survivor's worthlessness, (4) significant retardation of psychomotor activity, (5) prolonged and serious functional impairment, and (6) persistent hallucinations other than imagining the voice or the sight of the deceased.

Mourning

Mourning can be defined as culturally sanctioned acts and expressions that occur following the death of a loved one. As with grief, mourning is an overt manifestation of the bereavement process and is a useful marker of the individual's adaptation to the loss of a loved one. Specific expressions of mourning vary considerably depending on the culture or values and beliefs of an individual within a given culture. Western tradition dictates that survivors participate in a funeral ritual that usually includes a eulogy or a formal review of the individual's life. Immediate survivors are expected to express outward signs of deep sadness (such as wearing dark clothing) associated with the loved one's death.

In many cultures, the mourning process defines a series of duties or obligations expected of survivors. Such customs provide opportunities for survivors to (1) express their grief over the death of the loved one, (2) give emotional support to others in the deceased person's social network, (3) consolidate their memories about the lost loved one, and (4) reaffirm traditional beliefs (for example, "Dad has gone to Heaven where he is waiting for us").

The beneficial impact of mourning traditions is evident in a powerful and long-standing ritual embodied in the Mexican–American custom of *el día de los muertos* (the Day of the Dead). In his review of this mourning ritual, John West highlights the interrelationship between festiveness and sadness as a mechanism for reconciling the feelings of loss associated with the dead loved one.

Families with Mexican roots [take] with them rakes and hoes and water buckets, along with picnic lunches [to the family grave sites]. Prominent also are mounds of flowers in every color imaginable. . . . Graves have their weeds cut; mounds are re-molded and sprinkled with water. Names on wooden crosses . . . are straightened up. . . . Then the family, seated around the grave, has a picnic meal . . . for it is truly a family gathering, a [symbolic] visit with members of the family who have "gone ahead."

Mental health providers need to understand the cultural underpinnings of the mourning process for specific clients. For example, it is important to assess the degree to which bereaved clients have participated in mourning rituals they have experienced as meaningful and comforting. Part of empathizing with grieving older adults involves the counselor's learning about expectations and formal obligations that are part of the client's mourning process. Although mourning may be stressful, if a person is able to participate in culturally congruent mourning behaviors then she or he may be in a better position to reintegrate and adapt to the loss of the loved one. The illustration that follows shows how stressful mourning can be, particularly if a person is not able to participate in culturally congruent mourning behaviors.

> My son was missing in action for almost two years. Each night we would regularly leave the porch light on for him and even set an empty place at the dinner table. The hope was that he would some day miraculously return. Finally, at the urging of our relatives, we held a small funeral with a eulogy and a plaque that we dedicated to my son. Although the funeral was hard on me emotionally, shortly afterward we no longer felt the need to keep the porch light on or to set the empty place at our table. It seemed like it was easier, now, to get on with life.

In summary, we recommend that therapists encourage bereaved clients to participate in culturally congruent mourning experiences. When bereaved persons do not follow their culturally prescribed mourning rituals they often experience regret later.

SOME GENERALIZATIONS ABOUT BEREAVEMENT

In this section, we explore three questions of importance to mental health professionals who work with older bereaved adults, and we also offer some generalizations based on research findings tempered by our own clinical experience. The questions to consider with older adults are the following: (1) What are the relationships between losing a loved one to death and the person's subsequent mental and physical health? (b) What personal characteristics distinguish those at higher risk for poor adjustment from those who adapt positively? (c) What coping strategies are often associated with healthy adaptation in bereavement?

Bereavement Adjustment and Health

Several studies have highlighted the negative impact of bereavement on indices of psychological and physical health. There is little doubt that maladaptive bereavement is associated with increased mortality rates as well as a variety of chronic physical disorders including cardiovascular disease and cancer. There is also compelling evidence of relationships between persistent unresolved bereavement and significant decreases in immune system functioning. This may help explain why, during and following the bereavement process, older adults often report experiencing increased physical symptoms and exacerbation of chronic physical conditions (for example, arthritis) as well as emergent disease states.

As for psychological disorders, bereaved older adults commonly report symptoms of depression and anxiety that may or may not become chronic. Probably the most pervasive psychological symptom associated with bereavement, however, is a chronic sense of loneliness and the social isolation that often accompanies it. Some researchers have concluded that there is a reciprocal relationship between social withdrawal during bereavement, decline in immune function, and vulnerability to illness. Even when an older adult is involved in supportive social networks, loneliness can be persistent and debilitating; the individual can be busy enjoying many different activities, and doing things with other people but still feel terribly lonely and alone.

Individual Characteristics and Bereavement Adjustment

What stable personal characteristics are associated with a resilient response to personal loss? This is a question of interest to mental health providers and of importance in discriminating between "healthy" bereaved individuals and those in need of professional assistance. In general, women tend to show better social adjustment following bereavement than men, as do women and men who are more educated and are from higher socioeconomic levels. Obviously, there are many exceptions to these group generalizations. Additionally, higher levels of bereavement resiliency have been shown to be associated with individuals who have a clearer sense of personal identity and who live according to their own internal rather than external expectations. Lower levels of anxiety and depression have also been shown to be associated with better adjustment, but it is difficult to demonstrate cause and effect relationships. Also, those who have previously expressed higher levels of life satisfaction, who perceive themselves in relatively good physical health, or who are skilled in performing household tasks and independent living behaviors are more likely to adapt well to bereavement. Finally, men whose wives have previously taken primary responsibility for domestic, family, and social roles may be particularly vulnerable to loss. Women, on the other hand, are more often adversely affected by financial and economic strain, inability to do needed home repairs, and lack of experience in taking care of family financial and legal matters.

Coping Strategies in Bereavement Adjustment

A number of coping strategies have been studied with regard to bereavement adjustment. A foremost example is continuing involvement by the bereaved individual in a supportive social network that enhances emotional strength and also provides physical and, if needed, financial help. Although individuals who stay socially integrated are still likely to experience feelings of loss, inevitable stresses can be more easily ameliorated through involvement in a dynamic social system. Our collective experience has been that it is often very helpful to intervene clinically with family members and the bereaved older person rather than to do only individual counseling. Involvement with concerned and caring others may well be as fundamental during later stages of life as during the first few years.

Cognitively restructuring the loss is another helpful coping strategy. This may be as simple as reaffirming to oneself that death is part of the natural course of events, or it may entail developing a meaningful rationale as to why the loved one died ("My father lived a long and happy life, and he was ready to go"). It may also require these individuals to develop new attitudes and beliefs that help them maintain their independence, which in turn may lead to adaptive new behaviors and skills.

Several general themes, however, have emerged from research and clinical work that overlap a variety of specific coping strategies. These themes apply to most bereavement situations and are important to understand.

First, although most bereaved older adults experience decreasing difficulty and more positive adjustment over time, it is important to recognize that what people do with their time determines adjustment outcomes. Thus, successful adjustment requires active work and effort rather than a passive and resigned response. For most it is not enough to say that "time heals all wounds."

Second, being physically and socially active during bereavement can help a person reduce his or her feelings of loneliness, despair, and helplessness. Previously bereaved older people have frequently told us that it is most helpful to take one day at a time and to remain active, involved, and socially connected with others. They have emphasized the importance of having social support from others and opportunities for self-expression during the early period of bereavement. How a person copes with loss early on appears to be one of the best predictors of his or her long-term adjustment.

Third, as in other areas of life, past behavior is a useful predictor of potential future behavior. Bereaved individuals are often overwhelmed initially and, at least for a time, unable to use old skills and strategies that have served them well in the past. A major task of bereavement is to identify coping strategies that have previously worked well, reaffirm their continuing value, and then apply them vigorously to the new situation. The evidence is clear that bereaved individuals who are able to do this during the initial months following the loss of their loved one will adapt more readily and with fewer long-term problems.

Fourth, it is important for bereaved older persons to know that their reactions are common and that others will respect their feelings and care about their well-being. Self-expression and opportunities to learn about the similar experiences of others is an important factor in promoting optimal adjustment following bereavement. Self-help groups for bereaved older adults, for example, provide important opportunities for self-expression and sharing of important life experiences, particularly for those who do not already have someone in whom they can confide. The use of bereavement self-help groups is discussed more completely in a later section of this chapter.

In summary, we believe that people's beliefs and feelings about themselves, along with the skills they have developed for managing the many tasks of daily living, profoundly influence their adjustment to the death of a loved one. People with positive self-esteem and a variety of social, interpersonal, and instrumental competencies are more likely to have favorable bereavement outcomes. There is really no substitute for positive beliefs and feelings about oneself, motivation to learn new concepts and skills, and success in responding to the challenges of daily living. Individuals who either already possess such qualities or develop them during their time of bereavement will likely cope well with life as an older single adult. On the other hand, bereaved older adults who neither use nor develop personal coping resources will very likely experience long-term difficulties. Such individuals often believe that they deserve to remain depressed, to feel lonely, and to be continually overwhelmed, and they take few constructive actions on their own behalf.

The sections that follow describe intervention strategies many clinicians, including ourselves, have found effective in dealing with issues of bereavement. We also discuss how research findings about the nature of bereavement and the adjustment process influence the usefulness and applicability of these methods.

SUPPORT GROUPS AND PARAPROFESSIONAL COUNSELING

Self-help support groups are a commonly used intervention with older adults. Such groups generally consist of bereaved individuals who voluntarily meet to discuss issues and problems associated with their situation. There are many potential benefits for those who attend self-help groups. Participants can experience hope, learn new ideas and problem-solving strategies, improve skills for developing social relationships, become less lonely, explore new role definitions, discover that others have similar difficulties, and receive additional social support and encouragement. Belonging to a group and sharing feelings of fellowship and solidarity have been helpful to many older adults with whom we have worked. An example highlights how an individual might positively view a support group intervention:

> After my wife died all my friends who were with me during her illness and eventual death seemed to disappear. I was left feeling lonely and abandoned. This support group has filled the void that I was experiencing around her loss. I can share my ups and downs. I know that you will also listen to me and that you really know what it is like to grieve. I love every one of you.

Many of the general benefits of various self-help groups are especially relevant to bereaved older adults. Group members often discuss ways to alleviate the feelings of loneliness, social isolation, and hopelessness that accompany widowhood. Members also have opportunities to meet new people, participate in social activities, and form new friendships. In addition, many bereaved spouses with whom we have worked are experiencing difficulties managing tasks of daily living such as meal preparation, house cleaning, yard maintenance, and transportation that were performed previously by the deceased spouse. Group members regularly share information, advice, and resources about these common problems. Finally, self-help groups are less expensive than most alternative services and are often attractive to individuals who are reluctant to use the services of mental health professionals and agencies.

"Widow-to-widow" support is a frequently used bereavement self-help format. The model was originally developed by Phyllis Silverman in the late 1960s and early 1970s, has been applied widely in many contexts, and is generally considered to be an effective approach for dealing with common bereavement issues. It is based on the premise that not all people want to participate in large group interventions and that therapeutic benefits can be derived from informal visits with someone else who has experienced a similar loss. Widow-to-widow programs are time limited and usually involve eight to twelve meetings. They are generally limited to two widows, one of whom has successfully dealt with the bereavement process. Sometimes the widow–to-widow concept has been applied to small groups of widows. Both our own experience and recent outcome studies have supported the value and utility of this approach *if* the participating widows are able to share personal experiences and feelings and accept each other's issues. Detailed information on the widow-to-widow support group model is contained in the 1984 book *Bereavement: Reactions, Consequences, and Care* by Osterweis, Solomon, and Green.

The potential value of support groups is poignantly represented in the following recent anonymous posting on an international e-mail mental health bulletin board:

> Your [earlier message] struck a responsive chord with me. As a psychologist with a ninety-year-old widowed father in a rather plushy retirement community, I've been concerned with

the absence of ways for healthy older people to express and work through grief. These retirement communities are carefully marketed to create the illusion of carefree retirement living. Just go to one. Almost every day there is someone missing from the lavish dining room because of death or hospitalization. Infirmity is all around but no one is supposed to acknowledge it. The recreation director at my Dad's place won't hear anything about the need for support groups for members who have lost loved ones or for people living with a partner physically or mentally deteriorating. She views her mission sort of like Julie on *Love Boat*. This is a large void in the field and needs to be filled.

In summary, support group formats in various forms are important interventions in helping older adults cope with the loss of loved ones. Research evidence and our collective experience indicate that carefully selected paraprofessional leaders are effective in helping others deal with common bereavement issues. For the more serious bereavement issues, there is greater likelihood that a professionally trained leader will be needed.

FAMILY INTERVENTIONS

We have used family interventions extensively in our bereavement counseling. The loss of a loved one inevitably affects the entire family system. The example that follows is indicative of the kind of struggle that individual family members might wrestle with when the family system is altered by loss through death:

> When mother died, our whole world changed. My father was left at home alone and I immediately felt the need to care for him, or at least fill the void that remained after mother was gone. Although I was initially not aware of the impact of mother's death on my own children and husband, it was not long before conflicts started when my husband was less willing

than I to provide help to my father in his time of grief. Over the course of several months our marital relationship became more and more strained. When I suggested that father sell his house and move in with us because he wasn't able to deal with his grief alone, my husband vigorously objected and stated that father should work on getting a life of his own and I was standing in the way. I was hurt and angered by this ultimatum. I was so offended by his uncaring attitude that I took my children and went to live with my father during this time. At first, I thought it was the right thing to do. Now, it seems that our presence has not been that helpful to my father, and I may have lost my husband. I think it's ironic that mother's death broke up my own marriage.

Families are affected in a variety of ways when a member of the system dies. Stress levels typically increase dramatically, immediately before or after the loved one's death; then they decrease gradually but unevenly over the course of extended bereavement. Much of the professional literature in the area has focused on helping a specific bereaved individual, such as the surviving spouse. In reality, there are usually numerous survivors in the extended family, including adult children and siblings of the deceased, grandchildren and even great-grandchildren, and other close relatives. Not only must various family members deal with the loss of the loved one, but they often also are confronted with the challenges of providing new kinds of support to the surviving spouse.

The degree to which the family needs help or can be an important source of support to the surviving spouse depends obviously on the family's history, resources, and relationships. Following is a series of questions adapted from Bob Knight's book, *Psychotherapy with Older Adults*, that we have found useful for assessing family dynamics.

1. How is the family defined? What is the nature of extended relationships (in-laws, uncles, aunts)? How strong and interconnected are these relationships?

2. What were relationships like between the deceased and other significant family members?

3. Did the spouse and the deceased have a good marital relationship? How is this relationship presently viewed by family members?

4. What role does each member play in the family system? How is this role being acted out during the bereavement process?

5. What plans has the family made to deal with the loss?

6. What plans, if any, has the family made to support the bereaved spouse?

We have found that traditional approaches to family therapy, which involve key members in the therapeutic process, can be very helpful for families that are functioning well and are sometimes useful for more dysfunctional systems. Families with stable histories and healthy relationships can often begin working immediately on bereavement issues and strategies for assisting the surviving spouse. In dysfunctional families, skillful interventions may not only prevent the emergence of more difficult problems that could unduly complicate the bereavement process but may also create opportunities to work on issues directly related to the loss of the loved one.

COGNITIVE INTERVENTIONS

Bereavement counseling approaches that emphasize cognitive strategies (or *cognitive-behavioral* as they are sometimes called) are based on the notion that bereavement causes stress and that coping resources to deal with stress can be strengthened by changes in a person's thoughts, attitudes, and beliefs. When applied to bereavement issues, cognitive approaches seek to redefine the stressors and/or the individual's belief system associated with the stressors. An initial therapeutic goal is to identify irrational or maladaptive thoughts and beliefs that are exacerbating the client's experience of stress. Following is a typical cognitive-behavioral approach to grief counseling. In this instance, note how quickly the therapist identifies negative thought patterns.

> *Client:* When my wife died I thought my life had come to an end. I said to myself, "I just can't live without her love and support."

In this case, the psychological distress associated with the actual loss experience is heightened by a maladaptive interpretation that life cannot go on without support from the deceased companion. Cognitive interventions identify such faulty assumptions and attempt to provide the bereaved adult with alternate ways of construing the experience so as to optimize the person's coping resources.

> *Therapist:* Is it true that life has actually stopped since your wife died? What might be a more accurate way to describe your current life situation?
>
> *Client:* Well, life hasn't actually ended, but it has become much harder since she passed away.
>
> *Therapist:* So life still is going on. I'm glad to hear that, but can you see how badly you choose to feel when you frame your wife's death in such catastrophic terms? What are some other ways you might choose to speak about your reaction to your wife's death that could give you more strength to deal with this loss in your life?

Laurie Powers and Bruce Wampold recently assessed the assumptions and interpretations made by each of 164 widows about the loss of a partner. Their purpose was to explore the relationship between a person's beliefs about the bereavement experience and psychosocial adjustment. They concluded that maladaptive beliefs associated with the grief reaction were strong predictors of subsequent adjustment. An example of a maladaptive assumption is this: "When I think about my husband's death, I am unable to do anything else in my life." There is a subtle but powerful difference between bereaved individuals reflecting on the significance to them of their deceased spouse and their assuming that they cannot function without the assistance of the departed. The implications for bereavement counselors are obvious.

Cognitive interventions can also be useful in treating the depressive reactions of survivors who are suffering from chronic and unresolved grief. Aaron Beck's cognitive therapy for depression is, of course, well known among mental health professionals and has fared well in recent outcome evaluation studies. In addition, Mardi Horowitz and his colleagues have developed a cognitively oriented approach for working with chronically grieving older adults that we have found very useful in our work with depressed survivors.

BEHAVIORAL INTERVENTIONS

Behavior therapy has also been successfully used with survivors who continue to struggle with long-term effects of bereavement. Strategies designed to increase positive events and minimize negative events often work well when protracted bereavement is interfering significantly with an individual's day-to-day coping. Brief behavior therapy has also been suggested for older adults in an acute stage of grief when their coping resources are temporarily overloaded. Evidence for the value of behavioral interventions is less clear, however, when applied to individuals experiencing common issues of grieving and in the early phases of the process. For this reason, we have limited our discussion of behavioral interventions to pathological or chronically unresolved grief reactions.

Desensitization techniques have been successfully applied to difficult cases of protracted bereavement. The approach involves helping such individuals confront their losses systematically and repeatedly across varying exposure domains. In addition to individual sessions with a behavior therapist, a variety of other methods are utilized including paper and pencil assignments, small group interactions with others with similar issues, and in vivo exposure to situations and stimuli that elicit intense grief and aversive emotion. The purpose of the therapy is to reduce and ultimately extinguish the problematic emotional responses that are initially cued by a host of thoughts and external stimuli. The presumption is that the individuals will then be able to learn more adaptive coping strategies and skills. Isaac Marks and several of his British colleagues have reported positive results with their comprehensive desensitization programs for the chronically bereaved, including success in reducing the negative emotions associated with protracted grief. They recommend their procedures for clients reporting stress-related grief of at least one year's duration when there is often a complicating diagnosis such as major depression.

Chronic grief reactions are often conceptualized by behavior therapists as intensely negative and rigid feedback loops from which the bereaved individual has not been able to escape. Negative affect is maintained and reinforced by thoughts, memories, and emotionally provocative stimuli that intrude frequently into the individual's day-to-day routine. The goal of behavior therapy is to help the individual control his or her response to such stimuli through systematic exposure to aversive situations and development of more positive emotional and behavioral responses. Behavioral techniques may also be an important element in counseling if the grieving individual begins to engage in substance abuse or related maladaptive behaviors to deal with intense feelings of grief. Behavioral techniques are also sometimes useful for individuals who are attempting to reenter the social system and develop a new and satisfactory social support network.

Skills Training Interventions

We have repeatedly found that many older adults become overwhelmed after their loved one's death because they are not prepared to negotiate the daily tasks of living that their deceased partner had performed. For example, older men are often unprepared to cook meals, wash clothes, and perform other routine household maintenance tasks. Similarly, older women often lack skills necessary for making home repairs and maintaining financial records. In fact, many contemporary older adults find themselves ill prepared to do common tasks required of widows or widowers. When older adults are simultaneously struggling with emotional bereavement issues, the problems are further compounded.

We have found that individuals who possess adequate home and personal maintenance skills feel better about themselves, are more independent, and in general are more effective in dealing with their grief. Conversely, those who are deficient in daily living skills find bereavement adjustment more difficult. Older men and women not only have differential skills regarding many necessary tasks of daily living, but also have common deficiencies, such as keeping up with legal or home maintenance needs. Bereaved individuals may be helped by family members and close friends who provide them with specific training in how to accomplish daily living tasks. In general, women are more likely to seek external help whereas men more typically rely on trial and error.

Behavioral competency interventions that identify and provide specialized training in daily survival skills can be of great value for several reasons. First, such training equips bereaved individuals with the "special expertise" they need to manage the tasks that had been performed by their deceased loved one. Second, successful mastery of new skills builds self-esteem and reinforces beliefs about personal competence. Finally, the process of training provides informal opportunities for the individual to socialize and interact with others while learning important life skills. We are not aware of any prior research on skill training interventions; however, it is an innovative approach with promise for helping bereaved older adults cope with issues of grief and mourning and prepare for healthy independent living.

PASTORAL/SPIRITUAL
GRIEF COUNSELING INTERVENTIONS

How can personal religiosity help the grieving older adult? And what role does spirituality play in the bereavement process? The first issue involves determining an individual's level of faith and related religious beliefs, and the second addresses how such beliefs influence the person's bereavement adjustment. We have found the following questions suggested by Jim Fowler useful in assessing an individual's religious beliefs and commitments: (1) To what or whom am I committed in life and in death? (2) With whom or what group do I share my most sacred and private hopes and dreams? (3) What power (or powers) do I rely on and believe I can trust?

Thoughtful responses to such questions can reveal important sources of inner strength that will help bereaved older adults come to terms with their loss. Answers may also indicate a level of internal conflict likely to complicate the bereavement process and engender feelings of guilt, fear, or anger. In either case, spiritual counseling may be an important activity in helping older adults work through difficult and value-laden issues. In processing such issues, older adults will often seek out trusted advisers who are related in some way to specific belief systems (for example, a priest or minister). An appropriate role for the mental health professional is to support clients' involvement with their religious or spiritual adviser, work to understand their beliefs and values, and then interpret the loss of the loved one with sensitivity in the context of the individual's belief system. The Spiritual Care Work Group of the International Work Group on Death, Dying and Bereavement has developed a set of guidelines that we have found helpful in working with grieving older adults. A basic premise in the guidelines is that death has powerful spiritual and social meanings beyond the biological cessation of life. Accordingly, there are important matters to consider when you are dealing with spiritual issues related to death and loss. These include the following:

1. It is critical that counselors who deal with spiritual issues be as free as possible from personal bias; this requires awareness of one's own beliefs and a capacity for restraint so as not to impose them on others.

2. Given our highly diverse and multicultural society, no single approach to spiritual care can be prescribed for all.

3. Spiritual needs and issues can be processed only after a careful review of the client's spiritual experiences and beliefs.

4. Trustworthy and knowledgeable members of the individual's spiritual community should be consulted and involved in the spiritual counseling process.

REMINISCENCE AND LIFE REVIEW INTERVENTIONS

Reminiscence as a therapeutic intervention has a long history in mental health work with older adults. The guiding feature of this approach has been the use of life review or guided reflection to examine previous personal experiences and unresolved issues that are presumably related to current problems with which the person is struggling. Some authors have suggested that life review interventions are especially appropriate for older adults dealing with what Erik Erikson described as the later-life crisis of "ego integrity versus despair." Ego integrity, according to Erikson, involves accepting and valuing one's life and facing death without great fear. Despair, on the other hand, means experiencing ongoing regret and continually speculating about how things might have been different. Life review methods are designed to promote ego integrity and an integrated sense of meaning regarding one's life. Thus, progressing through the life review process is a way to make peace with oneself by putting experiences across the life span into meaningful perspective.

When applied to issues of bereavement, life review methods may be especially useful in helping older adults evaluate the meaning to them of the deceased and the role of the departed person in the survivor's ego development (such as intimacy versus isolation, integrity versus despair). Basic elements in life review therapy include these:

1. Crystallizing memories of the deceased individual.
2. Accepting death as a normal part of the aging process.
3. Understanding that coping with the loss of a loved one is an important developmental task of later adulthood.
4. Ultimately experiencing peace and comfort by using critical memories to face and work through issues of loss and personal meaning.

When life review techniques are guided by trained and caring professionals, they can be powerful tools for helping survivors lay to rest unresolved issues associated with the deceased. In addition to verbal reminiscence, life reviews can take the form of written journals or narrative stories. Although we are unaware of any attempts to test the life review approach empirically, it is intuitively appealing, particularly as an intervention for non-pathological grieving and as a method for helping survivors integrate positive and negative feelings and consolidate memories of the deceased. We believe that this process, selectively applied, will enable survivors to move forward with a more integrated sense of self in the absence of the lost loved one.

In this chapter we have provided an overview of the bereavement process and examined various therapeutic techniques for assisting older survivors cope with the psychological experience of loss. It is clear that the emotional upheaval associated with the loss of an intimate family member, especially when one is in the twilight of life, can be intense and even debilitating. It is important that professional helpers, trained to understand and handle bereavement issues, be available in these times. Some approaches to bereavement counseling emphasize traditional approaches (behavior therapy, cognitive therapy) focused on issues of bereavement, that is, coming to terms with grief. Spiritual grief counseling and skills training interventions are examples of emerging techniques that show promise but need additional validation. Increasing numbers of mental health professionals are becoming interested in bereavement counseling with older adults. This is fortunate, as issues of loss, grief, and bereavement are common among a very fast-growing segment of our society's population. There is a need for skilled practitioners and researchers who understand the bereavement process and are knowledgeable about developmental issues of older adults. We hope this chapter has stimulated your interest and understanding and helped in your preparation for making contributions in this important area.

NOTES

P. 45, *professional help may be important as, for example, with complicated bereavement:* Strocbe, M. S., Stroebe, W., & Hansson, R. O. (Eds.). (1993). *Handbook of bereavement.* New York: Cambridge.

P. 46, *1990 census:* U.S. Bureau of the Census. (1991). Marital status and living arrangements: March, 1990. *Current population reports,* Series P–20, No. 450. Washington, DC: Government Printing Office.

P. 46, *the fastest growing age groups:* Atchley, R. C. (1994). *The social forces in aging.* Belmont, CA: Wadsworth.

P. 46, *a worldwide trend:* Olson, L. K. (1994). *The graying of the world.* New York: Hawthorne.

P. 46, *when the bereaved individual lacks coping resources:* Kastenbaum, R. (1995). *Death, society, and the human experience* (5th ed.). Boston: Allyn and Bacon.

P. 48, *Grief diminishes over time:* Worden, J. W. (1991). *Grief counseling and grief therapy: A handbook for the mental health practitioner* (2nd ed.). New York: Springer.

P. 48, *the grieving process as including at least three partially overlapping phases:* Shuchter, S. R., & Zisook, S. (1993). The course of normal grieving. In M. S. Stroebe, W. Stroebe, & R. O. Hansson (Eds.), *Handbook of bereavement* (pp. 44–61). New York: Cambridge.

P. 49, *the absence of a grief response:* Sanders, C. M. (1989). *Grief: The mourning after.* New York: Wiley.

P. 49, *the recently published* Diagnostic and Statistical Manual of Mental Disorders: American Psychiatric Association. (1994). *Diagnostic and statistical manual of mental disorders* (4th ed.). Washington, DC: American Psychiatric Association.

P. 50, *a useful marker of the individual's adaptation:* Worden, J. W. (1991). *Grief counseling and grief therapy: A handbook for the mental health practitioner* (2nd ed.). New York: Springer.

P. 51, *Such customs provide opportunities for survivors:* Dershimer, R. A. (1990). *Counseling the bereaved.* Elmsford, NY: Pergamon Press.

P. 51, *the Mexican-American custom of* el día de los muertos: West, J. O. (1988). *Mexican-American folklore* (p. 152). Little Rock, AR: August House, Inc.

P. 51, *Families with Mexican roots:* West, J. O. (1988). *Mexican-American folklore* (p. 152). Little Rock, AR: August House, Inc.

P. 53, *negative impact of bereavement on indices of psychological and physical health:* Hofer, M. (1984). Relationships as regulators: A psychobiologic perspective on bereavement. *Psychosomatic Medicine, 46,* 183–197; Stroebe, M. S., & Stroebe, W. (1993). The mortality of bereavement: A review. In M. S. Stroebe, W. Stroebe, & R. O. Hansson (Eds.), *Handbook of bereavement* (pp. 175–195). New York: Cambridge.

P. 53, *relationships between persistent unresolved bereavement and significant decreases in immune system functioning:* Irwin, M., & Pike, J. (1993). Bereavement, depressive symptoms, and immune function. In M. S. Stroebe, W. Stroebe, & R. O. Hansson (Eds.), *Handbook of bereavement* (pp. 160–171). New York: Cambridge.

P. 53, *bereaved older adults commonly report symptoms of depression and anxiety:* Dershimer, R. A. (1990). *Counseling the bereaved.* Elmsford, NY: Pergamon Press.

P. 53, *relationship between social withdrawal during bereavement . . . and vulnerability to illness:* Jacobs, S., & Ostefeld, A. (1980). The clinical management of grief. *Journal of the American Geriatrics Society, 38,* 331–335.

P. 54, *women tend to show better social adjustment following bereavement than men:* Lund, D. A., Caserta, M. S., & Dimond, M. F. (1986). Gender differences through two years of bereavement among the elderly. *The Gerontologist, 26,* 314–320; Lund, D. A., Caserta, M. S., & Dimond, M. F. (1989). Competencies, tasks of daily living, and adjustments to spousal bereavement in later life. In D. A. Lund (Ed.), *Older bereaved spouses: Research with practical applications* (pp. 135–152). New York: Taylor & Francis/Hemisphere; Umberson, D., Wortman, C. B., & Kesler, R. C. (1992). Widowhood and depression: Explaining long-term gender differences in vulnerability. *Journal of Health and Social Behavior, 33,* 10–24.

P. 54, *a supportive social network:* Lund, D. A. (1989). *Older bereaved spouses: Research with practical applications.* New York: Taylor & Francis/Hemisphere.

P. 57, *many potential benefits for those who attend self-help groups.* Hopmeyer, E., & Werk, A. (1994). A comparative study of family bereavement groups. *Death Studies, 18,* 69–83; Lund, D. A. (1989). *Older bereaved spouses: Research with practical applications.* New York: Taylor & Francis/Hemisphere; Osterweis, M., Solomon, F., & Green, M. (Eds.) (1984). *Bereavement: Reactions, consequences, and care.* Washington, DC: National Academy Press.

P. 58, *"Widow-to-widow" support:* Worden, J. W. (1991). *Grief counseling and grief therapy: A handbook for the mental health practitioner* (2nd ed.). New York: Springer; Hopmeyer, E., & Werk, A. (1994). A comparative study of family bereavement groups. *Death Studies, 18,* 69–83.

P. 61, *Bereavement counseling approaches that emphasize cognitive strategies:* Lazarus, R. S., & Folkman, S. (1984). Coping and adaptation. In W. D. Gentry (Ed.), *The handbook of behavioral medicine* (pp. 282–325). New York: Guilford; Beck, A. T., Rush, A. J., Shaw, B. F., & Emery, G. (1979). *Cognitive therapy of depression.* New York: Guilford; Horowitz, M. J., Marmar, C., Weiss, D. S., DeWitt, K., & Rosenbaum, R. (1984). Brief psychotherapy of bereavement reactions. *Archives of General Psychiatry, 41,* 438–444.

P. 63, *Behavior therapy has also been successfully used:* Raphael, B., Middleton, W., Martinek, N., & Misso, V. (1993). Counseling and therapy of the bereaved. In M. S. Stroebe, W. Stroebe, & R. O. Hansson (Eds.), *Handbook of bereavement* (pp. 427–453). New York: Cambridge; Dershimer, R. A. (1990). *Counseling the bereaved.* Elmsford, NY: Pergamon Press; Mawson, D., Marks, I. M., Ramm, L., & Stern, R. S. (1981). Guided mourning for morbid grief: A controlled study. *British Journal of Psychiatry, 138,* 185–193; Kavanagh, D. G. (1990). Towards a cognitive-behavioral intervention for adult grief reactions. *British Journal of Psychiatry, 157,* 373–383.

P. 64, *many older adults become overwhelmed after their loved one's death because they are not prepared to negotiate the daily tasks of living:* Lund, D. A. (1989). *Older bereaved spouses: Research with practical applications.* New York: Taylor & Francis/Hemisphere; Worden, J. W. (1991). *Grief counseling and grief therapy: A handbook for the mental health practitioner* (2nd ed.). New York: Springer.

P. 66, *what role does spirituality play in the bereavement process:* Fowler, J. W. (1981). *Stages of faith.* San Francisco: Harper & Row; Spiritual Care Work Group. (1990). Assumptions and principles of spiritual care. *Death Studies, 14,* 75–81.

P. 67, *Reminiscence as a therapeutic intervention:* Lewis, M. I., & Butler, R. N. (1974). Life review therapy: Putting memories to work in individual and group psychotherapy. *Geriatrics, 29,* 165–173; Erikson, E. H. (1963).

Childhood and society (2nd ed.). New York: Norton; Knight, B. (1986). *Psychotherapy with older adults.* Beverly Hills, CA: Sage; Sanders, C. M. (1989). *Grief: The mourning after.* New York: Wiley.

FOR FURTHER READING

American Psychiatric Association. (1994). *Diagnostic and statistical manual of mental disorders* (4th ed.). Washington, DC: American Psychiatric Association.

Atchley, R. C. (1994). *The social forces in aging.* Belmont, CA: Wadsworth.

Beck, A. T., Rush, A. J., Shaw, B. F., & Emery, G. (1979). *Cognitive therapy of depression.* New York: Guilford.

Dershimer, R. A. (1990). *Counseling the bereaved.* Elmsford, NY: Pergamon Press.

Erikson, E. H. (1963). *Childhood and society* (2nd ed.). New York: Norton.

Fowler, J. W. (1981). *Stages of faith.* San Francisco: Harper & Row.

Hofer, M. (1984). Relationships as regulators: A psychobiologic perspective on bereavement. *Psychosomatic Medicine, 46,* 183–197.

Hopmeyer, E., & Werk, A. (1994). A comparative study of family bereavement groups. *Death Studies, 18,* 69–83.

Horowitz, M. J., Marmar, C., Weiss, D. S., DeWitt, K., & Rosenbaum, R. (1984). Brief psychotherapy of bereavement reactions. *Archives of General Psychiatry, 41,* 438–444.

Irwin, M., & Pike, J. (1993). Bereavement, depressive symptoms, and immune function. In M. S. Stroebe, W. Stroebe, & R. O. Hansson (Eds.), *Handbook of bereavement* (pp. 160–171). New York: Cambridge.

Jacobs, S., & Ostefeld, A. (1980). The clinical management of grief. *Journal of the American Geriatrics Society, 38,* 331–335.

Kastenbaum, R. (1995). *Death, society, and the human experience* (5th ed.). Boston: Allyn and Bacon.

Kavanagh, D. G. (1990). Towards a cognitive-behavioral intervention for adult grief reactions. *British Journal of Psychiatry, 157,* 373–383.

Knight, B. (1986). *Psychotherapy with older adults.* Beverly Hills, CA: Sage.

Lazarus, R. S., & Folkman, S. (1984). Coping and adaptation. In W. D. Gentry (Ed.), *The handbook of behavioral medicine* (pp. 282–325). New York: Guilford.

Lewis, M. I., & Butler, R. N. (1974). Life review therapy: Putting memories to work in individual and group psychotherapy. *Geriatrics, 165–173.*

Lund, D. A. (1989). *Older bereaved spouses: Research with practical applications.* New York: Taylor & Francis/Hemisphere.

Lund, D. A. (1993). Widowhood: The coping response. In R. L. Kastenbaum (Ed.), *Encyclopedia of adult development* (pp. 537–541). Phoenix, AZ: Oryx Press.

Lund, D., & Caserta, M. (1992). Older bereaved spouses' participation in self-help groups. *Omega: Journal of Death & Dying, 25,* 47–61.

Lund, D. A., Caserta, M. S., & Dimond, M. F. (1986). Gender differences through two years of bereavement among the elderly. *The Gerontologist, 26,* 314–320.

Lund, D. A., Caserta, M. S., & Dimond, M. F. (1989). Competencies, tasks of daily living, and adjustments to spousal bereavement in later life. In D. A. Lund (Ed.), *Older bereaved spouses: Research with practical applications* (pp. 135–152). New York: Taylor & Francis/Hemisphere.

Lund, D. A., Caserta, M. S., & Dimond, M. F. (1993). The course of spousal bereavement in later life. In M. S. Stroebe, W. Stroebe, & R. O. Hansson (Eds.), *Handbook of bereavement* (pp. 240–254). New York: Cambridge.

Mawson, D., Marks, I. M., Ramm, L., & Stern, R. S. (1981). Guided mourning for morbid grief: A controlled study. *British Journal of Psychiatry, 138,* 185–193.

Norris, M. L., & Murrell, S. A. (1987). Older adult family stress and adaptation before and after bereavement. *Journal of Gerontology, 42,* 606–612.

Olson, L. K. (1994). *The graying of the world.* New York: Hawthorne.

Osterweis, M., Solomon, F., & Green, M. (Eds.). (1984). *Bereavement: Reactions, consequences, and care.* Washington, DC: National Academy Press.

Parkes, C. M. (1972). *Bereavement: Studies in grief in adult life.* New York: International Universities Press.

Powers, L. E., & Wampold, B. E. (1994). Cognitive-behavioral factors in adjustment to adult bereavement. *Death Studies, 18,* 1–24.

Raphael, B., Middleton, W., Martinek, N., & Misso, V. (1993). Counseling and therapy of the bereaved. In M. S. Stroebe, W. Stroebe, & R. O. Hansson (Eds.), *Handbook of bereavement* (pp. 427–453). New York: Cambridge.

Sanders, C. M. (1989). *Grief: The mourning after.* New York: Wiley.

Shuchter, S. R., & Zisook, S. (1993). The course of normal grieving. In M. S. Stroebe, W. Stroebe, & R. O. Hansson (Eds.), *Handbook of bereavement* (pp. 44–61). New York: Cambridge.

Silverman, P. (1986). *Widow-to-widow.* New York: Springer.

Spiritual Care Work Group. (1990). Assumptions and principles of spiritual care. *Death Studies, 14,* 75–81

Stroebe, M. S., & Stroebe, W. (1993). The mortality of bereavement: A review. In M. S. Stroebe, W. Stroebe, & R. O. Hansson (Eds.), *Handbook of bereavement* (pp. 175–195). New York: Cambridge.

Stroebe, M. S., Stroebe, W., & Hansson, R. O. (Eds.). (1993). *Handbook of bereavement.* New York: Cambridge.

Umberson, D., Wortman, C. B., & Kessler, R. C. (1992). Widowhood and depression: Explaining long-term gender differences in vulnerability. *Journal of Health and Social Behavior, 33,* 10–24.

U.S. Bureau of the Census. (1991). Marital status and living arrangements: March, 1990. *Current population reports,* Series P–20, No. 450. Washington, DC: Government Printing Office.

West, J. O. (1988). *Mexican-American folklore.* Little Rock, AR: August House.

Worden, J. W. (1991). *Grief counseling and grief therapy: A handbook for the mental health practitioner* (2nd ed.). New York: Springer.

3

ANXIETY DISORDERS

Javaid I. Sheikh

During my psychiatry residency in the early 1980s, I became interested in anxiety disorders and was involved in several clinical trials of anti-anxiety medications in younger populations. In subsequent years of my fellowship training as I became more interested in working with older patients, it seemed natural to combine my previous interest in anxiety with the new fascination of working with older adults. Consequently, I turned to the mental health literature for guidance in assessment and management techniques of the anxious elderly. To my amazement, during a time period generally considered the "decade of anxiety" in the psychiatric literature, I could find precious little on anxiety in the elderly. This began a decade-long passion for me of clinical practice and research in the area of anxiety in the elderly. Although there has been a gradual increase in published literature in this area over the last several years, anxiety remains one of the most underaddressed psychiatric problems of the elderly. This inattention continues despite a six-month prevalence of 19.7 percent for all anxiety disorders (that is, the anxiety symptoms must have occurred within the prior six months) in the age group who are sixty-five and over. To try to explain this apparent neglect of anxiety in the elderly, I examine here some of the problems associated with accurate assessment of anxiety in the elderly that have led to underdiagnosis of this group of disorders.

The chapter begins with a few words about the usage of the words *anxiety* and *anxiety disorders* in clinical literature. This is followed by an introduction of the classification of anxiety disorders based on the *Diagnostic and Statistical Manual of Mental Disorders*, fourth edition (DSM-IV), of the American Psychiatric Association. Then I provide brief descriptions of the two anxiety disorders most commonly seen in clinical settings, using clinical vignettes for elucidation. Following is a discussion of the overlap of anxiety with depression in clinical situations, with attention to some of the complications that can be associated with chronic anxiety. Finally, I provide an overview of treatment methods particularly suited for anxiety in the elderly.

ANXIETY AND ANXIETY DISORDERS

Anxiety is a sense of apprehension or nervousness about some future event. It is a rather complex, normal human emotion that has adaptive value in that it helps one anticipate, prepare for, and possibly avoid undesirable events. Such noxious events can vary from mundane concerns to life-threatening situations, depending on one's perspective.

Anxiety, however, can take on pathological features if it becomes excessive, as in the morbid anxiety seen in clinical situations. Such clinically significant anxiety can manifest itself as unusual worry about everyday problems—for example, one's living situation (as in the constant fear of being robbed that limits a person's activities even though he or she lives in an upscale and quite safe neighborhood), relationships (as in a person's fear that his or her spouse will leave despite forty-plus years of marriage), health (as in continuous concern about having some dangerous illness, leading a person to call his or her physicians frequently for every little symptom despite extensive medical evaluations revealing no major problems), or finances (as in unrelenting dread of becoming destitute despite being very well off and having a good financial plan monitored closely by family members).

In the other extreme, clinically significant anxiety may appear in the form of intense episodes of fear (panic attacks), usually accompanied by a multitude of cognitive, behavioral, and physiological symptoms. Typically patients with such panic attacks believe that they are going to suffer from heart attacks or lose their minds and tend to develop avoidance behavior, as described in more detail under the section on panic disorder. A constellation of several such symptoms of anxiety for an extended period of time leading to psychic pain and dysfunction is typically termed an *anxiety disorder*. The word *anxiety* is used in this text to signify pathological or clinically significant anxiety unless a different definition is clearly specified. The terms *anxiety disorders* and *anxiety syndromes* are used interchangeably. Table 3.1 lists several examples of symptoms in the cognitive, behavioral, and physiological domains that might be experienced by patients with various anxiety syndromes.

The generally accepted norm of defining anxiety disorders based on criteria from the DSM-IV has several advantages

Table 3.1
Multidimensional Symptoms of Anxiety

Cognitive	*Behavioral*	*Physiological*
Nervousness	Hyperkinesis	Muscle tension
Apprehension	Repetitive motor acts	Chest pain or
Worry	Phobias	tightness
Fearfulness	Pressured speech	Palpitations
Irritability	Startle response	Hyperventilation
Distractibility		Paresthesias
		Light-headedness
		Sweating
		Urinary frequency

Source: Sheikh, J. I. (1994). Clinical features of anxiety disorders. In J.R.M. Copeland, M. T. Abou-Saleh, & D. G. Blazer (Eds.), *Principles and practice of geriatric psychiatry*. Chichester, England: Wiley. Copyright ©1994 by John Wiley & Sons, Inc. Reprinted by permission.

including standardization, consistency, and ease of reimbursement from third-party insurance carriers. There are, however, some potential problems with these criteria. For example, they make no provision for the valuable subjective impressions of the clinician, nor do they provide for the subtleties of communication between the therapist and the patient. The dynamics of the patient's relationships with family members, spouse, or friends and their effects on the patient's mental health are also ignored. Thus a strict adherence to these criteria has the potential of creating a "tunnel vision" whereby the therapist is focusing on trying to "fit" the patient into a certain preconceived picture to the exclusion of developing an empathic and genuinely caring relationship with the patient. Further, in many cases and especially in the elderly, anxiety seems to be accompanied by varying degrees of depression, making more difficult the task of looking for neatly defined categories. With these caveats, Table 3.2 is

Table 3.2
DSM-IV Anxiety Disorders

- Panic Disorder
  with Agoraphobia
  without Agoraphobia
- Agoraphobia without history of Panic Disorder
- Social Phobia
- Specific Phobia
- Generalized Anxiety Disorder
- Obsessive-Compulsive Disorder
- Acute Stress Disorder
- Posttraumatic Stress Disorder
- Anxiety Disorder due to a General Medical Condition and Substance-Induced Anxiety Disorder
- Anxiety Disorder Not Otherwise Specified (NOS)

Source: American Psychiatric Association. (1994). *Diagnostic and statistical manual of mental disorders* (4th ed.). Washington, DC: Author.

based on a classification of anxiety disorders as presented in the DSM-IV.

A few general remarks about treatment issues, especially the context of treatment settings, are in order here before I discuss specific anxiety disorders. It is not very common for an anxious elderly patient to contact a mental health professional directly and ask to be treated for anxiety. In fact, most of these patients are seen in medical settings, as somatic symptoms of anxiety typically seem to suggest physical problems. It is usually after an extensive medical workup has revealed no physical illness explaining the symptoms and/or a trial of tranquilizers has failed to stop the patient from frequently calling the physician for multiple complaints that these patients are referred to mental health professionals.

If mental health professionals are to serve these patients better, we must work in close collaboration with our medical colleagues, as in many cases patients' care will be shared between the therapist providing psychological treatments and the physician prescribing medications. In the next sections, I offer brief descriptions of the two anxiety disorders most commonly seen in clinical situations, illustrated with two relevant clinical vignettes.

Panic Disorder

Panic disorder is manifested by recurrent episodes of severe anxiety or fear (panic attacks) that are accompanied by multiple somatic and cognitive symptoms. For example, during a panic attack one may experience palpitations, shortness of breath, chest pain or discomfort, sweating, hot and cold flashes, tingling in hands or feet, fear of dying, and fear of losing control. The panic attacks can occur either unexpectedly (uncued) or can be situationally bound (cued)—that is, occurring in specific feared situations.

Many patients with recurrent panic attacks develop a fear of being in places from which escape might be difficult if they were to experience an incapacitating panic attack. Such a fear of panic may lead over time to multiple avoidance responses (agoraphobia). Panic disorder is typically chronic in its course with frequent recurrences and remissions.

Preliminary investigations in our program suggest that many older patients with onset of panic attacks in early life seem to continue with their symptomatology in later life, while receiving inadequate or no treatment over the years. Also, although most cases of panic disorder begin in a person's twenties or thirties, de novo cases do occur in people fifty, sixty, or older, though this is relatively infrequent. Data from ongoing studies in our program suggest that in older populations, late-onset panic disorder (LOPD) may be characterized by fewer panic symptoms, less avoidance, and lower scores on somatization measures compared to early-onset panic disorder (EOPD). Here is an example of such a late-onset panic disorder:

MR. JONES

Mr. Jones, a sixty-six-year-old white male, was referred to me by a cardiologist after extensive evaluation of the patient's symptoms of chest pain, difficulty breathing, and palpitations did not reveal any physical illness. During my initial interview, Mr. Jones described experiencing rather classic panic attacks for the last several years. On more detailed questioning, I learned that the onset of these attacks seemed to be related temporally to a business failure and severe financial difficulties he had experienced approximately ten years earlier. During that time, his relationship with his wife also began deteriorating as he tried to play the role of a "strong man" and did not share with her the extent of his psychic pain. He also lost interest in any kind of sexual intimacy, which his wife perceived as rejection and an indication to her that she was getting "old" and was no longer attractive.

Meanwhile, the panic attacks started occurring with increasing frequency leading, on his part, to several half-hearted attempts on the insistence of his wife (who by now had become aware of his problem) to seek medical help. Over the last two years he had become uncomfortable driving and at the time of my evaluation, had not driven on the freeway for several months. A round of rather comprehensive medical/cardiological evaluations was prompted by his expressing passive suicidal wishes to his wife a few weeks earlier and his belief that he was soon going to die of a heart attack.

It became rather obvious after talking to both Mr. Jones and his wife that he was quite depressed in addition to having recurrent panic attacks. He was started on a trial of the antidepressant sertraline (Zoloft) in conjunction with couples therapy sessions where he and his wife explored relationship issues. Mr. Jones was symptom free after four weeks, at which point he was referred back to his primary care physician for continued antidepressant treatment and to a marriage therapist closer to his home (it took him and his wife about two hours to drive to my office) for continuation of work on marital issues.

Mr. Jones's case typifies a rather common dilemma seen in clinical settings, whereby an older patient with an underlying anxiety disorder presents with a multitude of physical symptoms for evaluation in a medical setting. For obvious reasons, the physical complaints have to be evaluated thoroughly to rule out any life-threatening medical illness, though many times this evaluation leads to a rather serious neglect of mental health problems. The need for closer collaboration by mental health professionals with other clinical disciplines cannot be overstated in such cases.

Generalized Anxiety Disorder

Generalized anxiety disorder is manifested by excessive anxiety or worry (apprehensive expectations) on most days for six months or longer. The worry is pervasive in that it focuses on many life circumstances and the person finds it difficult to focus attention on tasks at hand. The worry is associated with six of the following symptoms of motor tension, autonomic hyperactivity, or hyperarousal:

1. Motor tension: trembling, muscle tension, restlessness, fatigability
2. Autonomic hyperactivity: shortness of breath; rapid heart rate; sweating or cold, clammy hands; dry mouth; dizziness; digestive disturbances; hot flashes or chills; frequent urination; trouble swallowing or "lump in the throat"
3. Hyperarousal: feeling on edge, exaggerated startle response, difficulty concentrating, insomnia, irritability

Many elderly patients with this syndrome usually also present with features of depression, and addressing only one or the other of these conditions frequently can leave a partially treated patient with residual symptoms. Here is an example of an elderly woman with predominant anxiety mixed with mild depression:

MS. SMITH

Ms. Smith, a seventy-eight-year-old white female, was referred by her internist for complaints of increasing anxiety and depression. Her husband had passed away approximately twenty years earlier from cancer of the lungs. She stated that after the initial grieving process, lasting approximately a year or so, she got quite involved in various civic activities and did fine on her own for several years. But in the past few years some of her friends had also passed away and she started being increasingly fearful of her own death. Her concern had reached a point that she was afraid of sleeping at night for fear that she would not wake up; she had developed chronic insomnia. Her physician prescribed sleeping pills, which she took only infrequently.

During her interview with me she seemed quite anxious and irritable. In addition, she seemed to have some underlying depression as she talked about feeling lonely and quite isolated. She also expressed fear of being robbed at night, though she lived in a rather upper-class, safe neighborhood. Two of her four adult children also lived in the area with their families, but she would not call them frequently for fear of imposing on them.

Ms. Smith made it quite clear that she was not looking for any therapy but wanted some medication to "fix" her insomnia and anxiety. I was able to convince her that she needed both medication and therapy at this time. She was started on a low dose, short-acting benzodiazepine while attending therapy sessions initially on a weekly basis that later became biweekly. Some of these sessions also involved her two children and their spouses. Over the next six months she was able to express some of her feelings of resentment and anger toward her children for not manifesting caring or concern for her. Meanwhile, her children were able to understand her concerns better; they became more involved in her care, with closer and more frequent contacts. She was also able to rejoin a group of women for social activities. Her medication was gradually tapered until she takes it very infrequently, not more than once a week. Therapy sessions have also been reduced to infrequent monitoring sessions.

Ms. Smith's situation reminds us of the importance of the context of presenting symptoms and the dynamics of family issues in such cases. In retrospect, one can make a valid argument that the primary reason for Ms. Smith's anxiety symptoms was her psychosocial concerns. These could have been addressed with therapy alone, without the use of medications. However, one has to be cognizant of the patient's expectations and be flexible about modifying one's therapeutic strategies. Our first and foremost task is to engage the patient in treatment. That often requires not adhering rigidly to one's own beliefs about the process and structure of treatment and making a patient an equal partner from the beginning in this evolving process. For a nonmedical therapist in this situation, it would have meant working closely with a physician for medication prescription while helping Ms. Smith identify and explore psychological issues in therapy and work toward their resolution.

ASSESSMENT OF ANXIETY

It is important for a nonphysician therapist to recognize that a proper assessment of an anxious elderly patient in an office-based practice can be confounded by several factors. Earlier in this chapter, I discussed the possibility that anxiety disorders could be neglected when the focus of the clinician is to look for a physical illness as the basis of anxiety symptoms. The converse is also quite true, as many medical conditions can masquerade as physical manifestations of anxiety. These may include cardiovascular problems (such as angina pectoris, cardiac arrhythmias), endocrine disorders (such as hyperthyroidism, hypoglycemia), pulmonary disorders (such as pulmonary embolism, chronic obstructive pulmonary disease), and neurological illnesses (such as temporal lobe epilepsy, movement disorders).

Remember that any major medical illness can produce anxiety as an expected response to a physical stressor. In addition, many medications can produce symptoms of anxiety. Examples of such medications include sympathomimetic compounds such as pseudoephedrine hydrochloride in over-the-counter drugs, thyroid replacement therapies, neuroleptics, antidepressants, and steroids, among others. Withdrawal from sedatives, hypnotics, or alcohol can also produce anxiety. Lastly, depression can be the possible principal disorder with concomitant anxiety as a co-morbid condition. Though these factors can be present in young patients as well, they are far more common among the elderly and thus more relevant to their care. A therapist should keep these caveats in mind during any evaluation of geriatric anxiety, which is usually accomplished in three major ways: clinical evaluation, assessment by rating scales, and laboratory investigations.

Clinical Evaluation

The clinical evaluation of anxiety includes a history of present and past illness (for example, panic disorder usually has remissions and relapses), medication usage (cold medications, anticholinergic medications, or others), drug (such as over-the-counter hypnotic or stimulant) and alcohol use, and a family history (such as panic disorder). A mental status examination may reveal some of the cognitive and behavioral signs and symptoms of anxiety including apprehension, distractibility, hyperkinesis, and startle response.

Psychometric Assessment

Clinical evaluation in itself may not be sufficient for a proper assessment of anxiety in some elderly patients and should be aided by the use of anxiety rating scales. In addition to serving as assessment tools, the anxiety rating scales can also serve as instruments to document effectiveness of various psychological and pharmacological therapeutic interventions when used before beginning and after completing the course of treatment. These are primarily of two kinds: observer-rated and self-rated scales. The most commonly used observer-rated scale is the Hamilton Anxiety Rating Scale (HARS). It has fourteen items consisting of eighty-nine symptoms measuring psychic and somatic components of anxiety, with each item rated on five levels of severity from "none" (0) to "very severe" (4). A rating of 18 or above is generally considered to be suggestive of clinically significant anxiety. HARS should, however, be used selectively, as many elderly people can be very fatigued by going through the entire list of eighty-nine symptoms. Also, many elderly tend to overendorse the somatic items, an observation you should consider in interpreting the score.

There are several self-rated anxiety scales including the State-Trait Anxiety Inventory (STAI), the Beck Anxiety Inventory (BAI), and the Symptom Checklist (90-Item)–Revised (SCL-90-R), which can be quite useful as adjuncts to clinical evaluation. The most frequently used self-rated scale is the STAI. The STAI consists of two twenty-item scales, the STAI-A-State scale measuring anxiety as an emotional state currently, and the STAI-A-Trait scale measuring anxiety as a relatively stable personality trait. In clinical situations, STAI-A-State seems preferable as it provides an avenue to measure changes in severity of anxiety in response to therapeutic interventions. Patients are instructed to check the responses correctly describing the intensity of their feelings for each item on a scale of 1 (not at all) to 4 (very much so). A modified form for geriatric populations is available. Other commonly used scales include the SCL-90-R and the BAI. A more detailed discussion of the advantages and disadvantages of various anxiety rating scales in the elderly is available in Sheikh (1991).

Laboratory Tests

Laboratory tests can aid in diagnosing anxiety disorders induced by underlying medical conditions and substance abuse. A complete blood count, electrocardiogram, vitamin B_{12} and folate levels, thyroid function tests, blood glucose levels, and a drug/alcohol screening can be helpful when used appropriately to rule out medical causes of anxiety. A nonmedical therapist needs to be aware of the value of these tests and should bring them up as points of discussion when sharing the care of an anxious elderly patient with a physician or when working as a member of a multidisciplinary treatment team in hospital settings. Note, however, that these tests are mentioned only as aids to diagnosis, to be used when properly indicated; in no way should they replace a good clinical evaluation supplemented by psychometric assessment.

Co-Morbidity of Anxiety

Anxiety in the elderly can be associated with several co-morbid conditions, both medical and psychiatric. It is important for the clinician to keep these conditions in mind as they can confound the symptom picture as well as complicate the treatment strategies.

Examples of medical illnesses associated with anxiety include chronic obstructive pulmonary disease (COPD), hypertension, and overactive thyroid (hyperthyroidism). There is also some evidence that anxiety might act as a predictor of future morbidity in cancer patients. Though knowledge is lacking about the specific mechanism by which anxiety and autonomic arousal can cause tissue damage, it is possible that the elderly accumulate deleterious effects of anxiety over many years and are thus at risk for the cumulative adverse effects of anxiety on physical functioning. Of relevance, there is some evidence that panic disorder increases mortality from cardiovascular causes among male patients.

In terms of psychiatric co-morbidity, clinicians working with the elderly need to be aware of high rates of co-morbidity between anxiety disorders and alcohol abuse. Some of the alcohol abuse in such cases may be related to attempts at self-medication. Thus, a careful evaluation of a history of alcohol abuse is important, and appropriate therapeutic referrals for that problem should be made when indicated.

Sleep disturbances are also very common in patients with anxiety. On the other hand, anxiety appears to be a common finding in patients with chronic insomnia. Specifically, anxiety disorders can create problems in initiating and maintaining sleep as well as significantly affecting its quality. Inquiry into the duration and quality of sleep should thus be an integral component of any management plans for geriatric anxiety. Such inquiry should take into account the common clinical observation that older people tend to go to bed early and may nap during the day, so a seemingly early wake-up time may not be so in reality and the total amount of sleep including nap time may be sufficient for many. For a detailed discussion of assessment and therapeutic approaches to insomnia in the elderly, please refer to Dr. Friedman's chapter (Chapter Four) in this volume.

Finally, anxiety disorders are very commonly accompanied by depression and seem to increase the risk of suicide. Thus the clinician assessing the extent of anxiety in an elderly patient should always inquire about any suicidal ideation or plan.

Clinical Differentiation of Anxiety from Depression

As mentioned elsewhere in this chapter, depression is a very frequent accompaniment of anxiety and vice versa. A recurring theme in the mental health literature is the unresolved and somewhat controversial issue of whether anxiety and depression lie on the same continuum or are separate conditions. Despite recent advances in our knowledge about the phenomenology and biology of these conditions, we do not seem any closer to resolving this controversy.

In clinical situations, it may be more common in the elderly to see a mixed-symptom picture of anxiety and depression rather than a pure anxiety disorder. For example, someone may present with a combination of excessive worrying (anxiety), insomnia (anxiety and depression), memory problems (anxiety and depression), lack of energy (depression), sad mood (depression), and a sense of helplessness (anxiety). In a situation like this, a therapist may not be able to tease apart anxiety from depression. In other instances, with some careful evaluation, a clinician can discern whether anxiety or depression is the primary disorder. Where possible, such differentiation is important, as therapeutic strategies for anxiety and depression can differ in their focus and scope. Table 3.3 summarizes some of the helpful distinctions between anxiety states and depressive syndromes.

Table 3.3
Differences Between Anxiety and Depression

Depression	*Anxiety*
Symptomatology	
Depressed mood	Anxious mood
Worse in A.M.	Worse in P.M.
Lack of energy	Agitation
Terminal insomnia	Initial insomnia
Feelings of guilt and anhedonia are more common.	Panic attacks, phobias, and symptoms of autonomic activation are more common.
Premorbid Personality	
Patients usually have better adjusted premorbid personalities, but variable. Usually more introverted, and during depression, patients might appear more dependent and clingy.	Patients tend to have poorly adjusted personalities. They appear to be immature, dependent, hypersensitive, and histrionic. Usually more avoidant with "anxious temperament."
Clinical Course	
Usually a history of regular cycles of depression with intervening periods of remission.	Irregularly recurrent with somewhat incomplete periods of remission.
Treatment	
Cognitive-behavioral therapy, antidepressant medications, electroconvulsive therapy (ECT)	Cognitive-behavioral therapy, benzodiazepines, buspirone, antidepressant medications

Source: Sheikh, J. I. (1994). Clinical features of anxiety disorders. In J.R.M. Copeland, M. T. Abou-Saleh, & D. G. Blazer (Eds.), *Principles and practice of geriatric psychiatry*. Chichester, England: Wiley. Copyright ©1994 by John Wiley & Sons, Inc. Reprinted by permission.

MANAGEMENT OF
ANXIETY

Anxiety can be managed by the use of either psychological or pharmacological approaches. As mentioned in the introductory section, such management usually entails a combination of the two approaches, with a therapist and a physician sharing care of a patient.

Irrespective of the specific treatment strategies, general principles of management remain the same. First, therapists working with the elderly need to be keenly aware of psychosocial issues unique to this group. These include, among others, a realistic possibility of multiple losses of family and friends, gradually deteriorating physical functioning with its psychological consequences of loss and apprehension about the future, fear of crime, and apprehension about driving long distances, including the drive necessary to come to the therapist. Second, clinicians need to show sensitivity to patients while inquiring about their symptoms, as many elders do not seem to be particularly comfortable about talking to therapists. Third, including the family members in the treatment plan whenever possible should be a priority, as this strategy can make the difference between treatment success and failure. Finally, educating patients in detail about the disorder, thereby making them partners in the treatment process and instilling hope that their suffering can be alleviated, is of paramount importance.

Psychological Treatments

Psychological methods of treatment can be broadly divided into traditional psychotherapy and cognitive-behavioral techniques. The following descriptions are presented with office-based practice in mind, though with some modifications they can be equally useful for a variety of settings, including hospitals and home-based visits.

Traditional Psychotherapy. Psychodynamic psychotherapy can be very useful in a broad context by providing patients with a framework to learn about their conflicts and to gain insight into their behaviors. However, targeting it specifically to achieve symptom resolution in anxiety disorders is generally not very successful. The mental health literature indicates rather clearly that with the possible exception of generalized anxiety disorder, traditional psychodynamic psychotherapy has shown limited usefulness in most other anxiety disorders. One reason may be the relatively open-ended nature of such therapy, which creates difficulty in targeting specific symptoms systematically. The role of traditional therapy in anxiety disorders thus appears to be mostly nonspecific and supportive.

Cognitive-Behavioral Therapy. Cognitive-behavioral therapy (CBT) is the cornerstone of psychological treatments for anxiety disorders in both young and old. Typically, this approach consists of ten to sixteen sessions, beginning initially on a weekly basis but usually spread to longer intervals after the tenth session. The basic premise of CBT for anxiety disorders is that faulty thinking patterns manifested by specific cognitions—with themes of fear of death, illness, or loss of control—underlie symptoms of anxiety and result in maladaptive and avoidant behaviors. Working with the elderly to identify such thinking patterns and replacing them with more adaptive thoughts and behaviors is the goal of treatment.

A number of cognitive and behavioral interventions are efficacious for the treatment of generalized anxiety, panic disorder, phobias, and obsessive-compulsive disorder. In our program, we typically use CBT techniques modified after two pioneers in the field, Beck and Barlow, whose books *Anxiety Disorders and Phobias* and *Anxiety and Its Disorders* we strongly recommend for therapists venturing into this field for the first time. CBT procedures for anxiety disorders generally fall into three main categories: cognitive therapy, relaxation training, and behavioral therapy. In the following sections, I describe these procedures using their application in panic disorder over a ten-session period as an example (see Table 3.4).

Cognitive therapy is based on the hypothesis that patients with panic disorder typically misinterpret bodily sensations associated with normal anxiety (such as increased heart rate) as being frightening, dangerous, or even lethal. These catastrophic cognitions in turn add to the physiologic sensations normally experienced during anxiety (see Table 3.1). The perceptions start a vicious cycle of escalating anxiety and autonomic activation leading to full-blown panic attacks.

Our goal, therefore, is to replace this tendency to misinterpret bodily sensations and to replace catastrophic cognitions with more adaptive thoughts. We typically begin the therapeutic process by providing education in the first session about physiological changes normally occurring during anxiety. This is followed by information about the maladaptive cognitions. During subsequent sessions we ask patients to identify their fearful cognitions and to start monitoring them. Patients are then taught cognitive restructuring techniques including thought stopping, refocusing, and reframing. They are given homework to practice these techniques and we monitor their progress during the sessions. This monitoring includes a discussion and analysis of both good and bad days that they might have had between the sessions.

Relaxation training consists primarily of tension-relaxation exercises of different muscle groups from head to toe. Typically, we begin with sixteen muscle groups and then gradually reduce them to eight and then to four. In addition, we teach cue-controlled relaxation as a coping strategy when patients may enter anxiety-provoking situations or are about to panic. We also teach the elderly to use diaphragmatic breathing to relax when they begin to panic.

Behavioral therapy in the form of exposure has been the mainstay for managing phobias for several years. This therapy can involve either real-life exposure (in vivo) to the phobic situation

Table 3.4
Cognitive-Behavior Therapy for Panic Disorder

Session	Cognitive Therapy	Relaxation Therapy	Exposure Therapy
1	• Present rationale and basic introduction of physical changes during anxiety and panic	• Present rationale and data collection techniques	• Introduction and treatment rationale
2	• Introduce techniques for monitoring cognitions • Further develop education of panic physiology	• Present eight-muscle group relaxation and assign practice of homework	
3	• Introduce faulty logic • Begin visualization • Assign homework practice	• Eight-muscle with discrimination training • Assign practice • Breathing retraining	
4	• Introduce cognitive coping skills	• Present four-muscle group training • Breathing retraining	
5	• Present logic and rationale for "ten rules for coping with panic" and "tips for effective practice" • Present self-statements, hypothesis testing and cognitive coping strategies	• Four-muscle group with discrimination training • Assign practice • Breathing retraining	• Present self-exposure rationale and guidelines • Assign imaginal exposure hierarchy
6	• Hypothesis testing and cognitive management procedures	• Four-muscle with discrimination "cue-controlled" • Breathing retraining "cue-controlled"	• Begin first self-exposure homework discussion and assignment

(continued)

Table 3.4 *(continued)*
Cognitive-Behavior Therapy for Panic Disorder

Session	Cognitive Therapy	Relaxation Therapy	Exposure Therapy
7	• Hypothesis testing and cognitive management procedures	• "Cue-controlled" muscle and breathing training	• Self-exposure homework
8	• Generalized practice • Present rationale for "good/bad" days and "setbacks vs. relapses" • Termination issues	• Generalized practice	• Generalized practice
9	• Generalized practice • Termination issues	• Generalized practice	• Generalized practice • "Troubleshooting"
10	• Generalized practice • Review of cognitive procedures and rationale • "Troubleshooting" • Planning ahead	• Generalized practice	• Generalized practice • "Troubleshooting" • Planning ahead

Source: Adapted from Barlow, D. H., & Cerny, J. A. *Psychological Treatment of Panic.* New York: The Guilford Press, Treatment Manuals for Practitioners, 1988, p. 86. Reprinted by permission.

or fantasy exposure (in vitro) using imagery to recreate the phobic situation. Some of the studies suggest that live exposure might be better than fantasy exposure whereas others document no difference. Both techniques usually require graded exposure over a period of a few weeks to the feared object or situation, whether in real life or in fantasy. We typically prefer a graduated in vivo exposure as it seems more efficient even if both are equally effective, as fantasy exposure would ultimately require transfer to real-life situations. The following case illustrates the implementation of psychotherapy and cognitive-behavioral therapy procedures in an integrated, multicomponent cognitive-behavioral treatment format.

MARIA

The patient, Maria, was an eighty-year-old married white female who presented with a long-standing history of panic disorder and agoraphobia. The patient clearly remembered the onset of her first panic attack at age thirteen in her school classroom. The incident was frightening and disturbing. Her panics continued. A few years later, in her sophomore year in high school, she was embarrassed by a teacher in class and experienced a major panic attack during this incident. She stopped attending school shortly thereafter. She further "educated" herself by reading. Later, in her early twenties, she married. Prior to her retirement some twenty years earlier, she had been a successful business administrator. In her advanced years she was still an avid reader with a very sharp mind.

Her interview revealed that she had periods when the symptoms were apparently in some degree of remission. However, this woman's panic disorder had been more or less chronic since that classroom event so long ago. Her severe generalized agoraphobia had likewise waxed and waned over time. At initial clinical diagnostic interview, Maria met DSM-III-R criteria for panic disorder (moderate) with severe agoraphobia. She requested cognitive-behavioral therapy for her condition.

PANIC-ASSOCIATED COGNITIONS

Maria's thoughts that occurred during panic attacks (and caused her moderate or greater levels of anxiety) included these: I may faint; people will stare at me; I may become hysterical; I may drive off the road and crash; I may scream; I may not be able to move from one spot; I may be put into a mental hospital; people will laugh at me; I may lose my balance and fall; I may die; I may lose control of my bowels; I will be trapped; others will think I am weird; I am going crazy; I may lose control (generally of myself).

PANIC-ASSOCIATED PHYSICAL SYMPTOMS

The typical physical symptoms Maria experienced during a panic attack were feeling unsteady and as if she might faint, shaking, hot flashes, shortness of breath, difficulty breathing, rapid heart beat, and feeling as if things around her were unreal.

PANIC-ASSOCIATED AVOIDANCE BEHAVIORS

Maria's agoraphobia (avoidance behaviors) was assessed and found to be generalized to a wide variety of situations, including the following, in which she avoided being alone at home, being alone away from home, crossing busy or wide streets alone, shopping alone in a big store, going to bed unless she was fully clothed (in case she needed to get out of the house in a hurry for help with panic), and taking a shower with the shower door or bathroom door closed (thus avoiding a "closed-in" feeling).

COGNITIVE THERAPY

Maria was given an extensive rationale concerning the etiology and maintenance of anxiety and panic, which stressed the essentially non-pathological, nondangerous aspects of the anxiety reaction (such as "the feelings of panic are not harmful; they are normal bodily responses 'gone a little haywire'"; "I don't have to be afraid of these physical symptoms any more"). The importance of inappropriate and maladaptive cognitions and their roles in initiating and maintaining attacks was discussed at length during all therapy sessions. Cognitive techniques such as the following were used:

- Thought-stopping ("There I go again thinking that I may die. STOP!")

- Refocusing ("I recognize that these symptoms of panic are extremely uncomfortable. However, I *can* sleep without my blouse and skirt.")

- Reframing ("It just looks like a small shower and bathroom; however, there really is sufficient room inside.")

- Changing self-statements (from "I just *can't* walk down this side-walk," to "If I just try I *can* walk, if even for a few steps at first.")

- Faulty logic analyses (certainties versus possibilities: "I am afraid that I will have a heart attack and die from these symptoms. But I have never actually had a heart attack as the result of having a panic attack. So, what really *is* the chance [probability] that I will do that now?")

RELAXATION THERAPY

Maria was trained to differentiate tension from relaxation and to use relaxation to decrease her general psychophysiological arousal. She also understood that she could use these techniques as a coping strategy for anxiety and panic attacks. Specific techniques included diaphragmatic breathing and cue-controlled relaxation. She practiced each newly introduced skill in session and subsequently as homework assignments. For example, Maria was instructed to use diaphragmatic breathing and cue-controlled muscle relaxation as coping skills whenever she took a shower. This technique facilitated her behavioral practices and ultimately enabled her to take a shower with both shower and bathroom doors closed.

BEHAVIORAL THERAPY

Out-of-session self-exposure "homework" allowed Maria to experience feelings of anxiety and to test and develop her growing abilities (skills) to remediate her dysfunctional (avoidance) behaviors and thoughts. She performed the behavioral homework assignments in a graduated hierarchical fashion; she approached the easiest situations first, then worked her way up to being in some of her most difficult situations using repeated self-directed in vivo exposure trials. These are practice sessions in specific situations that the patient does repeatedly and without the assistance or modeling of the therapist until he or she experiences little or no anxiety. The therapist discussed Maria's self-directed exposure practices with her after each homework trial and planned upcoming homework assignments at the end of each session.

For Maria, a specific example of the implementation of behavioral self-exposure to feared situations was learning to become comfortable taking a shower with both shower and bathroom doors closed. A graduated hierarchy of exposure was created that required Maria to initiate the behavior change by taking her shower as usual at first, then closing the door about six inches and letting any anxiety "peak and pass," then opening the door fully. After a minute or so, she was to repeat this trial and again note physical symptoms and thoughts related to her anxiety. She would repeat this small behavior until it no longer was arousing.

The next step during the same (or subsequent) shower was to close the door twelve inches and to repeat the procedure until she could remain in the situation with little to no anxiety. By extrapolation she learned to shower with the door closed. When this became "routine," she added to the procedure the closing of the bathroom door, using the same model. Eventually this too became the norm.

Throughout the repeated trials, she was to be cognizant of her panic-associated thoughts and physical symptoms, which she would record at the end of each trial. During each trial she would practice relaxation (breathing and cue-controlled muscle relaxation), panic-coping cognitions (for example, "My heart is pounding, but I have experienced this before; I will be all right") and strategies. Thus all elements of cognitive, relaxation, and behavioral therapies were used together to help her effect change.

TRADITIONAL PSYCHOTHERAPY

In Maria's case, traditional psychodynamic therapy was used in conjunction with the above-described procedures. Psychodynamic therapy was employed to elicit Maria's thoughts and feelings about the incidents that she believed initiated and maintained her panic-associated thoughts and consequent avoidance behaviors. Her degree of marital distress, her sense of dependence and independence, her feelings toward her situation and husband, and other issues were also explored. Thus, a more "traditional psychotherapy" combined with cognitive, relaxation, and behavioral therapies effected major positive changes in the life of this elderly woman.

Pharmacological Treatments

A detailed description of pharmacological strategies is beyond the scope of this chapter. However, in many cases, nonmedical therapists will be sharing patients' care with a physician in outpatient settings or working as members of a treatment team on an inpatient unit that may include physicians, nurses, social workers, and physical therapists. Thus a working knowledge of pharmacological strategies can be quite helpful.

As a general rule when prescribing any medications to the elderly, physicians need to consider age-related physiological changes in absorption, distribution, protein binding, metabolism, and excretion of drugs. In addition to significantly altering plasma levels of drugs, these changes can lead to excessive accumulation of medications in various body tissues, making elderly patients particularly prone to experiencing toxic side effects even at dose ranges average for the general population. Hence the adage, "Start low and go slow" for the elderly population.

As for specific treatment strategies, controlled clinical trials of anti-anxiety compounds (anxiolytics) in the elderly are scarce and thus the standard practice is to use anxiolytics based on effectiveness data in younger populations. Numerous compounds belonging to several different classes have been used as anxiolytics over the past few decades. These include alcohol, barbiturates, antihistamines, antidepressants, neuroleptics, beta blockers, benzodiazepines, and azapirones. The most commonly prescribed anxiolytics at present include benzodiazepines, antidepressants (particularly selective serotonin reuptake inhibtors [SSRIs]), and the azapirone, buspirone. In general, these are all well tolerated by elderly patients and quite effective if used judiciously.

ANXIETY AND AGITATION ASSOCIATED WITH DEMENTIA

When anxiety and agitation are accompanied by dementia, a unique set of problems occurs. A geropsychologist may be called for consultations by nursing home staff to deal with anxiety and agitation in a patient with dementia. This is a situation where a truly multidisciplinary approach is needed, with a physician prescribing medications to control anxiety and agitation, a geropsychologist designing and recommending behavioral strategies to minimize stimulation and to alleviate the patient's fears (ranging from suspiciousness to frank delusions), and the nursing staff implementing those strategies while monitoring changes in the patient's behavior. Anxiety and agitation in these patients can also reflect underlying depression and acute medical problems, though most commonly it appears to be a behavioral syndrome depicting a gradual progression of dementia.

Several classes of compounds have been used in the management of severe anxiety and agitation associated with dementia. These include benzodiazepines, neuroleptics, SSRIs, trazadone, buspirone, beta blockers, and anticonvulsants. Benzodiazepines appear to be useful in clinical situations as short-term measures, possibly because of their sedating effects. However, their long-term usage can lead to several complications including confusion, loss of coordination and risk of falls, and paradoxical reactions. If one chooses to use benzodiazepines, short-acting compounds such as lorazepam and oxazepam may be preferable because of their smaller risk of accumulation. A more detailed discussion of this problem and its management is presented in Dr. Streim's chapter in this book, Chapter Seven.

∾

Despite being among the most common mental health problems of the elderly, anxiety disorders are usually unrecognized by clinicians. There are two major reasons for this phenomenon. First, older patients with anxiety typically present with physical complaints and this tends to divert the attention of the clinician away from psychological issues. Second, many of these patients also have concomitant depression, which is usually better recognized among clinicians and thus tends to become the primary focus of assessment and treatment.

Although anxiety disorders mostly begin at a young age, they usually continue into old age if not treated properly. A typical older, anxious patient frequently visits his or her primary care physician over the years and usually gets prescribed sedatives of various kinds. Most of the time, the patient's compliance with these medications is not very good, as underlying psychological issues are not addressed in these treatment settings. This lack of compliance in turn leads to a relatively unsuccessful treatment response and a feeling in such patients of being misunderstood.

If anxiety is assessed properly, effective treatments are available that can minimize pain and suffering as well as prevent complications like alcohol abuse and physical co-morbidity. In practice, a combination of psychological and pharmacological strategies is usually needed. Examples of such combination approaches are described earlier in this chapter in the cases of both Mr. Jones and Ms. Smith. Thus, for a nonmedical therapist, an ongoing relationship with a physician or a group of physicians is necessary to provide the most effective care for such patients. Proper education of the patient and involvement of family members or other caregivers from the beginning of treatment is imperative to ensure the patient's compliance with the treatment regimen. Recent advances in treatment, both psychological and pharmacological, will continue to improve the outlook for these patients for better functioning and a more optimistic prognosis.

NOTES

P. 75, *a six-month prevalence of 19.7 percent:* Blazer, D., George, L. K., & Hughes, D. (1991). The epidemiology of anxiety disorders: An age comparison. In C. Salzman & B. D. Lebowitz (Eds.), *Anxiety in the elderly.* New York: Springer.

P. 76, *DSM-IV:* American Psychiatric Association. (1994). *Diagnostic and statistical manual of mental disorders* (4th ed.). Washington, DC: Author.

P. 80, *Data from ongoing studies in our program:* Sheikh, J. I., King, R. J., & Taylor, C. B. (1991). Comparative phenomenology of early-onset versus late-onset panic attacks: A pilot survey. *American Journal of Psychiatry, 148*(9), 1231–1233.

P. 85, *HARS:* Hamilton, M. (1959). The assessment of anxiety states by rating. *British Journal of Medical Psychology, 32,* 50–55.

P. 86, *STAI:* Speilberger, C., Gorsuch, R. L., & Lushene, R. (1970). *Manual for the State-Trait Anxiety Inventory.* Palo Alto, CA: Consulting Psychologists Press.

P. 86, *BAI:* Beck, A. T., Epstein, N., Brown, G., & Steer, R. A. (1988). An inventory for measuring clinical anxiety: Psychometric properties. *Journal of Consulting and Clinical Psychology, 56,* 893–897.

P. 86, *SCL-90-R:* Derogatis, L. R. (1977). *The SCL-90-R.* Baltimore: Clinical Psychometric Research Unit, Johns Hopkins School of Medicine.

P. 86, *A more detailed discussion of the advantages:* Sheikh, J. I. (1991). Anxiety rating scales for the elderly. In C. Salzman & B. D. Lebowitz (Eds.), *Anxiety in the elderly.* New York: Springer.

P. 87, *Anxiety in the elderly can be associated with:* George, L. K., Landerman, R., Blazer, D., & Melville, M. L. (1989). Concurrent morbidity between physical and mental illness: An epidemiologic examination. In L. L. Carstensen & J. M. Neale (Eds.), *Mechanisms of psychological influence on physical health, with special attention to the elderly.* New York: Plenum.

P. 87, *Of relevance, there is some evidence:* Coryell, W. (1988). Mortality of anxiety disorders. In R. Noyes, M. Roth, & G. D. Burrows (Eds.), *Handbook of anxiety: Vol. 2. Classification, etiological factors and associated disturbances.* Amsterdam, Netherlands: Elsevier Science Publishers.

P. 91, *Anxiety Disorders and Phobias:* Beck, A. T., & Emery, G. (1985). *Anxiety disorders and phobias: A cognitive perspective.* New York: Basic Books.

P. 91, *Anxiety and Its Disorders:* Barlow, D. H. (1988). *Anxiety and its disorders: The nature and treatment of anxiety and panic.* New York: Guilford Press.

P. 92, *In the following sections, I describe:* Swales, P. J., Solfvin, J. F., & Sheikh, J. I. (1996). Cognitive-behavior therapy in older panic disorder patients. *American Journal of Geriatric Psychiatry, 4*(1), 46–60.

P. 95, *DSM-III-R:* American Psychiatric Association. (1987). *Diagnostic and statistical manual of mental disorders* (3rd ed., rev.). Washington, DC: Author.

P. 99, *The most commonly prescribed anxiolytics at present:* Sheikh, J. I., & Salzman, C. (1995). Anxiety in the elderly: course and treatment. *Psychiatric Clinics of North America, 18*(4), 871–883.

P. 100, *These include benzodiazepines:* Salzman, C. (1992). Treatment of anxiety. In C. Salzman (Ed.), *Clinical geriatric psychopharmacology* (2nd ed.). Baltimore: Williams and Wilkins.

4

INSOMNIA

Leah Friedman

My introduction to working with older insomniacs consisted of a warning from a senior psychologist. He told me that most therapists don't like this kind of work because they find insomniacs difficult to work with and their sleep problems fairly intractable. Despite that inauspicious beginning, I have spent years working with older people who have trouble sleeping and I have found that with very few exceptions my patients are cooperative and pleasant; I've also found that their sleep problems are by no means intractable.

We have been called a sleep-deprived society. As many as one-third of all Americans have reported problems with their sleep. Magazines and the Sunday papers are full of articles suggesting ways to improve sleep. Topics range from how to deal with jet lag and shift work to just plain trouble sleeping. Older people are the most sleep-deprived group of our sleep-deprived society.

Many older adults appear to regard poor sleep as just another of the many assaults of the aging process on their well-being. A frequent comment is, "Well I'm older now so I shouldn't expect to sleep well. Besides older people don't need much sleep."

Wrong!—on both counts. It is not at all clear that older people require less sleep than younger people to feel good and function well. Poor sleep in both the young and old is associated with lower energy, reduced ability to concentrate, and a reduction in the sense of well-being. Happily, there *are* things that can be done to improve the sleep of older people and consequently to improve the quality of their lives.

PRELIMINARY CONSIDERATIONS

Aside from suggestions about how to change specific behaviors, there are two basic things that we do for our patients. The first is that we listen with understanding to their sleep complaints; most older patients have had years of feeling tuned out when they mention their sleep problems. They feel that nobody understands or believes how truly distressing and debilitating these problems are. This goes for friends, spouses, children, and even, sad to say, their physicians and therapists. The second is that we hold out hope that with some effort things can be done to improve their sleep.

What Complaints Are Older Poor Sleepers Likely to Bring to You?

Younger people with sleep problems usually complain about trouble *falling* asleep; older people, however, usually complain about *staying* asleep without waking during the night or about waking up in the morning long before they want to. In other words, their problem is generally not one of initiating sleep but one of maintaining a night of good consolidated sleep. Interrupted, unconsolidated sleep leads to dissatisfaction and a feeling of not being refreshed by the night's sleep. There are also some unfortunate older people who have problems both initiating and maintaining sleep.

I often encounter this very common complaint: "I have no trouble falling asleep—in fact, I fall asleep all too easily. I have a problem even staying awake through my evening television shows. But it seems that once I get into bed, I sleep only an hour or two and then I'm wide awake. It just doesn't make sense."

Which Older People Are Likely to Be Poor Sleepers?

There are no simple rules of thumb to determine the types of older people who have sleep problems. In a sense, insomnia is a great leveler; it happens for a wide array of reasons to an equally wide array of types of people. Nonetheless, I'll present the profiles of two general types of older persons I have frequently encountered who needed help with their sleep. The first type is super busy (even if retired): taking classes, working on church projects, jogging or walking, participating in social activities and the like. These persons are often highly conscientious and therein lies much of the problem. They're the people who have helped keep the community afloat—the salt of the earth. It is hard for them to let go day or night.

The second type of poor sleeper is less outgoing, staying increasingly at home; these people have less and less structure or routine in their lives. Often this situation occurs with retirement or after the loss of a spouse. One woman—whose days, when her husband was alive, were structured around household chores, the three meals a day she shared with him, and their busy social life—became fearful of going out at night in the years after he died and stayed home reading into the wee hours of the night. When she finally went to sleep, she woke several times and then had a terrible time getting up the next morning for doctors' appointments or even for lunch with friends. Gradually, her days and nights lost their shape. Sleep intruded into the day and wakefulness extended late into the night.

When Does Insomnia Start?

My own experience is that most older poor sleepers have had their problem for a long time. The average duration of insomnia in a group of forty-two older sleepers I worked with was a little more than sixteen years. Some cases of insomnia seem to be almost lifelong. These patients will say that they were poor sleepers ever since they can remember. Then they might add, "And my mother was always a poor sleeper, too." Other poor sleepers will report that their sleep problem came about because of their life situation—for example, something about the nature of the job they have.

One man I worked with was a supervisor of an emergency response team. He would be awakened on an erratic basis on any and all nights and could never predict how interrupted his sleep would be on a given night. Some women have reported that their poor sleep began when they had babies or small children who woke them during the night. Another woman said that she could handle the babies but her poor sleep began when she stayed awake listening for her teenagers to come home at night.

In many other cases, insomnia starts as a response to a crisis situation, such as a death or illness in the family. Unfortunately, for many people, a chain of maladaptive behaviors that is established at the time of crisis often remains long after the original situation that gave rise to the behaviors is gone.

Changing these maladaptive behaviors is the core of our work with insomniacs. My experience has been that using sleep hygiene—a package of techniques designed to promote adaptive sleep-related behaviors—is very effective with older poor sleepers. Perhaps its greatest asset as a treatment approach is that it makes sense to older people. It involves no fancy gimmicks, no medications with tricky consequences. I tell patients that the treatment is based on good common-sense principles—principles that both Ben Franklin and their grandmothers would have had no trouble endorsing.

A second great advantage of behavioral techniques for working with older people is that patients become collaborators in testing out what does and doesn't work for them. I always tell patients that we are co-investigators in an experiment to figure out the best sleep program for them. Older people rarely get a chance to make an input into the form of their treatment. In my experience, things go much smoother if they do.

EVALUATION ISSUES

As in all psychotherapy, it is essential to begin by taking a careful evaluation. In the case of insomnia, this should include a medical and sleep history. You can find useful examples to follow in books recommended at the end of this chapter.

Insomnia is a symptom, not a disease complex, and is associated with many different psychological and physical problems. In treating insomnia in older people there are several areas of special concern that alert the clinician to the need either for a medical/psychiatric consultation or for referral to a sleep clinic. A sleep clinic is a laboratory usually associated with a hospital or a medical center that is staffed by specialists in the diagnosis and treatment of sleep disorders.

Medical Problems

Most elderly people who seek your treatment will have a primary care physician. If they don't, you might suggest that they get one. It is a wise policy, in general, for older persons to have regular checkups and to build an ongoing relationship with a physician or clinic.

A behavioral treatment is not the first line of attack for the treatment of insomnia associated with acute or severe medical illness. A large number of chronic diseases associated with aging are accompanied by poor sleep: metabolic disorders such as thyroid disease and diabetes, musculoskeletal disorders such as arthritis and fibromyalgia, cardiovascular disease such as congestive heart failure, kidney disease, neurological disorders such as Parkinson's disease, respiratory disease such as asthma, digestive problems such as gastroesophageal reflux, and hormonal changes associated with menopause. I suggest that you get permission from your patients to consult with their physicians whenever there is doubt about their health or the suitability of your treatment for their sleep problem. It is important that any underlying health problems be addressed before you start your treatment.

My experience has been that most physicians are pleased that someone else will be working with their patients on their sleep problems. In particular, the recommendations made as part of a program of sleep hygiene treatment are benign and often can be adjusted to suit patients with physical limitations. When underlying medical conditions have been appropriately treated, residual poor lifestyle habits that may have developed over the course of illness can be treated to advantage by behavioral techniques. Behavioral treatments that aim at improved sleep can be a significant and beneficial adjunct to patient health care.

Medications

Unfortunately a number of the medications used to treat common chronic illnesses among the elderly have an arousal effect. The list includes some of the common medications for respiratory illness such as theophylline and cardiorespiratory illness such as beta blockers. Other medications, such as antihistamines, can have sedating effects. Sometimes after consultation with patients' physicians, substitutes can be found without these effects.

It is important to determine at the outset whether patients are taking sleep medications. In my experience, treatment works best when patients are weaned from their sleep medications before we start a behavioral program to improve their sleep.

Many older people who seek therapists for help with their sleep come because they are dissatisfied with the effects of their medications: "I feel groggy the day after," "After a while the medications don't seem to work anymore."

Most patients I have seen were taking their sleeping medications on a sporadic basis. I usually try to wean patients off their medication gradually, with the help and advice of their prescribing physicians. We start treatment when patients have been free of the medications for a period of two weeks.

Depression, Anxiety, and Major Psychiatric Disorders

Poor sleep is associated with a wide range of psychological disorders. In the case of older people, the overlap of poor sleep with depression needs to be carefully considered. Of course, the treatment of insomnia associated with depression can contribute to improvement of mood.

But this is a high-risk age group for the more serious consequences of depression; hence, it is important to screen for major depression. In addition to your interview, you can use standard depression rating scales such as the Hamilton or the Geriatric Depression Scale for these purposes.

Similarly, if any other major psychopathology is present, it is important to treat such disorders first. Thus, for example, schizophrenia is associated with heightened anxiety and disturbed sleep at night. Obviously, the underlying schizophrenia is the first order of treatment. Similarly the same would be true for patients with panic disorders. However, insomnia is frequently present in the less seriously anxious older patients, and treating the insomnia of these patients may well be a good way to reduce their anxiety.

Furthermore, many psychotropic medications impact sleep. Again, it may be necessary to consult with the prescribing physician.

Sleep Disorders Whose Incidence Increases with Aging

Several types of sleep disorders are known to increase as we age. Here are several you may encounter among your patients:

Sleep Apnea. Sleep apnea is a potentially life-threatening sleep disorder in which respiration is interrupted and accompanied by brief arousals. Cessations in breathing can be very brief or long enough to lead to dangerous drops in the level of oxygen saturation in the blood. You should look for the following signs: Are there complaints of excessive daytime sleepiness such as reports of dozing off at inappropriate times either from a safety or social point of view, accidents or near accidents while driving, inability to stay awake even while doing enjoyable activities? Is the patient obese? Do spouses complain of snoring that shakes the rafters? Are patients reported to stop breathing during their sleep? These are warning signals that your patient may be suffering from sleep apnea. It is very important to refer such patients to a sleep disorders clinic or to their physicians for diagnosis and treatment.

Restless Legs. If patients report having a creepy, crawling sensation in their legs that can only be assuaged by rubbing, or shaking, or getting up and walking around, they probably have restless legs syndrome. These symptoms tend to appear especially during periods of rest, such as when the patient is in bed trying to fall asleep at night. Patients with symptoms of this condition should be referred to a sleep specialist for treatment.

Periodic Leg Movements. Does the patient report experiencing jerking leg movements during the night? Often people are not aware of having these movements, but their partners, if they have them, can definitely tell. One man reported to me that his sheets would wear out from the sheer friction of his leg movements during the night. These people have frequent arousals during the night even if they are not aware of them and should also be referred for appropriate treatment.

What Are Patients' Current Sleep-Related Behaviors Like?

Information needs to be collected on patients' usual times in and out of bed. In addition, it is important to find out how long it takes them to fall asleep; how often they wake and for how long; what time they wake for the last time; when they do get out of bed, what their caffeine, tobacco, and alcohol habits are. The best way to collect this information is by means of daily sleep logs. A sample sleep log is shown in Exhibit 4.1.

I give patients a set of fourteen sleep logs and show them how to complete them. I explain that it is important to collect this information for a period of two weeks because sleep varies from night to night and even from week to week. One or two days is just too small a slice of people's sleep to get an accurate picture of what their usual sleep is like and what factors contribute to it. In sending off the patient with a set of sleep logs, I continue the theme of this being a co-investigative endeavor. I tell them that they will be performing a data collecting, self-observation task essential for us to get a good grasp of the factors that may be contributing to their poor sleep. I also tell them that many patients find keeping a sleep log very enlightening. They often make observations about their sleep that they have never noticed before.

SLEEP HYGIENE TREATMENT

Sleep hygiene is the name given to a set of sleep-related behaviors that, when followed, maximize a person's ability to get good sleep. These practices were first codified and given their current name by Peter Hauri. Although the core of these practices remains the same, some additions and modifications have been made over the years. The principles of sleep hygiene are widely accepted and are often used either independently or in conjunction with other behavioral sleep therapies. I have worked with sleep hygiene principles in a clinical research setting for a number of years and have found them to be a practical approach to treating insomnia in older people.

What We Do During the Day Affects the Night

The core concept of sleep hygiene treatment is that sleep at night is greatly influenced by what goes on during the day and evening. For example, what activities we do and when we do them or what we eat and drink and when all have an impact on

Night Time Report

Before turning out the lights at night, please review your day and complete the following:

Name:_____ Day:_____ Date:_____Time now:_____

1. Caffeine products only
   How much coffee, tea, cola or chocolate: _____ _____ _____

2. Alcohol   How many: beers   wine   shots of   mixed drinks
              One drink= 12oz   5 oz   liquor 1.5oz
   How much: ____   ____   ____   ____
   At what times: ____   ____   ____   ____

3. Medications: _____ _____ _____
   Dosage: _____ _____ _____
   How many: _____ _____ _____
   At what times: _____ _____ _____

4. Naps or dozing: (please report sleep of any duration)
	Nap 1	Nap 2	Nap 3
Time you lay down:	____AM/PM	____AM/PM	____AM/PM
Time you got up:	____AM/PM	____AM/PM	____AM/PM
Time asleep:	____min	____min	____min

5. Did you exercise today?   Yes/No   Type of exercise:_____
   Time and length of exercise_____

6. Has anything unusual or upsetting happened today?_____

7. Please describe the activities you have engaged in during the last hour before getting into bed:_____

8. Please circle the number below that best describes, overall, how sleepy you felt today:

1	2	3	4	5	6	7
not at all			moderately			very
sleepy			sleepy			sleepy

Exhibit 4.1
Daily Sleep Reports

Morning Report

When you wake in the morning, please fill in and report the following:
Your name: _____
Day of the week:_____
Today's date:_____
Time right now: _____
1. Time you got into bed last night:_____
   Time you began trying to fall asleep_____
   How long it took you to fall asleep:_____
2. The number of times you got out of bed to go to the bathroom: _____
3. Did you take any medications after completing the report last night?
   Yes/No
   Name: _____ _____ _____
   Dosage: _____ _____ _____
   How many: _____ _____ _____
   At what time: _____ _____ _____
4. Time you woke up for the last time this morning:_____
   How did you wake up this morning? (Please circle an answer below)
   with alarm   spontaneously   other (please specifiy)_____
   Time you got out of bed this morning:_____
5. Your estimate of the total amount of sleep you got last night (Please do
   not include the time you were awake): _____
6. Please circle the number below that best describes how rested you feel
   this morning:

1	2	3	4	5	6	7
not at all			moderately			very
rested			rested			rested

7. Comments_____
   _____
   _____
   _____

Exhibit 4.1 *(continued)*
Daily Sleep Reports

our night's sleep. In other words, our daytime (or waking) behavior influences our sleep.

Sleep hygiene treatment is designed to help patients change any of their current behaviors that could be expected to influence sleep negatively. The extent to which any given behavior is emphasized is determined by the information gained from patients' sleep histories and collected in the sleep logs they have completed.

Food and Drink. What we eat and drink often has a significant impact on how we sleep.

MEALS. We suggest that patients try to eat their meals at regularly scheduled times. Patients are advised *not* to eat heavy, spicy meals right before bedtime. On the other hand, a light snack may be helpful to many people: crackers and low-fat cheese, for example. Moderation is the theme: people should not go to bed either stuffed or starving. Either condition might disturb their sleep.

CAFFEINE. Even people who believe that caffeine has little effect on them may be susceptible to its sleep-disturbing qualities. Many people are also unaware that many soft drinks have high amounts of caffeine among their ingredients, as do tea, chocolate, and cocoa. One woman I treated sipped tea all day; it wasn't coffee, so she thought it was all right.

I suggest that people have no more than two cups of caffeinated beverages during a day and that these be limited to the morning hours. Patients need not feel deprived on this score as there are many flavorful decaffeinated coffees and teas available in restaurants and stores these days.

ALCOHOL. Although many people know that caffeine disturbs sleep, few are aware of the presence of the same effects from alcohol. There is a popular misconception that alcohol has a sedative effect. This is because alcohol has a tendency to make us drowsy.

In fact, alcohol has a soporific effect only at the beginning of the sleep period. As the night wears on alcohol has the unfortunate characteristic of being extremely disruptive of sleep. Consequently, I suggest that patients limit their evening drinking to one drink with dinner. In order for patients not to feel left out on special nights out, I suggest that they start dinner with some of the new fancy mineral waters, and then have their alcoholic drink. This way they can have their treat and participate with others but still limit themselves to one drink. There should be no alcoholic intake within three hours of bedtime.

FLUIDS IN GENERAL. For those older people who are troubled by frequency of urination, it is probably wise to cut back on the amount of fluids taken later in the evening to avoid waking to urinate. For those patients taking diuretics, consultation with their physicians can often lead to a revision of their daily medication schedule that alleviates the problem of excessive nighttime urination.

Light Exposure and Exercise.

Both exposure to light and physical exercise play an important role in our ability to sleep.

LIGHT EXPOSURE. Many less active older people spend a great deal of time indoors, often with the drapes drawn and in dim lighting. They live in a kind of twilight zone both day and night. This can be bad for sleep because our daily sleep/wake cycles are influenced by the alternation of light and dark.

I suggest to people that they pull the drapes open and turn on the lights if the day is dim or overcast. In addition, patients should try to get exposure to bright light shortly after waking in the morning. Many of my patients are rightly concerned about exposure to sun and skin cancer. I recommend using caps or hats with brims and a liberal dose of sunblock. The main objective is to bring bright light into the brain through the eyes. This bright light serves to establish waking during the daytime period.

EXERCISE. Daily moderate (or greater) exercise is encouraged. Most of my patients have generally elected for brisk walking. Ideally, exercise should be scheduled for thirty to forty minutes at roughly the same time every day. Here, as in most other sleep-related behaviors, regularity leads to maximum benefit. Sporadic exercise just doesn't do the trick. The late afternoon is suggested as the time to get the maximum sleep benefit from exercise. The rise in temperature caused by the exercise with a subsequent drop five to six hours later benefits sleep.

In general, an active lifestyle with some social contact helps establish a good sleep/wake cycle. It is not hard to see that people who spend their days indoors, alone, without much to engage their minds would be constantly dozing on and off. Indeed, it is easy to see how the practices that maintain good sleep also tend to advance good mental health.

How We Schedule Sleep Has a Major Impact on Its Quantity and Quality

There is evidence that the timing of the daily sleep cycle shifts forward with aging. This explains the oft-observed phenomenon of older people going to bed (and getting up) earlier and earlier. To some extent, we can make use of the shift in the sleep cycle by suggesting to our patients that they move their bedtimes forward somewhat—as long as bedtime is consistent.

My own experience, however, is that most independently living older people do not want to go to bed and get out of bed very early. They don't like to be out of sync with the rest of the world. They want to be able to go to social and cultural events scheduled in the evening. They don't want to miss their programs. A number of patients have said to me that they hated the idea of being up in morning when it is dark and everyone else is asleep, particularly in winter. This is all the more reason for them to follow good sleep hygiene practices.

Thus evening, or the part of early night that is not intended to be spent in sleep, is often a very difficult time for older people to stay awake. But they are not yet ready for bed. This is the time for which I suggest activities that help prevent sleep before it is scheduled or wanted.

A sure loser in this regard is watching television. But because so many older people are avid television fans it is unrealistic to prescribe TV abstinence, although I must confess that I have had to struggle against the temptation to do this many times. What I suggest, instead, is lots of bright ambient lighting when they watch TV. Many people turn the lights down or off when watching TV, which adds to its soporific effect. I also suggest that patients get up and walk around or stretch during programs as well as during commercials. Sitting upright instead of in a semi-reclining position also helps maintain alertness.

More active but nonarousing activities are a better method for staying awake. Social activities are best of all, and I encourage them. People are not likely to doze off in the midst of a conversation. Unfortunately, not all older adults have active evening social lives, and reasonable alternatives have to be suggested. One man who had a hard time refraining from dozing off in the evening switched his grocery and mall shopping to the evening. He thus freed daylight time for walking in the park near his home and playing tennis. Sometimes people get to take care of things they have postponed for years. Consider those boxes of unlabeled photographs or the task of sorting through piles of magazines saved for that special article long unread, or even organizing papers for the tax person in advance so that April is not always the cruelest month.

Accomplishing these tasks can be a positive side effect of the treatment. One woman was thrilled about her improved sleep after treatment but a close second benefit for her was that she got all her cupboards cleaned up, something she had been wanting to do for years. All these activities have the desired effect of not allowing people to doze off before their desired bedtimes.

Bedtimes. It is very important to establish a routine time for getting in and out of bed, seven days a week. Routine is one of the fundamental elements of sleep hygiene treatment and one of the basic factors contributing to successful treatment. I tell the people that I work with that the parts of the brain that regulate sleep prefer predictability. In effect, we are training the sleep mechanism in our brains to expect sleep at a certain time and to wake at a certain time. When we get off routine, we are confusing our sleep regulators. Jet lag provides a dramatic example of how powerful an effect routine has on sleep. When we change time zones we take with us our training to wake up at times that were adjusted to our time zone of origin. We can feel pretty miserable and get some terrible sleep when we make major rapid changes to our sleep routine.

Although many older adults hold fast to a certain amount of routine in their daily life, there are others who, after the structure of a job or life with a spouse has been disrupted, keep very irregular schedules; this can have devastating effects on their sleep.

I consider regular scheduling of sleep to be so important that I suggest setting an alarm to be sure that patients get up at approximately the same time every day, weekends included. Now, the problem with this aspect of sleep hygiene is that many older people say that one of the joys of aging is that they don't need to have a set schedule. They don't have to catch an 8:10 train, or make the kids' breakfast and pack lunch. All this is true, but they nonetheless need a wake-up schedule to sleep well. In fact, having a fixed morning wake-up time could be considered one of the cornerstones of the treatment.

I use the example of athletes in training. Athletes have to be at the top of their physical form. In addition to strict exercise regimens, they stick to strict routines about eating and sleeping. I tell my patients that they are similar to athletes in training and that I am serving as their coach.

Getting Out of Bed in the Morning. The times of waking and getting out of bed in the morning are critical to establishing the sleep routine. Notice, I said not only time of waking but also time of getting out of bed. This emphasis is because a lot of older people think that one of the luxuries of aging is being able to loll around in bed after waking in the morning. I try to discourage this. This is not a moral judgment. The culprit here is not self-indulgence but what happens when people lie about in bed. Without realizing it, they frequently doze off again, maybe for just a few minutes or more. This can start to nibble at their sleep/wake schedule.

Special Late Night Events. What happens when you go out and stay up late for a party or an event? This is a common problem. One woman who was an opera buff could stick with her sleep schedule pretty well except during opera season. Every Friday night during the season she would stay up much later than her usual routine. Not surprisingly, she wanted to sleep in the next morning. Here, the kindly therapist became firm. No matter what time she went to bed the night before, it was important that she get up at the regular time. If she were to sleep in the next morning, say till ten o'clock, the next evening she would not be sleepy when it came time for bed. But if she got up at her regular time she would certainly be ready to go to sleep by her regular bedtime the following night. This is a good example of how what you do one night and morning affects the next.

To Nap or Not to Nap? This is a real question. People seem to divide into two groups on this one. In my experience, napping or non-napping appears to be almost as strong as a character trait. There are nappers and there are non-nappers and the two can be pretty adamant about not wanting to change their behavior. People seem to divide like the difference between siesta cultures and non-siesta cultures. In the case of cultures, geography and climate play a role, but it is not clear what causes some people to be nappers in our society, and some not. I have found that if I tried to change people in either direction I was almost doomed to fail.

One very elderly woman said to me, "I have managed very nicely all these years taking my daily nap and I don't see why I should give it up now." On the other hand, one woman got quite angry at the thought of an afternoon nap. She said, "It reminds me of having to take a nap at summer camp. I hated it then and I'd hate it now." "OK, OK," says the wise therapist and then goes with the path of least resistance.

If a nap *is* going to be part of the program, some important limitations need to be instituted. These limitations all have to do with time. First, the nap should be scheduled at a consistent time of day. Second, naps should be for a limited amount of time. In fact, an alarm should be set to make sure that there won't be oversleeping. I have found that for most people, thirty to forty-five minutes is a practical amount of time for napping. Third, the nap should be placed at the time of day of maximal sleepiness. For most people, this appears to be midday—from one to about four o'clock at the latest. This is the time for naps in siesta cultures. Naps scheduled late in the day or in the evening take away from the pressure to sleep at night.

I often make an analogy to eating sweets before dinner (another one of those things grandmother seems to have been right about) and point out that our "hunger" for sleep is diminished when we nap later in the day, just as our hunger for food is diminished when we snack on candy before dinner.

Bedtime Routine. Establishing a pleasant bedtime routine has at least three purposes. First, going to bed becomes a negative experience for many poor sleepers. Sleep and thinking about sleep raise negative thoughts and emotions. I try to tell patients that our goal is to make sleep and all the factors that surround it a pleasant thing. It is one of the few basic recurring activities of our daily lives. We do it every day of our lives. So if it isn't enjoyable, a large hunk of our lives isn't enjoyable—surely that's not a good thing. Sleep adds to a sense of well-being if it has pleasant associations. But for poor sleepers, sleep often takes on such a negative cast that in a way we need to detoxify it.

One way to do this is to establish a pleasant bedtime routine. That is, after taking care of their personal hygiene, patients should have a set routine of pleasant activities. These might include sitting in a comfortable chair reading a chapter in a book they enjoy, doing relaxation exercises, putting on perfume, using some new skin cream, listening to pleasant music, or whatever else would be cozy and pleasing. Of course, those who have significant others could incorporate lovemaking into this routine. In my experience, poor sleepers as a group tend not to indulge the sensual sides of themselves nearly enough.

A second function of a bedtime routine is that it's a way of making a transition from wakefulness to sleep. Notice that all the pleasant activities I have suggested are of a relatively quiet, calming nature. No listening to rock and roll or doing calisthenics right before bed! The point is that the routine should provide a bridge or transition between the state of alertness and arousal required for daytime activities and its opposite, that required for sleep.

Few of my patients have ever done much in preparation for bed. They go right from their nighttime activities: talking to people on the phone, playing bridge, listening to the latest horrors on the news; then they give themselves five to ten minutes to brush their teeth, wash their faces, go to the bathroom, pop off their daytime clothes, and get into their bedclothes. They then expect to lie down and fall into a deep satisfying sleep. It is easy to point out to them that they have done nothing to discharge the tensions of the day and that the stage has not been properly set for them to sink into blissful oblivion.

A third function of a bedtime routine is to serve as a stimulus for sleep. Elementary learning theory tells us that if a routine is established on a nightly basis, it will become a learned stimulus for sleep. Thus, if practiced enough, the bedtime routine in itself reinforces a response of increased sleepiness.

The Sleep Environment

The setting in which sleep takes place also plays an important role in enabling people both to fall asleep and to maintain that sleep without interruption.

1.   Bed should be a locale strictly limited to two activities, sleep and lovemaking. The idea again has its roots in basic learning theory. The bed should be a cue for sleep. It should not be the setting for conflicting, wake-inducing activities. Unfortunately, many older people spend a great deal of time in bed not sleeping. For some older people, their beds become their home office: they watch TV, do their correspondence, write bills, and complete their income tax forms in bed. Small wonder that such beds often don't serve as cues for sleep.

2.   The room should be neither too hot nor too cold. Sometimes this is not easy for older people to arrange, especially if they do not have an individual thermostat. Some collective problem solving between you and your patient can generate solutions such as using electric blankets, opening and closing windows, and so on.

3.   The room should be dark and quiet, and the mattress firm but comfortable. The darker and quieter the room, the better for sleeping. Some people don't realize that the light from such things as digital clocks can disturb their sleep. Also, for many people, very little intermittent noise can disrupt their sleep. Not everyone can arrange for quiet, especially those who live in apartment houses. For these people, something like using a white noise machine or running a small fan would be a good idea.

4.   Clocks should be turned around so that the sleeper cannot look at them during the night. Night clock watching often heightens anxiety and diminishes patients' ability to fall asleep.

5.   The sleep setting should also feel as safe as possible. A number of older people (particularly divorced or widowed women) have mentioned that part of their sleep problem comes about because they feel unsafe sleeping alone. To the extent practicable, we discuss ways of making them feel more secure during the night, such as sleeping with the phone next to their beds, getting bolt locks for doors and windows, having a buddy system with a neighbor they can call if they are worried about safety during the night.

What Should One Do When One Wakes
During the Sleep Period?

Much of the time older, poor sleepers spend awake in bed is when they wake and cannot fall back to sleep. If sleep does not come, I advise patients to be sure not to try too hard to sleep; relax, and let sleep come rolling in. If it doesn't, they should avoid the stress that comes with too great an effort. Trying too hard to sleep is almost guaranteed to produce sleeplessness.

I have found one activity at which many of my patients are quite adept that has disastrous consequences for their sleep: worrying. Lying in bed worrying is almost synonymous with insomnia. It is a major reason patients should get up and get involved in a pleasant nonarousing activity. It's very important to block out worrying thoughts. As I tell my patients, nighttime is a bad time to think about things. Everything looks worse in the dark of night. Often the same problem in the light of day seems to vanish or certainly diminish in terror. I tell patients to get their minds engaged with something else. If they find they absolutely cannot stop worrying, I suggest that they write a list of their worries on a pad so they can look at it in the morning. Their model should be Scarlett O'Hara, who said, "I'll think about it tomorrow."

One worry in particular that poor sleepers should avoid is worrying about sleep itself. Poor sleepers frequently get quite agitated thinking about how they are going to make it through the next day if they don't get a good night's sleep, and this is often why they try too hard to sleep. Although we obviously think good sleep is important to well-being, we are thinking about the big picture. One or two nights does not have a dramatic effect on the next day's function. Mother Nature has so arranged things that if people stick with their regular sleep routines, they will be sleepy enough on subsequent nights to sleep better and things will straighten out. If anything is counterproductive for sleep, it is worrying about sleep.

We encourage patients to get out of bed during all wakeful periods lasting longer than twenty minutes. One gentleman complained of getting out of his nice warm bed into the cold winter evening (not an unreasonable complaint). We arrived at the solution that he would have a warm robe and slippers laid out on a chair right by his bed. Patients are encouraged to get involved in a quiet, nonstimulating activity and told not to return to bed until they are feeling sleepy again.

What patients do when they get out of bed makes a difference as well. Clearly they should do something that is restful and non-stimulating, something that gets them ready to go back to bed and fall asleep. A number of people have told me that they listen to talk shows when they wake up. In fact, after working with many older poor sleepers, I have developed an image of late-night America with a whole cohort of insomniacs wide awake, listening to talk shows, becoming increasingly electrified and agitated at what they hear, and, of course, less and less able to fall back to sleep.

FURTHER CONSIDERATIONS

There are, of course, other well-defined behavioral treatments such as stimulus control, relaxation, cognitive-behavioral, and sleep restriction treatments. Sleep hygiene treatment includes elements of these and makes somewhat fewer demands on the patient. That is why I have found it a good place to start with older subjects. It is always possible to add these treatments to the treatment program if sufficient success is not achieved with the program outlined above. It is a good idea to tell the patient at the very beginning that there are a number of approaches to the improvement of poor sleep, and that you will try various approaches until the patient's sleep is improved.

Tailoring the Treatment to the Individual

In this chapter, I have enumerated a long list of behaviors to work with. It is a list you should shop from by selecting those factors that both you and the patient feel are appropriate. Peter Hauri has made the point that one man's elixir can be another man's poison. I encountered a good example of this principle when I was encouraging an elderly man to try relaxing before going to sleep and he told me that relaxing made him nervous.

After selecting the behaviors that you feel should be changed, work on a few of them at a time; otherwise you and the patient can get quite overwhelmed and not know what's working and what isn't.

Some Logistical Issues

How long should treatment last and how frequent should appointments be? This varies with the patient, but six to eight weeks of weekly sessions is generally sufficient time for signs of improvement to show. Neither the therapist nor patient should be discouraged if it takes somewhat longer. As I tell patients, it took years to develop their package of sleep problems; we can't be expected to turn things around overnight. However, if the patient continues to complain of excessive sleepiness in the daytime that does not seem to be responding to your treatment after about four weeks, it is possible that the patient has a physiologically based sleep disorder such as sleep apnea and should be referred for an evaluation at a sleep disorders clinic.

What about follow-up? I highly recommend scheduling follow-up sessions. Patients often find scheduled follow-up sessions reassuring and they benefit from touching base with the therapist. Knowing that they will be seeing you in a fixed period of time serves to encourage their continued compliance with the treatment elements. At follow-up, patients can review how their sleep has gone and what they have (or have not) practiced in the time since you last met. Taking stock often serves as positive reinforcement; patients can see how well sticking with the program has paid off. Follow-up can serve as a mini-refresher course and can also be an opportunity to discuss any new problems that may have developed.

NOTES

P. 105, *As many as one-third of all Americans have reported:* Karacan, I., Thornby, J. I., Anch, M., Holzer, C. E., Warheit, G. J., Schwab, J. J., & William, R. L. (1976). Prevalence of sleep disturbance in a primarily urban Florida county. *Social Science and Medicine, 10,* 239–244.

P. 105, *not at all clear that older people require less sleep:* Dement, W. C., Miles, L. E., & Carshadon, M. A. (1982). "White paper" on sleep and aging. *Journal of the American Geriatric Society, 30,* 25–50.

P. 107, *duration of insomnia:* Friedman, L., Brooks, J. O., III, Bliwise, D. L., Yesavage, J. A., & Wicks, D. S. (1995). Perceptions of life stress and chronic insomnia in older adults. *Psychology and Aging, 10,* 352–357.

P. 109, *useful examples to follow:* Lacks, P. (1987). *Behavioral treatment for persistent insomnia.* Elmsford, NY: Pergamon Press; Morin, C. M. (1993); *Insomnia: Psychological assessment and management.* New York: Guilford Press.

P. 109, *insomnia associated with . . . illness:* The Harvard Health Letter. (1995). *Sleep disturbance.* Boston: Harvard Medical School Health Publications.

P. 110, *a number of the medications used to treat common chronic illnesses:* Wincour, M. Z. (1993, May). Restful sleep: The pharmacotherapy of insomnia. *US Pharmacist,* 47–78.

P. 111, *Hamilton:* Hamilton, M. (1967). Development of a rating scale for primary depressive illness. *British Journal of Social and Clinical Psychology, 6,* 278–296.

P. 111, *Geriatric Depression Scale:* Yesavage, J. A., Brink, T. L., Rose, T. L., Lum, O., Huang, V., Adey, M., & Leirer, V. O. (1983). Development and validation of a geriatric depression screening scale: A preliminary report. *Journal of Psychiatric Research, 17,* 37–49.

P. 111, *other major psychopathology:* Espie, C. A. (1991). *The psychological treatment of insomnia.* West Sussex: Wiley.

P. 111, *Sleep apnea . . . potentially life-threatening:* Guilleminault, C. (1994). Clinical features and evaluation of obstructive sleep apnea. In M. H. Kryger, T. Roth, & W. C. Dement (Eds.), *Principles and practice of sleep medicine* (pp. 667–677). Philadelphia: W. B. Saunders.

P. 112, *jerking leg movements during the night:* Montplaisir, J., Godbout, R., Pelletier, G., & Warnes, H. (1994). Restless legs syndrome and periodic movements during sleep. In M. H. Kryger, T. Roth, & W. C. Dement (Eds.), *Principles and practice of sleep medicine* (pp. 589–597). Philadelphia: W. B. Saunders.

P. 113, *practices . . . given their current name:* Hauri, P. J. (1977). *Sleep disorders: Current concepts.* Kalamazoo, MI: Upjohn.

P. 118, *sleep cycle shifts forward with aging:* Miles, L. E., & Dement, W. C. (1980). Sleep and aging. *Sleep, 3,* 119–220.

P. 126, *other well-defined behavioral treatments:* Spielman, A. J., Caruse, L. S., & Glovinsky, P. B. (1987). A behavioral perspective on insomnia treatment. In the Psychiatric Clinics of North America, *Sleep disorders* (pp. 541–553). Philadelphia: W. B. Saunders.

P. 127, *one man's elixir . . . another man's poison:* Hauri, P. (1991). *Case studies in insomnia* (p. 66). New York: Plenum.

FOR FURTHER READING

Espie, C. A. (1991). *The psychological treatment of insomnia.* West Sussex, England: Wiley.

Hauri, P. J. (1991). *Case studies in insomnia.* New York: Plenum.

Hauri, P. J. (1992). *Sleep disorders: Current concepts.* Kalamazoo, MI: Upjohn.

Hauri, P. J., & Linde, S. (1990). *No more sleepless nights.* New York: Wiley.

Lacks, P. (1987). *Behavioral treatment for persistent insomnia.* Elmsford, NY: Pergamon Press.

Morin, C. M. (1993). *Insomnia: Psychological assessment and management.* New York: Guilford Press.

The Harvard Health Letter. (1995). *Sleep disturbance.* Boston: Harvard Medical School Health Publications.

Webb, W. B. (1992). *Sleep, the gentle tyrant.* Bolton, MA: Anker.

CHAPTER

5

SEXUAL PROBLEMS

Diane Morrissette, Antonette M. Zeiss, and Robert A. Zeiss

Cocoon, a popular movie of a few years ago, offers a fascinating portrayal of some basic cultural expectations about aging. In this film, several older men (roughly age sixty-five to seventy-five) find their swimming pool occupied by cocoon-like pods; unknown to them, these cocoons hold life forms that are being revitalized by their benign and friendly planetary kin. Swimming in the pool imparts new youth and vigor to the aging men, who leave their swim feeling mysteriously cheerful and energetic. They start talking about their equally mysterious firm erections ("boners"), and the married men rush home intent on finding their wives. The wives, who have not had any invigorating life-force swim, are receptive to intercourse but somewhat baffled by their husbands' behavior, since no sexual activity had occurred for a long time. Meanwhile, the one unmarried man finds the courage to ask out the woman he has secretly longed for, and their relationship proceeds fairly rapidly to one including intercourse. At first blush, many consider this a positive presentation of older adult sexuality, but we find it to be full of problematic stereotypes about the sexuality of the elderly.

Our experience in working with sexual concerns of the elderly has come mainly through our work with the Andrology Clinic, a sexual dysfunction clinic at the Veterans Affairs Palo Alto Health Care System. This interdisciplinary clinic, which has been operating since 1984, is staffed by physicians and psychologists and provides training to physicians, psychologists, and counselors. Two of us (RZ and AZ) are clinical psychologists who are co-directors of the Andrology Clinic. We began training as sex therapists in 1972, while in graduate school, and have been actively involved in research, clinical work, and training in sex therapy since then. The third author (DM) is a sexologist and marriage, family, and child counselor intern. She began graduate training in 1978, followed by a fellowship in sex research; she is respecializing in sex therapy and was a trainee in the Andrology Clinic.

SEXUAL CHANGES WITH AGING

Based on our experience, we noticed the following problems with the depiction of sexuality in the movie *Cocoon*. First, male erection is presented as impossible for this group of mostly healthy older men without a mysterious "youth infusion." Second, their wives are presented as strictly passive partners—they didn't need to swim in the life force to be able to receive sexual attentions, presumably since their role is simple and strictly receptive. Third, the unmarried man could not even date a woman unless he had the capacity to have an erection and initiate sexual intercourse. Finally, as suggested by all the above, the most basic assumption is that sex is simply intercourse, and that if older adults cannot have intercourse, they have no sexual interest or other sexual activities.

The messages of the film mirror many of the stereotypes our culture holds about sexuality and aging. How well do these stereotypes hold up against what we know about normal age-related changes in sexual function and behavior?

Hormonal and Physical Changes with Aging

We want to emphasize that aging is a gradual and highly individual process. None of the effects described in this chapter can be associated with a specific age; they tend to occur gradually.

For example, some women may enter menopause at age forty and others at fifty-five; some men may have changes in ejaculation at age fifty and others at eighty. The processes described here are intended as guidelines for what a clinician might attend to in working with older people, not a fixed set of norms.

Starting with women, there is a marked shift in hormones during menopause that may result in concerns about changes in their sexual response. One menopausal woman we treated, when asked, complained about pain with intercourse. This was likely caused by her loss of estrogen with menopause, resulting in her vaginal walls becoming thinner. She may also experience pain from decreased vaginal lubrication or because lubrication occurs more slowly in response to sexual stimulation. Taking more time for foreplay can compensate for the slower sexual response. Educating women about artificial lubricants, such as Astroglide or Replens, or hormone replacement therapy can address these problems caused by reduced estrogen.

Elderly women sometimes also find vaginal penetration is more difficult or even painful. This is likely caused by folds of skin covering the vaginal entry, the vaginal lips or labia, that no longer fully elevate during sexual arousal to create the funnel-like entrance toward the vagina seen in younger women. In addition, if the cervix has descended into the vagina, cervical bumping during intercourse can be painful. In our experience, most aging women say clitoral response remains, and clitoral stimulation continues in importance as a prelude to orgasm.

Women seen in our clinic, like those seen at other centers, also report changes with orgasm. They say orgasm itself may be shorter, with weaker and fewer vaginal contractions and shorter duration of general body involvement in the orgasmic experience. But they also say they retain their multiorgasmic ability.

Although aging men do not experience a marked change like menopause, they report gradual changes similar to those experienced by women. Men say they need more direct stimulation of the penis for an erection and that it takes longer to become erect. They also say the erection may be less than 100 percent—

say, 80 percent to 90 percent, compared to their younger years. Combined with the woman's reduced lubrication and limited labial elevation, this may make penetration for intercourse difficult. We tell couples this can be easily solved by using a hand to guide the penis into the vagina and a vaginal lubricant for ease and comfort of intercourse.

In older men, we find that stimulation usually must continue for a longer period to reach orgasm (a potential boon for men who had very rapid ejaculation). These men also say orgasm consists of fewer and weaker contractions as well as reduced general body response. In addition, the ejaculatory force may be reduced—some men tells us their ejaculate just seeps out—and the amount of semen is reduced. One man we saw believed that a woman feels the ejaculate as it spurts into the vagina and that this contributes greatly to her sexual satisfaction. He worried that the ejaculate lacked the volume and full expulsion needed to excite his partner. We first educated the man that these were normal age-related changes. Then we taught him about female sexuality, including the lack of sensation in the inner two-thirds of the vagina and the primary role of the clitoris in a woman's sexual satisfaction. The patient left the session saying he had much to think about.

After ejaculation or orgasm, both older men and women say they return to the pre-aroused state more rapidly than when younger, and men typically report a time period when they cannot be restimulated to erection, called the *refractory period*. In younger men, the refractory period may be just a few minutes, but in older men it may last hours or even days.

Use It or Lose It

Both men and women are subject to the "use it or lose it" phenomenon. As a preventive measure, clinicians may want to advise patients of the sexual health benefits of remaining sexually active. We tell couples that women over sixty who continue partner sexual activity are likely to experience vaginal lubrication as rapidly as younger women. In addition, postmenopausal women having intercourse three times a month or more are less likely to have a vagina that becomes smaller (shorter and narrower) than their sexually inactive counterparts. Women without a partner who masturbate regularly may also experience fewer physical changes in the vagina and more rapid vaginal lubrication.

While age-related changes are significant and meaningful, they do not, in themselves, cause a person's sex life to end. Older adults may need to plan for more time in a sexual encounter; they may need to be sensitive to changes in their own bodies and their partners', and they may need to use aids such as lubricants or vibrators to increase stimulation. They may want to emphasize sexual activities other than intercourse. For example, oral stimulation may be an excellent prelude to intercourse by increasing genital lubrication, or it may be an end in itself, especially for a woman who has pain during intercourse because the cervix gets bumped. Older adults need to talk about these changes, be flexible in their thinking about the timing and nature of sexual contacts, and be creative in working out activities that fit their own unique pattern of age-related changes.

Behavioral Changes with Aging

While it's easy to say what healthy older adults might do to maintain sexual satisfaction, it's not always easy to do these things. Many of us, at all ages, are uncomfortable talking candidly about sex and have not been encouraged to think creatively and flexibly about sexuality. It would not be surprising, then, if the sexual behavior of older adults showed more change than one would expect solely from the physical changes described above. The most commonly reported pattern for older couples is to maintain a steady level of sexual activity, whatever that level had been. The second most common pattern is couples who maintain sexual activity until a point of sudden, dramatic decline or cessation of sexual activity. These declines generally result because of changes in the man. When men die, their wives often cease all sexual activity. When men develop a medical problem that interferes with erectile function, the couple often ceases all sexual activity. We hear this all too often in our clinic. But reversing the genders does not have the same result. When wives die, their husbands often remain sexually active, either in masturbation or with a new partner. When wives develop medical problems that make sexual activity more difficult, most couples remain sexually active.

This second most common pattern sounds suspiciously like the *Cocoon* scenario. Both genders act as if they believe that men must have erections for older adults to have satisfactory sexual lives. When health problems affect erection, many couples do not communicate, plan, or change their behavior; instead they give up on sex. Clearly, medical problems, especially in men, play a major role in sexual function in older couples, but the changes in behavior are also the result of a psychosocial construction of sexuality that emphasizes the passive, receptive role of women and the centrality of intercourse.

SEXUAL DYSFUNCTION

We turn now to a more careful analysis of how older adults might develop sexual problems. We recall a married couple, Jane and Adam Geront (not their real names; all names of patients in this chapter are pseudonyms and identities are thoroughly disguised), whom we saw in our clinic. Here's their story.

ADAM AND JANE

Adam (seventy-two) and Jane (seventy) have been married for forty-six years and have two adult children, now aged forty-four and forty. Adam has a history of depression, high blood pressure, and lung disease. Jane went through menopause at age fifty-one and has never been on hormone replacement therapy. Medically, she has a history of arthritis. Adam complains that he cannot get an erection better than about 60 percent, which allows penetration only with difficulty. Often he loses his erection after penetration. He says, "I guess I'm just getting too old. Things just don't work the way they used to. This isn't fair to my wife; I'm worried she's missing out on something. Why should she stick around with such a useless husband?" Jane responds, "My husband thinks about sex all the time. I don't see what the big deal is. Why can't he just understand that I'm not upset with him if he can't get an erection? It's kind of a relief anyway—intercourse is pretty difficult for me these days."

As with Adam Geront, the most frequent complaint of the aging male is erectile dysfunction. Although figures vary considerably depending on age and specific population, the prevalence of this difficulty ranges from 55 percent to 95 percent of men over the age of seventy. Incidentally, in our clinic we avoid the term *impotence*, an outdated label. Much like the old label *frigidity* for female dysfunction, *impotence* is an imprecise, pejorative, and value-laden term. We recommend using *erectile dysfunction* or *erectile disorder*, or, even better, being more specific, for example, diagnosing *difficulty obtaining erection* or *difficulty maintaining erection*.

In older women, as with Jane Geront, the most common sexual complaint is painful intercourse, a condition called *dyspareunia*. This is a problem for about one in three sexually active women over sixty-five. As with the Geronts, a level of interest in sex discrepant from the partner's is also a cause for complaint. This often reflects a change in level of desire for one of the partners, such that a long-standing equilibrium becomes destabilized. Sexual desire disorders can represent as many as 50 percent of sexual complaints, often in conjunction with other problems, such as loss of erection or dyspareunia.

Although less common, we see older adults with other sexual dysfunctions, including rapid ejaculation, delayed ejaculation, lack of orgasm, and orgasm without pleasure, to name a few.

Causes of sexual function problems are many and include relationship issues, intrapersonal issues such as difficulties accepting aging, psychopathologies, grief, adjustment to illness or loss of a partner, and medical problems, including treatments such as surgeries and medications. None of these problems are exclusive to older patients, but their prevalence increases with age. In working with older adults, it's important to be knowledgeable about the range of conditions that may occur.

PSYCHOLOGICAL ISSUES

Psychological issues are seldom the sole cause of serious sexual dysfunction in elders, particularly those in a stable, long-standing relationship. In a review of 195 people with sexual dysfunction referred to our clinic, we identified only 10 percent with *solely* psychologically caused sexual complaints. Psychological issues, however, do seem to play *contributing* roles in the development, maintenance, and resistance to treatment of sexual problems in older adults.

Ageism and Anxiety

Barriers frequently associated with sexual problems in the elderly include cultural stereotypes, intrapersonal issues, and changes in roles. Chief among the cultural stereotypes is ageism—particularly the notions that older adults are not sexually attractive, that older adults are not sexually active or even interested, and that there is something wrong with those who are. Images of sexuality in elders are often derogatory—a "dirty old man," for example, or a "wealthy old lady duped by a gigolo."

We frequently see older men with erection problems who are otherwise healthy, vibrant human beings but who avoid social or romantic relationships and fear that no woman could ever be interested "if I can't have sex the right way." Such pervasive cultural norms interfere with normal sexual interests and desires older adults might experience and seriously impair their abilities to express sexuality or even affection.

Anxiety is one of the intrapersonal issues that has the biggest impact on sex. For example, many men who have one experience of difficulty getting or maintaining an erection develop the fear that this will occur in every future sexual encounter. This creates a self-fulfilling prophecy: it becomes almost impossible for them to respond with interest and arousal because all attention is diverted to worrisome thoughts. Anxiety is also an issue for older individuals, often women, for whom pain is a sexual problem. Fear of pain often develops in response to the pain itself, exacerbating tension in the encounter and possibly even increasing the level of pain.

Both sexes experience changes in body image with aging. Some of these coincide with aging, such as wrinkling skin, loss of hair, sagging breasts, or loss of muscle tone. Changes related to disease may be more dramatic, involving function and appearance. Illnesses such as heart disease or lung disease, for example, can lead to loss of stamina, while cancer might necessitate a mastectomy. With the cultural definition of sexuality as being for the young and healthy, it is not surprising that an older person, especially someone medically compromised, would find it difficult to overcome changes in body image and maintain an identity as a sexually active person.

A pattern of erectile dysfunction has been described as a *widower's syndrome*, in which a man still in the grief process after losing a partner feels pressure to be sexually active with a new potential partner, often a long-term personal friend. When a man gives in to such pressure before he is emotionally ready, he can experience erectile difficulties, setting off a vicious cycle in which he defines himself as "impotent," with all the negative connotations of that label.

A final psychological barrier has to do with changes in roles, through changes in health status or the assumption of a patient or caregiver role. The transition from an equal partnership to one of caregiver and patient is never easy and, particularly if there is a lack of communication around sexual issues, sexual relationship changes may never be adequately worked out. The loss of a partner may require the survivor to use skills that have been long missing or dormant. Establishment of a new romantic or sexual relationship may require frank discussion of sexual interests, habits, and needs with potential new partners—a difficult task for anyone.

Psychological Disorders

Psychological disorders go beyond common sexual worries and self-doubts to reflect more pervasive concerns. Fifty-two percent of patients in our sexual dysfunction clinic had a psychological disorder that was diagnosable by DSM-III-R standards. Some disorders, particularly depression and alcohol abuse or dependence, provided such extensive interference with sexual function and its treatment that we insisted they be treated before we could treat the sexual problems that had brought the patients to our clinic.

Somewhat to our surprise, the prevalence of diagnosable anxiety disorders, severe psychopathology, personality disorders, and dementia was fairly low in this population. This may not reflect the population as a whole, but it was certainly true of the group referred to our particular clinic.

Considering psychological barriers with the Geronts, Adam seems to be particularly affected by depression and performance anxiety. His depression is expressed in statements that he is a "useless husband" while his anxiety is expressed in his fear that his wife might not "stick around" because he cannot satisfy her. He holds these beliefs tenaciously, despite her assertion that she is uninterested in sex and glad not to be approached for intercourse. Thus, there also seems to be some difficulty for this couple in talking openly to each other about sex.

Jane overemphasizes her husband's concern about sex: "He just thinks about sex all the time." This may reflect her acceptance of sexual stereotypes that older people should no longer be interested in sex. In addition, either of them may be having body image problems related to aging and their health problems.

We have emphasized the idea that sexual problems in older adults almost always result from a combination of factors, both psychological and medical. This is certainly true for our example, the Geronts, where we have seen that psychosocial factors, menopause, and medical problems all combined to create the final set of sexual complaints. We turn now to an assessment strategy designed to elicit multifactorial causes and then to a consideration of treatment modalities.

ASSESSMENT OF
SEXUAL PROBLEMS

Assessment and treatment of sexual problems in the elderly are best accomplished in an interdisciplinary team setting where psychosocial and medical expertise can be integrated. When this is not possible, it is important to develop a network of colleagues who are knowledgeable about sexuality in the elderly. Patients seen in a counseling context should be referred for a medical workup, and release of information should be obtained so that information will be available to the psychotherapist.

Assessment depends on the ability to skillfully and sensitively elicit sexual information from patients who are often embarrassed, deeply distressed by their sexual "failures," unaware of basic sexual information or even misinformed, and unsure whether it is appropriate to discuss sexual concerns.

Studies have consistently shown that patients with sexual problems expect and hope that health care professionals will raise the issue, rather than having to bring it up themselves. Unfortunately, many professionals fail to raise sexual issues, reasoning that patients will bring it up if they are concerned. This approach gets the professional off the hook if he or she is uncomfortable discussing sex, but the result is often that sexual difficulties are overlooked. We strongly advocate that all health care providers discuss sexuality openly and that they include it in their basic interviews for all patients.

Assessment information to be obtained follows naturally from the causes of clinical problems. Information should be obtained regarding mood, anxiety, mental health problems, relationship issues, knowledge about basic sexuality and age-related changes, body image, adaptation to grief, and role changes. In addition, sexuality should be evaluated over the complete arousal cycle to establish whether there are sexual problems in addition to the presenting complaint.

The Interview

In our clinic, we follow a standard semistructured format that provides complete information but allows a natural interview style. We try to interview the couple together if the identified patient has a regular partner. Sometimes the person is unwilling to bring a partner to the first interview, so we try to educate him about the reasons for involving both partners. In the following sections we present our procedures as if we are interviewing one person, to make the presentation simpler. The logic of the interview, however, would follow the same pattern when we interview a couple.

We begin validating that the individual may feel uncomfortable with the frankness of our questions and with giving us such personal information. We assess whether the person has ever talked openly about sexual concerns with anyone before and how anxious he feels talking with us. We then get general information about life situation, such as age, relationship status and history, family, and work status and history. We shift then to information about patterns of sexual expression, including ways of expressing affection, foreplay and intercourse patterns, and other preferred sexual activities. We also ask about use of alcohol, tobacco, and other drugs.

By this point, the patient generally feels more comfortable, and we begin to discuss the concern that brought him to the clinic. We try to get a complete description of the current experience of desire level and responses during the arousal process and orgasm. Usually the person will emphasize that part of the arousal cycle where his difficulties occur, but it is not uncommon to find problems in other portions of the arousal cycle when he is specifically asked about them. For each problem, we try to get information about how frequently it occurs and whether the problem is a total lack of response (no orgasm ever) or whether there is more variability (sometimes getting a full erection, sometimes getting none, sometimes getting an erection but not being able to maintain it). We especially try to find out whether the problem happens in all sexual activity or just in some circumstances—for example, with one partner but not everyone, or with a partner but not in masturbation.

After obtaining a clear picture of the current pattern (or patterns), we shift to questions about the history of the problem. We try to establish a baseline—the last time the person remembers when there was no problem with sexual activity. We then ask whether the problem(s) began abruptly or gradually and what life changes were associated with the development of the problem. These might be psychological or relationship events, or they might be medical events or medications. We also ask how the person and partner(s) have tried to handle the problem.

We find it important to get more information about the context of the sexual problem as well. For example, we ask about sexual values and beliefs and about how the person's attitudes compare to the partner's attitudes about sex. We try to understand the meaning of sexuality in the context of religious background. We also want to understand how important sexuality is in defining the relationship between the couple (for people with steady partners), and we explore the ability of the couple to discuss sex openly and engage in problem solving about sexual concerns.

We always ask about the person's goals; the answers to these questions can bring surprises. For example, it seems natural to assume that the goal is the opposite of the problem: if there is no erection, the goal is erection; if there is no orgasm, orgasm is the goal. However, people sometimes have other goals in mind, or there are big differences in the goals of one partner compared to the other. We saw one couple in their seventies who had been married for three years, a second marriage for both. The man's goal was to get better erections in order to have intercourse so that his wife would have orgasms, just like his first wife used to. His current wife had never had orgasms during intercourse and thought the couple were coming to the therapist because her husband felt desperately unhappy because he couldn't have an erection. She was orgasmic with manual and oral stimulation, so they needed to redefine their goals and the importance (or unimportance) of an erection in relation to these goals.

Finally, we generally end our interviews by checking on the patient's hypotheses for the sexual problems. We may be developing hypotheses about the problem which, for example, emphasize the role of widower's syndrome and performance anxiety in the new relationship but discover that the patient is convinced that his medication caused loss of erection and is only interested in treatment based on that hypothesis. In such cases, the first phase of treatment is designed to open the patient to consideration of a broader range of possible causes of his difficulties.

ASSESSMENT OF MEDICAL PROBLEMS

Many physical systems are involved in sexual function; thus, a huge array of illnesses and treatments can disrupt it. Specific medical conditions are commonly associated with particular sexual dysfunctions, but causes can't be definitively determined. Instead, educated guesses are made, based on the information available. We've seen cardiovascular diseases, including hypertension, coronary artery disease, arrhythmias, and heart failure, affect sexual function in both sexes. Psychotherapists need to obtain information about medical problems, surgical history, and medications to identify problems that may contribute to the presenting complaints and then make the necessary referral for a detailed evaluation. But keep in mind that the initial causes of problems may not be the maintaining factors. For example, an erection problem may start with blood pressure medication but be maintained because of psychosocial problems after the initial medication is stopped.

Vascular Disease and Reduced Blood Flow

In men, vascular disease can contribute to decreased blood flow to the penis, accounting for as much as a third of erectile dysfunction cases. Sex therapists and researchers assume that the increased blood flow responsible for penile erection is also responsible for vaginal lubrication, but we know of no data on the effects of atherosclerosis on women's sexual functioning.

Diabetes

Diabetes is notorious for its link to erectile dysfunction, and we see a lot of such cases in our clinic. Erectile problems can occur at any stage of the illness. We sometimes hear diabetic men say they no longer experience ejaculation. Although they report continued pleasure from orgasm, they're concerned about the lack of ejaculate. We explain that diabetes can cause ejaculation into the bladder, a condition called *retrograde ejaculation*, rather than through the penis. In our assessment, we also ask about rapid ejaculation, which can be associated with diabetes, but find orgasm typically unaffected. In our experience, diabetic men and their partners often do not attribute these sexual side effects to diabetes, and many couples give up reaching sexual satisfaction once erection is inconsistent. We find that couples who continue to provide each other sexual pleasure to orgasm despite the impact of diabetes have a better prognosis for working out an effective solution to the erection problem.

Diabetes in women may be associated with sexual problems also, including desire disorders, reduced vaginal lubrication, and painful intercourse. Because these are common problems for older women, the role of diabetes is not clearly understood; the incidence of these problems actually may be no greater than in the general population.

Testosterone

Decreased amounts of the hormone testosterone are typically associated with diminished sexual desire in both sexes and, to some extent, with decreased erections for men and decreased orgasmic capacity for women. While age normally brings a decrease in testosterone, the level ordinarily remains within the normal range, and it is uncommon to see older men with testosterone at abnormally low levels. When we supplement testosterone in men with abnormally low levels, we frequently see a dramatic increase in sexual desire and general well-being. These men usually have true *hypogonadism*—that is, testosterone deficiency. One man described the effects of testosterone injections this way: "Not only do I now have more sexual desire, I now think about sex every second!" But some men may also have additional factors causing erectile problems, such as cardiovascular disease or diabetes. For them, injections will not improve erectile capabilities. Treatment must include other components for these men and their partners (discussed in the section on treatment).

Testosterone also seems to be responsible for sexual desire in women, and supplementing low levels of testosterone in women can lead to dramatic renewal of interest in sex as well as resumption of preexisting orgasmic responsiveness. Some practitioners, particularly in Europe, have begun recommending judicious testosterone replacement for postmenopausal women.

Prostate Cancer

For men, the likelihood of developing prostate cancer increases directly with age. Unfortunately, men we see treated for prostate cancer are likely to have serious sexual effects, including erection and ejaculation problems. Even more common for older men is enlargement of the prostate without cancer, a condition known as *benign prostatic hypertrophy*. A common surgical treatment, called *transurethral resection of the prostate*, is to enter the urethra with a flexible instrument and slice away sections of the prostate. This usually results in ejaculation going back into the bladder rather than out through the urethra.

Few men are well prepared for this outcome and, in our experience, many find it very upsetting when not given a forewarning or explanation of why it occurs. Such men need education and reassurance to help them accept this change, since it is irreversible. It is generally argued that this type of surgery should not cause erectile difficulties, but many men and their clinicians believe it sometimes does. Erectile dysfunction after such surgery may sometimes be psychogenic, but about 4 percent of men have physically based loss of erectile capacity following the surgery.

Dyspareunia, or painful intercourse, in the aging woman is most often associated with the postmenopausal changes discussed earlier, such as the vagina becoming smaller, loss of elasticity of the vagina, delays and decreases in vaginal lubrication, and thinning and impaired elevation of the vaginal lips. It also can be psychologically mediated or associated with medical conditions, including diabetes, endometriosis, pelvic adhesions after surgery, and pelvic tumors.

Multiple Simultaneous Causes

Many health problems that occur more frequently in the older population do not directly affect sexual organs or function, but they have an indirect affect. Two that are particularly common are arthritis and lung disease. Arthritis, with its stiffness and joint pain, interferes with sexual activity itself, as well as with pleasure and satisfaction. One woman described the frequency of partner sexual activity when first married as "daily and twice on Sunday." But with age her activity had dwindled to almost nothing because of arthritis. We recommended alternate positions to ease the strain of painful joints. For example, the spoon position allows both partners to lie on their sides, the woman in front of the man, so he can enter her vagina from behind and neither needs to support his or her weight.

Lung disease, such as emphysema, asthma, and bronchitis, results in shortness of breath and reduced energy, which interfere directly with sexual activity and enjoyment. In extreme cases we recommend that the healthy partner take over much of the physical movement, allowing the person with shortness of breath to continue to participate at a level that is physically comfortable.

Although all these medical considerations can have important effects as single factors, it would be difficult to overemphasize the importance of the cumulative effect of multiple simultaneous causes for sexual dysfunction in the elderly. It is quite common for us to see an older patient with a long history of smoking and lung disease, a history of alcohol abuse, long-standing vascular disease, and obesity who did not lose adequate erectile functioning or, for women, lubrication and sexual desire, until developing an additional disease, such as diabetes. The physical basis of our sexual responses is vulnerable (in that it is dependent on many systems), but it is also resilient. Often, multiple problems must be present for that innate resilience to be overcome.

We saw one case, John and Daisy Sutton, in which John's problems with erection seemed to have been in part a result of his diabetes. He also had high blood pressure, another possible cause of erectile dysfunction. Daisy's problems may have been related to postmenopausal pain with intercourse, with an additional possibility of loss of desire due to reduced androgen production. This helped us begin to develop a diagnosis, but it didn't capture all the information or provide a complete explanation. Next, we turned to how medications might also be affecting their sexual function, and we address these issues next.

MEDICATIONS

Many medications have a negative impact on sexual function, and, in general, the more medications a person is using, the greater the likelihood of negative effects. Because older adults metabolize medications more slowly and are more likely than younger adults to take multiple medications, the impact on elders is particularly heavy.

Antidepressants

The most common mental health problem for older adults is depression, and antidepressant medication is the most commonly offered treatment. Of the three classes of antidepressants in general use, each has different effects on sexuality. It's hard to determine whether sexual difficulties are a result of depression itself or a side effect of a drug treatment. A defining symptom of depression, for example, is loss of sexual interest, and loss of interest can also be a result of some antidepressants.

We sometimes see people on tricyclic antidepressants like Elavil say they experience decreased desire, decreased arousal, and/or delayed orgasm. In fact, some 10 percent to 43 percent of people on this type of antidepressant make these reports. And people on the monoamine oxidase inhibitors (MAOIs) such as Nardil and Parnate report even higher rates of sexual dysfunction. Another antidepressant, Trazodone, has been associated with rare cases of priapism, a painful erection that will not subside and, if untreated, can result in serious and permanent damage to the penis.

The newer antidepressants, the selective serotonin reuptake inhibitors (SSRIs), which include Prozac, Zoloft, and Paxil, are associated with reduced desire and a different type of sexual dysfunction—delayed or absent orgasm. Both men and women report this in our clinic. Because these medications are new, we're unsure of the exact frequency of orgasm problems, but other clinics have reported their occurrence in 10 percent to 75 percent of patients. Some users say these sexual side effects dissipate after a few months or when the dose is reduced, but the predictability of improvement is yet unclear.

Older patients commonly receive medications to treat anxiety, such as Ativan, Valium, Xanax, and Librium. Although we've had some reports of problems in desire, arousal, and orgasmic capacity, we haven't seen a consistent pattern.

There aren't a lot of geriatric patients on medication for bipolar disorder (manic depressive illness). When they are, lithium, the typical treatment, has been associated with erectile dysfunction, but it's rare. We don't know the effects on women's sexual function.

Antipsychotics

Many older patients, especially those living in hospitals or nursing homes or whose behavior has been disruptive, receive antipsychotic medications, such as Haldol or Prolixin. Although Thorazine, Mellaril, and Prolixin are the most widely cited culprits, all the antipsychotic medications can disrupt sexual interest, arousal, and orgasm, and we see both men and women with these problems. They can be tough cases to treat because continuing the offending medication is necessary, so we treat the sexual side effect. Sometimes a switch to a different drug will result in fewer sexual effects. It's our understanding that Prolixin, Trilafon, and Mellaril also cause ejaculatory disturbances in more than 50 percent of men using them; effects on orgasm in women are unknown. And occasionally men report priapism when on antipsychotics.

High Blood Pressure Medication

Many of the elderly take at least one high blood pressure medication. Diuretics such as Maxide are often used as the first-line treatment of elevated blood pressure, but they are associated with erectile dysfunction. Less frequently associated with problems are the alpha-blockers, such as prazosin and terazosin. Finally, newer medications that have not yet been implicated in sexual difficulties include calcium channel blockers and ACE (angiotensin converting enzyme) inhibitors. It's quite possible that this type of medication, in addition to diabetes, contributed to lack of full erection in the previously mentioned case of John Sutton. If an older woman on blood pressure medications told us she was experiencing reduced vaginal lubrication, we might suspect the drugs.

Digoxin, disopyramide (used to treat heart arrhythmias), and clofibrate (for treatment of elevated cholesterol levels) have been associated with erectile dysfunction and decreased interest in sex. Tagamet and Zantac, medications used to treat upset stomachs and soothe the effects of other medications on the digestive tract, have been associated with erection problems, decreased sexual interest, breast enlargement, and breast pain. We saw a fifty-year-old woman who reported low desire for the preceding four years. Coincidentally, she had been started on Tagamet four years earlier. Although after she stopped the medication she continued to experience decreased desire, it appeared that the problem started with Tagamet and was being maintained by other factors, including anxiety from a high-stress job. Anticonvulsants are associated with a decrease in sexual interest in men, possibly because they reduce testosterone levels, but effects in women are unknown. Anabolic steroids and estrogens, antiandrogens, and cancer chemotherapy agents are also associated with reduced desire and arousal.

Drug Abuse

We often see drugs of abuse, including alcohol and tobacco, disrupt sexual function, and their impact increases with patients' age. Although small amounts of alcohol may disinhibit men and women, we find that larger quantities lead to reduced response of the vagina and reduced erection, as well as reduced sex drive and orgasm. Chronic alcohol abuse has been associated with erection problems, as high as 54 percent in some studies, and dysfunction may not be reversible even if the former drinker becomes abstinent.

Tobacco use can make getting an erection more difficult and possibly decrease vaginal lubrication because it reduces blood flow to the genitals. These effects take time to develop, so they are more likely to be seen in older people who are lifelong smokers.

TREATMENT OF SEXUAL PROBLEMS

Treatment of sexual dysfunction in the elderly often involves more than one component. Our interdisciplinary approach includes brief or intensive individual or couples therapy in conjunction with medical treatment. Medically based interventions that colleagues can provide or for which patients can be referred include hormonal and surgical treatment, vacuum constriction devices, oral medications, and changes in pharmacological regimens.

Psychologically Based Interventions: The PLISSIT Model

A standard model of sex therapy, the PLISSIT model, is especially appropriate for the elderly population. The PLISSIT model is a four-level conceptual model that guides the therapist from simple to more complex interventions. If problems are not resolved with a simple intervention, the therapist adds more complex interventions as needed. PLISSIT is an acronym for the four progressive levels of sex therapy: *P*ermission, *L*imited *I*nformation, *S*pecific *S*uggestions, and *I*ntensive *T*herapy.

Permission. In the first level, Permission, the therapist acts as an authority, giving endorsement to sexual activities and fantasies and reassuring the person that he or she is normal. For instance, we often see older men who need permission to masturbate as an alternative to intercourse when a wife is uninterested or ill. One man in our clinic associated self-stimulation with adolescence and believed it reflected sexual inadequacy rather than seeing it as appropriate regardless of age or relationship status. We gave him permission to consider resuming this activity, especially in light of his wife's decreased desire to be sexual.

Limited Information. In the next level, Limited Information, a clinician provides factual information specific to the individual's problem. Such psychoeducational interventions can be quite successful with the elderly. People rarely know about normal, age-related changes in sexual function, let alone changes due to illness or medications, so they may misinterpret these changes. Here's an example:

A fifty-two-year-old divorced diabetic man was experiencing decreased erections, achieving about 60 percent of a normal erection. The last two women he dated each believed that his lack of full erections meant he didn't find them sexually desirable. During short-term therapy with an interdisciplinary team, the man began to understand that his decreased erections were physically caused and that he was not alone in experiencing this problem. As he considered treatment options, he began to feel more confident and started dating again. He also began to discuss in therapy how and when to tell a potential sex partner about the quality of his erections before initiating a sexual relationship.

Specific Suggestions. The third step of the model, Specific Suggestions, involves simple problem-solving interventions. For example, an older couple who used to have sex after romantic evenings out will need to change their pattern if they can no longer drive after dark. Older couples who have always considered the man's erection to be the signal to begin sexual activity will also need specific suggestions on changes in the initiation and orchestration of sex, as the older man will likely need direct penile stimulation to obtain an erection.

Couples may need to utilize new positions for sexual intercourse that are less stressful to arthritic joints or place fewer energy demands. An excellent pamphlet is available from the Arthritis Foundation for this purpose. We frequently see men and women experiencing decreased desire unrelated to medical changes, so we give suggestions on ways to augment flagging interest, including sexually explicit videos, magazines, books, sexual fantasy, and sexy lingerie.

Intensive Therapy.   Intensive therapy, the fourth level of intervention, is used when brief therapy is ineffective or when specific suggestions are not carried out because of intrapersonal conflict. A specific program unique to that person's or couple's needs and circumstances is developed.

Couples therapy techniques are also appropriate at this level, such as couple communication. Basic to effective communication is managing the anxiety experienced when a partner is anxious, agitated, or upset. It also includes managing one's own anxiety when talking with one's partner. The key is for the listener to maintain boundaries, avoid reacting in kind, and avoid taking personal affront—that is, to keep in mind that what the partner is saying is a reflection of that person, not the listener. Granted this is difficult to do and doesn't come easily, but the benefits are enormous. A listener who maintains boundaries is better able to understand and empathize with a partner. And differentiation allows the initiator to fully explore his or her feelings.

Even when medical problems initiated the sexual dysfunction, psychological factors may play an important role in the treatment plan. For one couple we saw, both partners were given permission to express their honest worries and wishes regarding sex. Jose was assured that he could express his own interest in continuing a sexual relationship rather than expressing vague fears that this was something his wife "needed." He was also given permission to express his worries about achieving only a partial erection, likely a result of cardiovascular disease. Maria was encouraged to express her waning desire since going through menopause, and it was suggested that she didn't need to be more sexually active than she wanted to be. Both were provided information about normal age-related sexual changes and the impact of medical conditions on their situation. This process helped them to communicate more comfortably about sex as well as to challenge their perceptions that they were "just too old" to care about sex any more.

We also gave Maria and Jose specific suggestions. We began the couple on a series of whole-body stroking exercises to help each focus on pleasure and sensuality. We also worked with them on using a mechanical device (described in more detail later) to help Jose get and keep an erection, and how to use it in a sensual way as part of love play. Maria had already been provided estrogen cream as part of the medical aspect of the interdisciplinary care plan. In this part of therapy the couple planned how to use the cream in a sensual way as part of foreplay, rather than having Maria apply it on her own before sex.

Intensive therapy was brief in this case, and took the role of coordinating all the interventions and providing some additional training in sexual communication. For example, both believed that only men discuss sex, only men initiate sex, and men should always be ready for sex. While these beliefs had not presented major problems when they were younger, they were clearly affecting their ability to make flexible adaptations to age-related changes. With therapy, they were able to develop a new pattern in which Jose could express both interest in sex and disinterest if timing was wrong. Maria was able to express interest, which did return when she felt closer to Jose. Both could talk intimately about the physical aspect of their relationship and how important it remained as they faced other losses with aging.

Medically Based Interventions

When a medication-induced dysfunction is suspected, it's important to consult with the patient's primary care clinician, who may choose to discontinue the medication, reduce the dosage, or try an alternate drug. In some cases, the person can be left on the medication and the dysfunction can be treated or an antidote may be available (Periactin or Yocan, for example, may effectively treat lack of orgasm caused by SSRIs). Geriatric patients with multiple medical problems often have no viable medication adjustments; in our clinic, we generally treat the secondary dysfunction rather than manipulating drugs that are otherwise effective.

Our team physician recommends hormone replacement therapy (HRT) to increase vaginal lubrication and decrease vaginal dryness (and thus, dyspareunia). For women unable to use HRT, we recommend artificial lubricants, such as KY Jelly, Astroglide, and Probe. For aging women with decreased sexual desire, we would consider testosterone replacement therapy, although little research has been done to confirm its clinical impact.

One woman in our clinic began using a topical estrogen cream to reduce vaginal dryness. This helped reduce the vaginal pain she experienced with penetration, increasing her interest in sexual intercourse. For another woman, changing medications proved helpful. Benja's arthritis medication was changed to one less upsetting to her stomach, so she greatly reduced her use of Zantac, used to treat her upset stomach. When the Zantac was reduced, her sexual interest increased.

Decreased Desire

Decreased libido, the second most frequently reported sexual problem we hear from older men, can be treated with testosterone enanthate injections when low levels of testosterone are the cause. Men reporting increased sexual desire following a trial of testosterone are placed on a treatment regimen with regular medical monitoring for potential adverse affects, specifically increased production of red blood cells, which can increase the risk of a stroke, and proliferation of prostate cancer. Testosterone injections don't increase the likelihood of prostate cancer but may cause it to progress if it develops for other reasons.

Erectile Dysfunction

Surgical treatment for erectile dysfunction includes vascular surgery and penile implants. Less invasive interventions are also available and are usually chosen by our patients. There are two widely used nonsurgical treatments: the vacuum pump and penile self-injections. Both have high success rates in creating satisfactory erections for intercourse.

Pharmacological agents, such as prostaglandin-E$_1$, injected into the penis result in an erection. The success rate with injections in the elderly population is equivalent to that in a younger population, though older men may require a larger dose—up to 50 percent more—than younger men. But there are at least four potential problems with injections. First, they can result in priapism; users must be aware of the need for immediate medical attention if this occurs. Second, the injections are sometimes described as painful. Third, scar tissue may develop at injection sites, causing a curved, sometimes painful, distortion of the erect penis. But the main problem with injections is the abhorrence, expressed by many men, to the idea of sticking a needle into their penis. They just can't imagine doing it.

The vacuum constriction device has gained considerable acceptance as a noninvasive treatment for erectile problems. The systems, available from various manufacturers, all consist of a clear plastic cylinder, a vacuum pump, and rubber or elastic rings; we prefer the Osbon ErecAid System. Use of the pump and cylinder create a vacuum, drawing blood into the penis and mimicking a natural erection. The man or his partner then slips a band from the cylinder onto the base of the penis, restricting the outflow of the blood and maintaining the erection until the ring is removed. We demonstrate the device to each individual in privacy to assess his response and train him in its use. In our experience, it is important for each man's partner to attend the session if at all possible; success is much more likely for men whose partners are actively involved in training and use of the system. In fact, for elderly men with decreased manual dexterity, the partner may have to apply the device or assist in its operation.

Following the demonstration, we do regular follow-ups to reinforce successful use or to problem solve if the system isn't used regularly or properly. Typically, the psychologists on our team do the follow-up. Problems with the pump system can generally be resolved and have, in our experience, never created serious problems for those using them.

A number of men report "graduating" from the pump; that is, they begin to get erections spontaneously. Some men have a very rapid return of spontaneous sexual function, which they attribute to reduced performance anxiety as they know they can always get an adequate erection with the pump.

In the case of one sixty-three-year-old man, testosterone injections were not needed as his sexual desire remained strong and his testosterone levels were normal. Because changing his medications was not feasible as these effectively controlled his high blood pressure and depression, he decided to try the ErecAid pump. The ErecAid produced erections of 95 percent of normal strength for him, and he and his partner incorporated its use into their lovemaking.

INTERVENTIONS FOR SPECIFIC POPULATIONS

We now turn to two select populations, women who have had mastectomies and people with dementia, who have special needs in sex therapy. We address both the particular concerns they may experience as well as treatment interventions.

Women Who Have Had Mastectomies

We encourage couples to return to sexual activity as soon as possible after the woman has undergone a mastectomy; otherwise, sexual avoidance may become a well-established pattern and more difficult to treat. Timing needs to be sensitively determined so that the return to sexual activity is not impaired by the arousal-reducing impact of chemotherapy. Many women fear that a breastless and scarred body will be a turn-off to a partner. Typically their partners say this is untrue, but unless the partners talk about their concerns, the woman may avoid sexual contact, fearing rejection. This, in turn, may provoke apprehension in her partner, leading to performance anxiety and related sexual difficulties, such as erectile problems.

Sexual difficulties of the mastectomy patient, such as low desire caused by depression, need to be addressed. Effective interventions have been developed for individual and couples counseling. For example, women may need to refocus concerns that partners will reject them, shifting instead to the pleasures of sensual touching by partners. This can be accomplished by basic sensate focus exercises.

It has been argued that loss of sexual interest in a woman who has had a mastectomy was indirectly caused by change in body image and fear of rejection by her partner. While these indirect affects are typically present, decreases in sexual desire and orgasmic capacity often have a physical basis as well. In particular, chemotherapy after mastectomy for breast cancer decreases testosterone levels, lowering sexual drive. Sex therapist Helen Singer Kaplan has successfully treated such women with testosterone without the adverse effects of virilization. This seems a reasonable treatment to consider.

People with Dementia

Dementia has serious sexual implications for both patient and caregiver. We often hear, for instance, that people with Alzheimer's disease experience sexual dysfunction, or caregivers may feel hesitant to have sex with partners who are unable to express either consent or refusal. Yet both may continue to have sexual thoughts, feelings, and desires. We've also seen men with early Alzheimer's who find resulting erectile problems alarming. Sex therapy can be helpful in these cases, particularly when both partners want to continue sexual activity.

We give permission to caregivers to honor their decision to discontinue sexual activity because their partners no longer recognize them, and instead, to satisfy their own sexual desires through self-stimulation. If a demented partner initiates unwanted sexual activity, we suggest the caregiver distract the patient or focus him or her on more acceptable sexual contact, such as massage, hugging, cuddling, and kissing. The need for touch by both patient and partner caregiver can also be met through these activities. We assure caretakers concerned about inappropriate sexual behavior—masturbation in public, for example—that this is unlikely. Demented males demonstrate little public sexual behavior of any kind, either appropriate or inappropriate. For the occasional patient who does demonstrate this problem, we train caregivers to handle the behavior calmly and to provide privacy or distraction.

Although aging is associated with a general decline in various factors related to sexual function, sexual satisfaction can, and most typically does, remain stable. Couples who place a high value on sexual intimacy regardless of age are able to make the necessary adjustments that allow them to continue to be sexually active. However, sexuality can be placed at risk in older adults by a number of health issues, by negative stereotypes about aging, or by lack of flexibility for making needed adjustments.

Willingness to experiment with alternatives and the involvement and attitudes of both partners in a sexual relationship are just as important in maintaining sexual activity as are physical changes related to aging. When working with sexual concerns of the elderly, we advocate an interdisciplinary approach to evaluating, diagnosing, and treating sexual dysfunction. This approach avoids arbitrary classification of sexual problems as "biomedical" versus "psychogenic" and instead recognizes the complex, interrelated roles of both factors in the development of sexual dysfunction and in its successful resolution.

NOTES

P. 135, *The most commonly reported pattern:* George, L. K., & Weiler, S. J. (1981). Sexuality in middle and late life. *Archives of General Psychiatry, 38,* 919–923.

P. 137, *In older women:* Kaiser, F. E. (1994). Sexuality. In P. D. O'Donnell (Ed.), *Geriatric urology* (pp. 493–502). Boston: Little, Brown.

P. 138, *In a review of 195 people:* Zeiss, R. A., Delmonico, R. L., Zeiss, A. M., & Dornbrand, L. (1991). Psychologic disorder and sexual dysfunction in elders. *Clinics in Geriatric Medicine, 7,* 133–151.

P. 138, *Images of sexuality in elders:* Schover, L. R. (1986). Sexual problems. In L. Teri & P. M. Lewinsohn (Eds.), *Geropsychological assessment and treatment: Selected topics.* New York: Springer-Verlag.

P. 139, *A pattern of erectile dysfunction has been:* LoPiccolo, J., & Heiman, J. R. (1988). Broad spectrum treatment of low sexual desire. In S. R. Leiblum & R. C. Rosen (Eds.), *Sexual desire disorders* (pp. 107–144). New York: Guilford Press.

P. 140, *Fifty-two percent of patients:* American Psychiatric Association. (1987). *Diagnostic and statistical manual of mental disorders* (3rd ed., rev.). Washington, DC: Author.

P. 146, *Testosterone also seems:* Sherwin, B. B., Gelfand, M. M., & Brender, W. (1985). Androgen enhances sexual motivation in females: A prospective cross-over study of sex steroid administration in the surgical menopause. *Psychosomatic Medicine, 7,* 339–351.

P. 147, *Erectile dysfunction after such surgery:* Bolt, J. W., Evans, C., & Marshall, V. R. (1986). Sexual dysfunction after prostatectomy. *British Journal of Urology, 59,* 319–322.

P. 149, *In fact, some 10 percent to 43 percent:* Balon, R., Yeragani, V. K., Pohl, R., & Ramesh, C. (1993). Sexual dysfunction during antidepressant treatment. *Journal of Clinical Psychiatry, 54,* 209–212.

P. 150, *Because these medications are new:* Walker, P. W., Cole, J. O., Gardner, E. A., Hughes, A. R., Johnston, J. A., Batey, S. R., & Lineberry, C. G. (1993). Improvement in fluoxetine-associated sexual dysfunction in patients switched to bupropion. *Journal of Clinical Psychiatry, 54,* 459–465.

P. 150, *Although Thorazine, Mellaril, and Prolixin:* Sullivan, G., & Lukoff, D. (1990). Sexual side effects of antipsychotic medication: Evaluation and interventions. *Hospital and Community Psychiatry, 41,* 1238–1241.

P. 152, *Chronic alcohol abuse has been associated:* Wein, A. J., & Van Arsdalen, K. N. (1988). Drug-induced male sexual dysfunction. *Urology Clinics of North America, 15,* 23–31.

P. 152, *A standard model of sex therapy:* Annon, J., (1974). *The behavioral treatment of sexual problems: Vol. 1. Brief therapy.* Honolulu: Enabling Systems.

P. 157, *Both have high success rates:* Turner, L. A., & Althof, S. E. (1992). The clinical effectiveness of self-injection and external vacuum devices in the treatment of erectile dysfunction: A six-month comparison. *Psychiatric Medicine, 10,* 283–293.

P. 157, *The success rate with injections:* Kerfoot, W. W., & Carson, C. C. (1991). Pharmacologically induced erections among geriatric men. *Journal of Urology, 146,* 1022–1024.

P. 159, *Sex therapist Helen Singer Kaplan:* Kaplan, H. S. (1992). A neglected issue: The sexual side effects of current treatments for breast cancer. *Journal of Sex & Marital Therapy, 18,* 3–19.

P. 159, *We've also seen men with early Alzheimer's:* Davies, H., Zeiss, A., & Tinklenberg, J. (1992). 'Til death do us part: Intimacy and sexuality in the marriages of Alzheimer's patients. *Journal of Psychosocial Nursing, 30,* 5–10.

P. 160, *Demented males demonstrate little:* Zeiss, A. M., Davies H. D., & Tinklenberg, J. R. (submitted for publication). An observational study of inappropriate sexual behavior in demented male patients.

6

COGNITIVE IMPAIRMENT

Greer M. Murphy, Jr.

Disorders of cognition are extremely common among the elderly. By some estimates, 5 percent of the population over the age of sixty-five suffers from some form of chronic cognitive impairment. In those over eighty, the frequency may be as high as 20 percent. Thus, all health care providers who work with the elderly should be familiar with the basic principles and techniques for evaluation and management of cognitive impairment. Because many of the assessment procedures and treatments for cognitive impairment require specialized training, clinicians with a variety of backgrounds are usually involved in the care of these patients using a "team" approach. I feel it is important that each member of the team be familiar with all phases of the assessment and treatment process so as to encourage communication among team members and coordinate treatment goals. Although the team approach is often used in a hospital setting, it can work equally well among medical and nonmedical members of a group practice or among an informal network of solo practitioners of different backgrounds.

My hope is that this chapter will provide an introduction for nonmedical clinicians interested in cognitive impairment and stimulate further study. Personally, I learn from each new elderly patient with cognitive impairment I see, and I try to identify something about each patient that is new or unfamiliar to me. I then use this new finding as the basis for further reading and study. Such an approach is really necessary in this complex and rapidly changing field.

In the elderly, the term *cognitive impairment* is often used interchangeably with the term *dementia*. Dementia is a syndrome, meaning that it can be caused by a variety of disease processes and is characterized by a chronic impairment of cognitive functioning that may or may not be reversible. In this review, I focus primarily on evaluation and management of dementia or chronic cognitive impairment. However, not all elderly persons with cognitive impairment suffer from dementia; some cognitive impairment is acute and is termed delirium, as is briefly discussed below.

EVALUATION OF COGNITIVE IMPAIRMENT

A variety of techniques have been developed for clinical assessment of cognitive impairment in the elderly. Two broad categories of these are the mental status examination and formal neuropsychological testing. In this chapter, I discuss some of the techniques I use in mental status testing and some of the neuropsychological tests we administer in our clinic. However, the reader not acquainted with these techniques is encouraged to refer to books devoted entirely to these topics as examination of cognition is a complex but fascinating field deserving a therapist's in-depth study before he or she approaches the patient for evaluation.

Mental Status Examination

The mental status examination has been described by many authors. The book by Strub and Black contains an especially clear and complete description. Following their technique, the clinician can determine the patient's status on the key dimensions of cognition.

Briefly, these dimensions include level of consciousness, attention, orientation, memory, language, calculations, abstraction, praxis, and constructional ability. *Level of consciousness* refers to the degree of central nervous system activation observed in the patient. This is determined by observation of the patient during the interview and is described as hyperalert, alert, lethargic, stuporous, or comatose. *Attention* refers to the patient's ability to attend to relevant stimuli in the environment without being distracted by either internal or irrelevant external stimuli. Testing attention depends in part on the patient's having a sufficient level of alertness to process the information being presented. Attention is usually assessed by simple observation of the patient or tasks such as digit repetition. *Orientation* refers to the patient's ability to state his or her identity, physical location, and the date and time. In order to be fully oriented, the patient must be alert and attentive to his or her surroundings.

Memory is the ability to retain and recall information previously presented. Many ways of subdividing the various aspects of memory function have been devised. One simple dichotomy is between material learned in the past prior to the examination and material presented by the examiner that the patient must recall later during the examination. To test material learned during the past, the examiner often queries the patient about personal information such as date of birth, address, phone number, or historical facts and dates. When a patient is tested for previously learned material, a corroborating source such as a spouse is invaluable, as patients may confabulate information to avoid embarrassment. To test the ability to learn and retain new information, the examiner usually presents three words and asks the patient to recall them three minutes later. However, much more sophisticated testing such as recall of a standardized story can be performed by the examiner without special testing materials. As with all aspects of the mental status examination, for the patient's memory to be tested adequately, he or she must be able to attend to the stimuli being presented so as to store the material for later recall.

Language refers to the patient's ability to receive and transmit information using words and sentences. Language function is usually divided into comprehension, production, and repetition. Comprehension is tested by asking the patient to follow a three-step command, or if that fails, by asking questions that require a simple yes or no response. Production is assessed by observing spontaneous speech, asking the patient to name objects, or asking the patient to produce a simple sentence about the weather. Repetition is tested by asking the patient to repeat a word or phrase. Deficits in any of these areas may indicate dysfunction of specific regions of the brain. Consultation with an expert is usually indicated if the screening language examination is abnormal.

Testing *calculation* is straightforward and involves asking the patient to perform progressively more difficult tasks involving arithmetic operations. Calculation ability is dependent on education, so the examiner must tailor the tasks to the patient's level of training. Often a spouse or other relative can provide information on the patient's prior skill level.

Abstraction is a higher cognitive function that is usually tested by asking the patient to interpret proverbs or to explain conceptual similarities between two objects, such as a piano and a violin. This cognitive function is to some extent dependent on education, but the complexity of the task can be tailored in some degree to the patient's background. In my experience, subtle deficits in abstraction are difficult to detect, but a severe inability to abstract is usually apparent on the mental status examination.

Praxis, sometimes also called ideomotor praxis, refers to the ability to perform complex learned movements or motor acts. For praxis to be tested, language comprehension and muscle strength and coordination cannot be grossly impaired. In this test, the patient is asked to demonstrate, for example, how he or she would blow out a match or comb his or her hair. Praxis is a higher cognitive function, and deficits can sometimes be related to dysfunction of important association areas of the brain.

Constructional ability, also sometimes called constructional praxis, is a higher cognitive function involving the ability to reproduce spatial information such as shapes and angles. This is usually tested by asking the patient to produce a drawing of an object such as cross, or copy a model provided by the examiner, such as a diagram of a cube. I have found tests of constructional skill to be very sensitive to even mild brain dysfunction in the elderly and recommend that these tests always be included in the mental status examination.

With elderly patients, it is particularly important to consider any complicating factors that might impair performance in any portion of the mental status examination. For example, the elderly often have difficulties with hearing so they may not hear instructions clearly, and as a result their performance may suffer. In hospitalized patients, pain, fatigue, medications, or even an unfamiliar environment can impair performance on the mental status examination. The examiner should make every effort to minimize these extraneous factors, but sometimes the only alternative is to delay complete examination of the patient until more suitable circumstances can be arranged.

Quantifying the Mental Status Examination

A central problem with the mental status examination is the difficulty of quantifying the degree of cognitive impairment present in a consistent way from patient to patient. From examining many patients with varying degrees of cognitive impairment, I have developed an informal sense of what is appropriate for patients of a particular age and educational background. Strub and Black provide "normative" patient responses for many of the tasks I have described above. Yet, I find that many times I want to "put a number" on the degree of cognitive impairment in a patient, particularly for communication with colleagues.

Many attempts have been made to develop psychometric instruments that can be administered rapidly and without special training but that yield a quantitative score of cognitive function. The most widely used is the Folstein Mini Mental Status Examination. Advantages of the Mini Mental exam are that it is easy and quick to use and that it has been used in a great many research studies of dementia over the years. Thus, norms exist that take into account age, education, and ethnic background. The principal disadvantage is that it is not sensitive to mild cognitive impairment. Patients complaining of memory problems may do well on the Mini Mental, but more challenging testing may reveal subtle deficits. Another disadvantage is that the questions and tasks on the Mini Mental tap a variety of brain functions, making it difficult to sort out exactly where the deficit exists. Nevertheless, the Mini Mental remains useful as a screening test for cognitive impairment, especially when used in conjunction with other instruments.

Another widely used examination for detecting cognitive impairment in the elderly is the Neurobehavioral Cognitive Status Examination (NCSE). This examination takes somewhat longer to administer than the Mini Mental exam but it is more comprehensive and more sensitive to mild cognitive impairment. The test consists of a series of screening questions for a variety of cognitive functions similar to items on the Mini Mental. However, if a patient fails a screening question, the NCSE provides a more in-depth examination of the affected cognitive function to determine the degree of the deficit. The NCSE generates scores for individual cognitive functions that can be compared to profiles typically seen in a wide variety of neuropsychiatric disorders.

Another useful method for quantifying impairment is the Global Deterioration Scale (GDS). This easily administered instrument takes into consideration not only cognitive deficits but deficits in activities of daily living and psychiatric disturbances that are common in elderly patients. Progressive deterioration of time can be documented with serial GDS scores.

Neuropsychological Testing

In many cases, the clinician may want more comprehensive testing of cognitive functions than can be obtained with mental status testing or screening exams. When I see that a patient has a mild deficit in a particular area on a screening exam, I often wonder whether this result represents early impairment or simply suggests that the patient didn't do well on that particular item on that particular day. For example, if a patient has deficits in language production skills on the Mini Mental, I might want to follow up with an instrument such as the Boston Naming Test to acquire more information on the severity of the problem as well as give the patient another chance to perform optimally. At the Stanford Alzheimer's Center, we routinely supplement the Mini Mental with the Alzheimer's Disease Assessment Scale, the Blessed-Roth Dementia Scale, the Boston Naming Test, the WAIS-R block design, the WAIS-R digit symbol, the WMS-R logical memory, the Fuld Object Memory Test, and Trail Making Test, parts A and B. Many other excellent tests of varying degrees of complexity are available.

If formal neuropsychological testing is required I invariably consult a colleague with specialized training in this area. Although it is possible to administer these tests using forms and manuals, I believe interpretation and integration with other data require special training. It is worthwhile to find a colleague in neuropsychology with experience in working with the elderly. Interpretation of deficits on neuropsychological tests in elderly and in younger patients will differ because of differences in the prevalence of neurologic disease in the two populations.

DIFFERENTIAL DIAGNOSIS

It is important to have a clear notion of the common causes of cognitive impairment in the elderly. This will allow you to formulate a "differential diagnosis," a list of possible causes for a set of symptoms. Then the various possibilities can be systematically eliminated until the most likely cause is defined.

A good way to subdivide patients with cognitive impairment is on the basis of whether the impairment is chronic or acute. Chronic cognitive impairment is called dementia. Acute cognitive impairment is called delirium. Common causes of chronic, progressive cognitive impairment in the elderly include Alzheimer's disease, vascular dementia, depression, and chronic intoxication with alcohol or prescription drugs. Common causes of acute cognitive impairment (delirium) in the elderly are strokes, alcohol and drug intoxications or withdrawal, head trauma, and systemic medical illnesses such as pneumonia, heart disease, or urinary tract infections. By knowing the common causes of cognitive impairment, a therapist has a good idea right away of what the problem might be.

When a patient presents with complaints related to memory, orientation, or other higher cortical functions, the first and most important information to be obtained is the history. If the change is acute, then it is likely that the patient is suffering from a delirium, which is best defined as a clouding of consciousness. The key feature of delirium is a fluctuating level of awareness. One minute the patient may be hyperalert, and the next drowsy and hypoalert. Orientation is impaired and the patient may suffer vivid auditory or visual hallucinations. Because of the impaired state of awareness, other cognitive functions are also impaired. For example, memory function is abnormal because sensory information necessary for establishing new memories is distorted by the delirium. Many cases of delirium are caused by underlying medical conditions that are reversible, resulting in full recovery. However, some cases of delirium, such as that caused by alcohol withdrawal, are life threatening if not treated. All patients with delirium require prompt medical evaluation to prevent complications.

Sometimes a family member or another clinician will report that the cognitive impairment is acute but on careful investigation the clinician will determine that the impairment is long-standing. However, because acute changes in cognition can be associated with life-threatening illnesses, it is wise to consider the change as acute until serious underlying medical conditions have been excluded. As an example, an elderly patient may be brought to the emergency room in a confused state. The history may suggest that the patient has been like this for some time.

After a routine medical examination shows normal results, the patient is returned to the nursing home. Several days later, the patient becomes comatose and then dies from bacterial meningitis, which had been missed because signs of infection in the elderly are often subtle.

If the impairment is found to be chronic, the patient is likely to have a dementia, which may or may not be reversible. Before beginning a workup to determine the cause of the dementia, however, it is important to rule out two common reversible disorders that can result in chronic cognitive impairment: depression and alcohol and drug use.

Impairment Due to Depression

Elderly patients with severe depressive episodes can appear very similar to patients with dementias due to degenerative brain diseases such as Alzheimer's disease. This syndrome has been called "pseudodementia," but it more properly should be called the "dementia syndrome of depression" as these patients really appear demented. The situation is complicated by the fact that up to 25 percent of patients with degenerative dementias such as Alzheimer's disease also have depressed mood. Thus, when an elderly cognitively impaired patient expresses depressive symptoms, there is no assurance that the cognitive impairment is entirely due to the depression. It could be a symptom of an underlying neurodegenerative disorder.

A frequently cited way of distinguishing patients with cognitive impairment due to depression from those with other dementias is that the depressed patient is apathetic and disinterested in the examiner's questions, whereas the demented patient is interested and makes an effort but fails. Another purportedly distinguishing feature is that demented patients have loss of recall primarily for recent events whereas depressed patients show more global memory loss. In practice, these dichotomies are of little use. Indeed, until there are objective physiological tests that can distinguish the dementia syndrome of depression from other dementias, there is only one real option in dealing with depressed, cognitively impaired patients; that is, to treat the depression, usually with combined psychotherapy and pharmacotherapy and see whether the cognitive impairment improves. If the depression lifts and the cognitive impairment abates, then an underlying degenerative dementia is less likely. However, if the depression improves but the patient remains demented, other causes must be sought for the cognitive impairment.

In practice we also see patients with severe anxiety disorders who may appear to have cognitive impairment. Deficits in memory, attention, and even orientation may be seen. This is generally caused by anxiety interfering with normal information processing by the nervous system. Anxiety reduction by behavioral or pharmacologic means usually results in an improvement in cognition. Bear in mind, however, that patients with degenerative dementias such as Alzheimer's disease occasionally present with anxious mood.

Impairment from Alcohol or Drug Use

Chronic cognitive impairment secondary to alcohol or drug use is common in the elderly. The rare Korsakoff's disease seen in chronic alcoholics resulting from thiamine deficiency is classically described as a pure amnesia in the absence of other cognitive impairments. In practice, deficits in other areas of cognition are also seen. The more common "alcoholic dementia" affects all cognitive functions and results from the toxic effects of years of ethanol abuse on the nervous system. At present, there is some controversy as to whether alcoholic dementia is reversible if the patient abstains from alcohol use. However, if the history strongly suggests long-term excessive alcohol intake, every effort should be made to encourage abstinence, and cognitive evaluation should be repeated at a later date. The acute effects of heavy ethanol use on the nervous system last at least two weeks, so little is to be gained from formal reevaluation of the patient until after the initial detoxification period.

A wide variety of prescription drugs have side effects that can cause cognitive impairment in the elderly. Metabolism of drugs often slows with aging, and drug levels in the blood may slowly rise over time despite constant dosing. I advise non-medical clinicians to refer elderly patients for review of their medications whenever there is new onset or worsening of cognitive impairment.

Alzheimer's Disease

If depression or alcohol use do not appear to be important factors in the chronic cognitive impairment, there is a wide variety of other neuropsychiatric disorders that must be considered. Statistically, the most common cause of dementia is Alzheimer's disease (AD).

Up to 70 percent of elderly persons with dementia are ultimately found at autopsy to have Alzheimer's, although this number varies among epidemiologic studies. Thus, when a demented patient enters the clinic, there is a good possibility that he or she has Alzheimer's disease. Because the incidence of Alzheimer's disease increases substantially with age, the oldest elderly, those over eighty-five years of age, are especially likely to suffer from this disorder. Unfortunately, at the time of this writing, there is no convenient definitive antemortem test of Alzheimer's. The only way to definitively make the diagnosis of AD is by examining brain tissue at autopsy or by doing a brain biopsy antemortem, which is rarely undertaken.

Because there is no convenient definitive antemortem test for AD, the diagnosis is made by exclusion. This means that other conditions that could cause cognitive impairment are excluded, making the diagnosis of AD most likely. The experienced clinician is usually accurate in making the diagnosis of AD about 75 percent to 90 percent of the time.

The way I approach the diagnosis of AD by exclusion is first to try to exclude common conditions other than AD that cause cognitive impairment. Depression and substance abuse as causative factors were discussed previously. After AD, the most common cause of cognitive impairment in the elderly is vascular or multi-infarct dementia, which probably accounts for 10 percent to 20 percent of cases. This condition results from events (infarcts) in which blood supply to brain tissue is temporarily or permanently impaired, resulting in the death of nerve cells. If the infarcts are small, usually many must be present in order for cognitive impairment to be clinically apparent. However, even large single infarcts often do not result in a global cognitive impairment; rather they cause deficits in a specific cognitive function such as aphasia, depending on their location.

In making the diagnosis of vascular dementia, clinical history can be important. For example, patients with vascular dementia often have a history of an abrupt onset and stepwise clinical deterioration rather than the slow, steady decline seen in AD. This is because cognitive function deteriorates with each new infarct, and the patient remains essentially unchanged until the next event. Beware, however, that AD patients can show precipitous declines in cognitive function if they develop a relatively mild medical illness such as a bladder infection, or experience an environmental challenge such as placement in a nursing home. This change can introduce and complicate diagnostic confusion.

Certain clinical features are suggestive of vascular dementia. The most important are the presence of neurologic changes suggestive of prior infarcts, such as deficits in vision and other sensory functions, difficulty in swallowing or speaking, or weakness in an arm or a leg. If such changes are present, the patient should be referred for a neurologic examination to determine the nature and extent of these changes. Cognitive testing may show patchy rather than global deficits. However, a similar pattern may be seen in early Alzheimer's disease.

The greatest asset in making a diagnosis of vascular dementia is brain imaging. The most frequently used method is computerized tomography, or CT. A more advanced and considerably more expensive technique is magnetic resonance imaging, or MRI. These techniques allow visualization of infarcts and other cerebral pathology in the living patient. Whenever I suspect vascular dementia, I order a brain imaging study.

There are published criteria for the diagnosis of vascular dementia that can be of assistance, such as those devised by the State of California Alzheimer's Disease Centers. These criteria provide guidelines for the clinician in interpreting brain imaging data and other clinical information. However, there is no sure way of knowing whether the infarcts visualized on brain images are sufficient to account for cognitive impairment. In the end, clinical experience in assessing patients with cognitive impairment provides a sense of what is sufficient brain injury to be significant.

Other Causes of Cognitive Impairment

When cases of Alzheimer's disease and vascular dementia are excluded, the remaining 10 percent to 15 percent of cases in the elderly can be attributed to a variety of reversible and irreversible causes. Among the irreversible causes, prior head trauma, especially trauma that occurred repeatedly over a number of years, may account for 1 percent of dementia cases. The classic "dementia pugilistica" seen in boxers is representative of this disorder. History is key in making this diagnosis.

Probably another 2 percent to 4 percent of dementias result from neurodegenerative conditions such as Pick's disease, Huntington's disease, and Parkinson's disease. Huntington's disease and Parkinson's disease can usually be diagnosed antemortem on the basis of the neurologic exam, but Pick's disease may be difficult to identify without autopsy data.

In younger patients, human immunodeficiency virus (HIV) encephalitis is a major cause of dementia, but this is of less importance in the elderly due to the lower frequency of acquired immune deficiency syndrome (AIDS) in this population. Nevertheless, if symptoms of immunocompromise are present in an elderly demented patient, a workup for HIV-induced dementia should be pursued.

The remainder of cases of cognitive impairment in the elderly fall into the category of so-called reversible causes, meaning that with proper treatment the patient may recover some or all cognitive function. These include infectious etiologies such as neurosyphilis, nutritional causes such as B_{12} and folate deficiencies, structural pathologies including normal pressure hydrocephalus, metabolic disorders such as hypothyroidism, and inflammatory conditions such as autoimmune disease. These conditions are uncommon in relation to Alzheimer's disease or vascular dementia. However, because they are reversible, every patient undergoing initial assessment for dementia must be evaluated for these conditions. It is wise to seek the collaboration of a physician with experience in the diagnosis of reversible causes of dementia. Although the actual procedures involved are not difficult, considerable experience is required to interpret the clinical history, physical examination, and laboratory data.

If vascular dementia, substance abuse, depression, and reversible causes of dementia have been excluded, then the diagnosis of Alzheimer's disease is usually justified. Criteria have been developed for the diagnosis of Alzheimer's disease. The most widely used are the criteria of the National Institute of Neurological and Communicative Disorders and Stroke (NINCDS). In essence, the diagnosis of *probable* Alzheimer's disease is made if other possible causes of dementia are excluded, if there are deficits in at least two areas of cognition, if the disease is progressive, and if delirium can be excluded. If patients do not meet all these criteria, a diagnosis of *possible* Alzheimer's disease can be made. The diagnosis of *definite* Alzheimer's disease is reserved for autopsy-proven cases.

MANAGEMENT OF COGNITIVE IMPAIRMENT

Management of cognitive impairment largely depends on the etiology. If the problem is reversible, for example due to a vitamin B_{12} deficiency, then correcting the deficiency is the highest priority. If depression is thought to be contributing, then psychological or pharmacologic treatment of the depression should be pursued aggressively. If alcohol use is a factor, abstinence would be an immediate priority.

Unfortunately, epidemiologic data show that in most cases of cognitive impairment in the elderly, the underlying etiology is AD or vascular dementia. Neither of these disorders is reversible at present. However, a number of interventions are available that can improve patient function and decrease troublesome behaviors.

First Steps

An important first step in the management of Alzheimer's disease and vascular dementia is to discuss the diagnosis, prognosis, and treatment options with the patient, family, and other clinicians involved in the case. My own feeling is that patients have the right to know about their diagnosis and options for treatment, and that most patients in the early and middle stages of dementia can comprehend this information.

In my experience the majority of patients are aware of their impairment and do not respond to this information with catastrophic depression or anxiety. Some clinicians, however, feel that hearing information on diagnosis and prognosis of dementia is very painful for a majority of patients and that providing patients with this information does more harm than good. According to this point of view, management should be planned by the clinician and the family with minimal input from the patient. Although this course of action may make sense for patients with advanced disease, the ethical basis for this approach is questionable in patients who are capable of comprehending their illness.

My approach is to have an initial discussion with the patient in which I go over the diagnosis and prognosis. If it is clear that the patient is not comprehending what he or she is being told or is reacting in a very negative way, I terminate the discussion.

Usually, however, the immediate result is that patients want to know what will happen to them and what can be done to treat their disease. The honest answer regarding prognosis is that for both Alzheimer's disease and vascular dementia the prognosis is difficult to predict with precision.

For Alzheimer's disease, the time between diagnosis and death varies between two and twenty years, with seven being the average. Vascular dementia generally progresses at a rate correlated with the rate of new infarctions. General medical condition plays a large role, as demented patients with serious coexisting medical conditions tend to die sooner than those who are healthy otherwise.

The combination of multiple medical problems plus dementia generally carries a grave prognosis. I believe that patients and their families should not be deceived about the seriousness of such a situation. On the other hand, I always try to explain positive steps that can be taken to maximize survival. Thus, if a patient's medical problems seem to be poorly controlled, I go directly to the primary care physician and try to learn why this is. If I learn that at least part of the difficulty is poor patient or family compliance with prescribed treatment, then I do my best to educate them about the importance of following up on treatment recommendations for the sake of the patient. If the patient has been receiving no regular care for medical problems, which is unfortunately surprisingly common among the elderly, I encourage the family to arrange for such care as soon as possible.

Minimizing Disability

In treating any elderly patient with cognitive impairment I always try to optimize the patient's remaining cognitive skills by removing factors that exacerbate the disability. Thus, if a demented patient has a hearing disability, obtaining a hearing aid can result in an improvement in function as speech and sounds previously missed are now received. If poor dentition contributes to an inadequate nutritional status, then dental consultation is necessary. If mobility problems mean that the patient is usually left in his or her room most of the day with little social interaction or stimulation, providing a walker or wheelchair can be beneficial. I sometimes find myself in the combined role of care coordinator and patient advocate in helping to arrange for the many care modalities elderly patients require. Ignoring these ancillary causes of disability may substantially impair efforts to treat the cognitive impairment directly.

Other practical steps can be taken to minimize disability in cognitively impaired patients. The patient's day can be organized and structured into a routine that is familiar and easy for him or her to recall. Efforts can be made to avoid abrupt changes in routine that can be disruptive. Also, the patient should be given assistance with complex tasks which when failed cause frustration or loss of self-esteem. In the early stages of dementia, this usually means turning over financial matters to a family member. As the disease progresses, the patient may need supervision with tasks such as dressing. However, I generally encourage patients to continue as many of their prior activities as possible as long as this does not cause difficulties for the patient or family.

Providing a safe environment for the patient is an important way of preventing additional disability brought on by accidents. Some patients may tend to wander away from home, so physical barriers or monitoring by caregivers may be necessary. In the home the patient's activities may need to be restricted to prevent accidents. For example, the stove may need to be off limits because of the risk of burns or fires. This restriction can often be difficult for patients who pride themselves on their cooking. The clinician can work with the patient to formulate alternative activities that provide some satisfaction but less risk of injury.

Working with the Family

Regardless of what information is provided to the patient, a family conference is vital. I always ask the patient's permission before initiating this conference, and few refuse. As many concerned members of the family should attend as is feasible. An important function of the family conference is to educate the family about the causes of the cognitive impairment, the course of the disorder, and treatment and placement options. If the family has not previously considered these issues, a follow-up conference may be necessary after they have had an opportunity to consider the options.

Another valuable function of the family conference is to allow the clinician to assess family dynamics that may be important in planning patient management. Often a leader or spokesperson can be identified; this member can be the contact person for the clinician in the future. When faced with the stress of planning for the care of a demented relative, some families may revert to previously established negative patterns of interaction. Referral for family counseling may be necessary in some cases. Other families may rally to new levels of cooperation.

Many family members will seek information from the clinician regarding their chances of developing Alzheimer's disease or other dementing illness if a parent has been diagnosed with one of these disorders. For Alzheimer's disease, the correct answer at present is that the risk to first-degree relatives is greater than that in the general population (which is about 2 percent over a lifetime), but less than 50 percent. A small number of families, probably numbering in the hundreds worldwide, have rare heritable forms of Alzheimer's disease in which about 50 percent of the offspring contract the disease if one parent is affected. The vast majority of families do not fall into this category. Because of this uncertainty, genetic counseling does not play a large role in the management of cognitive impairment at present.

There has been discussion in the scientific literature and the popular press about genetic tests for Alzheimer's disease. Many families are aware that one form of the apolipoprotein E (Apo E) gene may increase risk for Alzheimer's disease, and requests that either the patient or family members have a genetic analysis for Apo E are increasingly common. At present, the best thing to tell families is that while on a population level Apo E genotype is associated with Alzheimer's disease, it is not useful in predicting whether individuals will develop the disease. Additional epidemiologic data and longitudinal studies of persons with the various forms of the Apo E gene may in the future increase the utility of this marker in predicting individual cases.

Medications

One of the first questions patients and families often ask concerns the pharmacologic treatment options for dementia. For Alzheimer's disease, the only FDA approved medication available in the United States at present is Tacrine (Cognex®). This medication increases the availability of the neurotransmitter acetylcholine at synapses in the brain. In some patients with Alzheimer's disease, the drug may temporarily slow the progression of the disease for six to nine months. However, the effect is temporary as the underlying neurodegeneration continues, and eventually the drug has no effect. Further, up to 35 percent of patients treated with Tacrine develop liver toxicity, which necessitates decreasing the dose or stopping the medication altogether. For these reasons, thus far Tacrine has not made a major impact on the treatment of patients with Alzheimer's disease.

In some patients with vascular dementia it may be possible to slow the course of the disease by reducing risk factors for additional ischemic injury to the brain, such as hypertension, high cholesterol, and cardiac arrhythmias. Treatment with aspirin or other medications to reduce the risk of further infarcts may be indicated in some cases. Consultation with a physician with specialized knowledge of stroke prevention and treatment is recommended.

Treating Agitation

Many patients with Alzheimer's disease or vascular dementia show behavioral disturbances that may be more troubling to patients and caregivers than the actual cognitive deficits. These behavioral changes are often referred to as "agitation." Patients may become loud and easily excited. Hostile, aggressive, or even assaultive behavior is not uncommon. Inappropriate sexual behavior may be present. In addition, varying degrees of uncooperative behavior are seen ranging from mild stubbornness to consistent refusal of feeding, toileting, medications, or other basic nursing activities. Wandering, pacing, and other forms of increased locomotor behavior are seen.

In many cases, these disruptive or uncooperative behaviors can be managed by changes in environment or in the approach of the caregiver to the patient. Noisy, cluttered, or excessively stimulating environments often induce agitation in demented patients. Most patients do well in a quiet, constant environment with regular, predictable periods of social interaction, feeding, and other caregiving activities. A regular day-night cycle of light and dark is also important. Gentle redirection of wandering patients is far more effective than angry scolding or threats. Physical barriers that limit the distance patients may wander are also effective.

Patience is a great asset in caregiving with demented individuals. If uncooperative behavior and resistance are present, it is important to take the time to determine the cause. Some patients with progressive cognitive impairment experience fear, a sense of loss, or a blow to personal pride that may be manifested as uncooperativeness. These reactions are frequently seen in patients suffering from any illness, although with cognitive impairment the situation is complicated by the fact that the diseased organ is the brain, which may impair patients' ability to discuss their emotions. Nevertheless, sympathetic listening, empathy, negotiation, and problem-solving techniques often yield good results. Condescending or patronizing behavior should be avoided, even with patients who have significant cognitive impairment. Most elderly, whether demented or not, have a lifetime of experience and accomplishment behind them and rightfully feel they deserve at least a modicum of respect. A kind but straightforward attitude on the part of clinicians and caregivers is often most successful.

Hostile and Uncooperative Behavior

In some cases, however, even extremely patient caregivers encounter a demented individual who remains consistently hostile or uncooperative. When the spouse is the principal caregiver, previously existing negative interaction styles may be exacerbated in the presence of cognitive impairment. In such cases, it is worthwhile, if feasible, to have another person attempt caregiving with the patient. Even patients with moderately advanced cognitive impairment may show behavioral improvement when provided with a new caregiver with a different personality style. This phenomenon is often seen in nursing homes and hospitals where a patient may be uncooperative and hostile during one nursing shift yet quite manageable when personnel change with a new shift.

Sometimes uncooperative or hostile behavior can be traced to delusions or hallucinations that compel the patient to act in ways that may appear incomprehensible to caregivers. Patients commonly suffer from delusions, often paranoid in nature. Hallucinations, both auditory and visual, are also frequently present. Peculiar forms of psychosis are sometimes seen, such as the "phantom boarder syndrome" in which the patient believes a stranger is living in the home.

Reassurance, negotiation, and redirection may be helpful in some cases, but pharmacologic intervention is often necessary for psychotic symptoms. However, the first critical task is to determine that the psychosis in a cognitively impaired patient is not due to a general medical condition or a medication effect. For example, psychosis and confusion can be induced by a urinary tract or respiratory infection in a patient with Alzheimer's disease, and the patient may be unable to clearly relate the symptoms of the infection to the clinician. Thus, new onset psychosis in a demented patient requires a reevaluation of the patient's medical condition, even if a thorough workup for reversible causes of dementia has already been performed. Further, when a behavioral change occurs in a demented patient, current medications should be reviewed. Many times a medication the patient has been using for some time for a condition unrelated to the dementia may have slowly built up to a high level in the blood and may now adversely affect brain function. Or a new medication with side effects on the nervous system may have recently been added to the patient's current regimen. Referral to a physician knowledgeable in geriatric pharmacology is important in these situations.

A key to avoiding medication-induced worsening of dementia is communication among clinicians of different backgrounds and specialties who are treating the patient. All should be aware of any changes in treatment. Very often the spouse or other caregiver can be very helpful in coordinating care by different clinicians. However, one should never assume that the spouse will report all changes in treatment initiated by another clinician. Elderly caregivers are usually under great emotional and physical stress and are unable to mentally juggle all the various aspects of the patient's care.

Antipsychotic Medications

Although the nonmedical clinician will not directly prescribe medications for psychotic elderly patients, it is critical that he or she be aware of the basic principles of antipsychotic use, as patients coming for assessment or behavioral management will often be taking these medications. In my experience, nonmedical practitioners who are aware of the side effects of antipsychotic medications and who see the patient on a regular basis are often the first to notice a change in the patient's behavior that is possibly due to medication side effects. Thus, for example, if an elderly patient comes to the office with a new onset of apparently involuntary tongue and mouth movements, the astute clinician aware of antipsychotic medication side effects will request that the patient be reevaluated by the physician prescribing the medication.

In general, low doses of antipsychotic medications such as haloperidol or risperidone are typically used to treat psychosis in cognitively impaired patients. It is important that antipsychotic medications be used at the lowest possible dose in the elderly because these drugs have serious side effects. At low doses that would not adversely affect a young adult, antipsychotic medications can induce Parkinsonian symptoms such as tremor or rigidity (so-called extrapyramidal reactions) in elderly cognitively impaired patients. In a younger patient an anti-Parkinsonian medication such as benztropine would be added to control these side effects; but in the elderly, this is generally not done because benztropine and related medications can worsen dementia or even induce a delirium. Antipsychotic medications also block the action of the neurotransmitter acetylcholine in the brain, an action that can increase confusion and disorientation in demented patients.

Antipsychotic medications also often cause blood pressure to fall when a patient moves from a sitting to a standing position; this drop can induce light-headedness or even transient loss of consciousness. The reaction is often exacerbated in the elderly in whom the normal vasomotor compensatory responses to upright posture are frequently impaired. Elderly patients on antipsychotic medications are at risk for falls if their blood pressure drops dramatically when they stand up. Sitting and standing blood pressure should be monitored carefully when the cognitively impaired elderly are treated with antipsychotic agents. Finally, elderly demented patients seem to be at particular risk for developing tardive dyskinesia, an involuntary movement disorder that may not be reversible, even when the medication is discontinued. Patients should be monitored regularly for the stereotypic movements of the mouth and tongue seen with tardive dyskinesia. To reiterate, the clinician who is aware of these side effects, even if he or she lacks formal training or experience in assessment of drug side effects, knows when to refer the patient back to the prescribing physician for reevaluation.

A wide variety of other medications has been used in an attempt to control agitation in cognitively impaired individuals. These include the anti-manic agents carbamazepine and lithium, the anti-anxiety agent buspirone, the benzodiazepine class of hypnotic sedatives, and beta adrenergic blocking agents such as propranolol. Although there are many anecdotal reports of success with these agents, we lack convincing scientific proof of their efficacy in treating agitation in the cognitively impaired elderly. This is an important point, as all these medications have side effects that are magnified in the elderly, so they should not be prescribed without clear indications and careful monitoring. Most clinicians, however, do resort to careful trials of these agents when antipsychotics fail.

Many times delusions and hallucinations become worse at night in demented patients, a phenomenon called "sundowning" or "nocturnal agitation." A mild confusional state or delirium may occur at night in some cognitively impaired patients during which they become transiently disoriented. These symptoms may relate to the disruption in sleep cycle and other biological rhythms that occurs in some patients with dementia. Treatment should include a regular cycle of light and dark, and restriction of caregiving activities to daytime hours as much as possible. Avoiding naps and other sleep hygiene measures may also help. Low doses of antipsychotics or benzodiazepines given at bedtime may also be of some help.

Managing Caregiver Stress

An important part of the treatment of cognitive impairment is managing caregiver stress. Caregivers of demented patients are usually under tremendous emotional, physical, and financial stress. Especially when caregivers are elderly spouses or relatives, they often have medical disabilities that may limit their adaptive abilities. The physical and emotional stress of caregiving may exacerbate medical conditions. Further, caregivers may be the targets of angry or even assaultive behavior from patients that may threaten their physical safety. As a result of these factors, significant depression and anxiety are frequent in elderly caregivers. Despite physical and emotional pain, many caregivers motivated out of a combination of love, self-sacrifice, and sometimes guilt will push themselves to the limits of endurance.

A key point to impress on patients and caregivers is that the well-being of the caregivers is essential for the well-being of the patients. If caregivers become disabled physically or emotionally, the patients will certainly suffer. Therefore, the clinician must encourage caregivers to attend to their basic needs despite the burdens of caregiving. Two important concepts in maintaining caregiver well-being are group support and respite.

Expressing shared emotions, comparing experiences, and empathetic listening are important functions of support groups for caregivers. Local chapters of the Alzheimer's Association, Veterans Affairs hospitals and clinics, HMOs, senior centers, and other organizations often run support groups for caregivers of demented patients. If these are not available, groups can easily be organized.

Respite care is also important for maintaining the well-being of caregivers. In respite care, patients are temporarily placed in a setting outside the home for a period ranging from hours to weeks to give caregivers a chance to attend to their needs. Respite care may be provided by a senior center day care program, a formal respite unit offering medical and skilled nursing care, or in other settings. Even a few days of respite care out of the month may be important for the overextended and burdened caregiver. The patient may also benefit directly in the respite environment from additional social contact and by regular reassessment by trained clinicians for changes in behavior or medical status.

Another form of respite care that may be useful in some cases is in-home care by a nursing assistant or health aide. Most mild to moderately cognitively impaired patients do not require skilled nursing care unless another medical illness is present. Home health aides are considerably less expensive than skilled nursing care. They are able to assist with functions such as eating, dressing, bathing, transfers from chair to bed, and toileting. They also can monitor patients who have a tendency to wander. Although many families cannot afford twenty-four-hour in-home care, even a few hours a day may greatly relieve the burden on the primary caregiver, which may ultimately improve the functioning of the patient, too.

Residential Care

Ultimately, however, many patients will require long-term care in a nursing facility. Sometimes a patient in the early-to-middle stages of a dementing illness may need placement in a nursing facility because of behavioral problems that require a secure locked unit or because there is no caregiver able to manage the patient at home. In the late and end stages of a dementing illness, skilled nursing care is usually required. The patient in the end-stage of Alzheimer's disease or vascular dementia is mute, nonresponsive to commands and questions, has lost control of the bowel and bladder, and usually does not ambulate. If the patient is nonambulatory, special care may be necessary to prevent decubiti (bed sores) and muscle contractures. The end-stage patient often will not take food by mouth even if he or she is hand-fed. For this reason, placement of a nasogastric feeding tube or gastrostomy tube may be necessary to sustain life.

It is wise, however, to reach a decision as to whether feeding tubes or other measures will be employed prior to reaching the end-stage. Often the patient in the early stages of cognitive decline will have an opinion as to whether he or she wishes to have a feeding tube placed. It is always easier from both ethical and legal points of view not to initiate tube feeding based on the patient's previously expressed wishes than it is to terminate feeding on the decision of the family or clinician. Likewise, the patient in the early stages may express an opinion as to whether measures such as intravenous fluids and antibiotics are to be used to treat the pulmonary and urinary infections that frequently occur in the end-stages of dementia. If the patient's prior wishes are unknown, then end-stage care must be based on a consensus among family members and clinicians as to the best course of action.

Financial aspects of the management of cognitive impairment are beyond the scope of this chapter, but the clinician should be aware that nursing home care for a demented individual may cost as much as $40,000 per year in a metropolitan area. Many families are unaware that Medicaid will not assist in nursing home payments until the patient and spouse have exhausted most of their personal resources. Consultation with an accountant or attorney with specialized knowledge of financing long-term care should be initiated early on to avoid potential financial ruin.

Legal Aspects

Legal aspects of the management of cognitive impairment are complex and vary from state to state. However, most states provide a means whereby a patient can be deemed legally incompetent to make decisions about his or her personal, medical, and financial affairs due to cognitive impairment. Often a court or other government agency will appoint a relative to manage the patient's affairs. If no competent relative is available, the state will usually assume decision making for the patient. An attorney specializing in geriatric law should be consulted regarding local procedures.

The clinician may be called on by relatives or state agencies to make decisions about the competency of cognitively impaired individuals. My personal philosophy is that patients should maintain their independence and right to control their fate as long as possible, but when a patient's behavior threatens his or her own health or safety or that of the caregiver, intervention is mandatory. Although a paternalistic attitude toward competency evaluations should be avoided, the clinician should act decisively and firmly; time is often of the essence in securing the legal means to place demented individuals in a facility where they can be prevented from harming themselves or others.

Often a patient who resists moving to a facility with a higher level of care will acquiesce when the move is backed up by a legal decision. Occasionally, however, a demented patient will demand a formal court hearing regarding his or her competency. For this reason, the clinician should carefully document in the clinical records evidence of cognitive impairment and the reasons the patient is judged to be incompetent. Documented examples of behaviors that demonstrate inability of the patient to meet his or her basic needs or behaviors harmful to the patient or others are very helpful in competency hearings.

Hospitalization of cognitively impaired elderly patients can raise legal issues. If the patient suffers from a superimposed delirium in addition to a baseline dementia, most states consider this a medical emergency, and the patient's care is usually left to the discretion of the physician until the emergency has resolved. However, it is always wise to seek the advice of a second clinician and also the patient's family, and to document these consultations in the chart. When the patient is hospitalized for behavioral changes of dementia, such as delusions, but there is no delirium present, the situation is more complicated. In California, this is technically not considered an emergency, so the patient should not be held, medicated, or subsequently placed in a nursing facility against his or her will. On the other hand, if it were necessary for every case of dementia to be heard by the courts before treatment could be commenced, the system would collapse from the sheer volume of cases.

In practice, a rational approach is that if the patient can present a consistent and clearly verbalized desire to leave or to refuse treatment, and this desire is articulated on several occasions, then the clinician is obligated to seek legal authorization to proceed with treatment or placement. On the other hand, if the patient is moderately or severely demented and makes random attempts to leave the hospital unit but at other times is cooperative, then it is probably safe to proceed with treatment after consent has been obtained from family members. However, advice from local legal and state authorities should be sought as rules vary among localities. Unless the patient is at the end-stage of dementia in essentially a vegetative state, it is usually necessary to seek legal authorization for long-term permanent placement in a nursing facility if the patient refuses to go voluntarily. Many times this can be avoided by negotiation with the patient and finding a facility that is acceptable to the patient.

The frequency with which family members take advantage of demented patients for their own personal gain is much lower than is portrayed in literature, movies, and television. Nevertheless, the clinician should be aware that occasionally some family members may not have the patient's best interests in mind. In these cases it may be necessary to involve state agencies such as adult protective services. However, many times these agencies are reluctant to act unless there is frank physical or psychological abuse.

More subtle cases of financial manipulation are difficult to assess and prevent. The clinician should be aware that personal intervention in such cases may result in involvement in lengthy and acrimonious legal proceedings. If the clinician feels that intervention is necessary, it is often wise to seek the assistance of a sympathetic relative and hope for an informal negotiated settlement among all those involved. Fortunately, most relatives, despite being under high levels of stress themselves, earnestly try to lessen the suffering of the cognitively impaired individual and are of great assistance to the clinician.

Driving

The prospect of a cognitively impaired individual driving an automobile is always of concern. In California, clinicians are required to report the diagnosis of Alzheimer's disease and related disorders to the state, which then usually schedules a driving test for the identified individual. Most clearly demented patients fail the test, but occasionally one passes. Indeed, there is currently a debate in the scientific literature as to whether mildly demented patients are actually a hazard on the road. This issue is of great importance to patients, who may find loss of driving privilege a hardship or a blow to self-esteem. On the other hand, many families are relieved when the driving privilege is suspended as they correctly fear for the safety of the patient behind the wheel. Clinicians should be aware that they may face liability if they do not notify the appropriate authorities when a clearly impaired patient continues to drive. A more efficient system for driver testing of patients with cognitive impairment needs to be developed, and more data are needed about the actual risk they pose on the road.

Assessing and treating cognitive impairment in the elderly is complex and demanding. Knowledge of the specialized medical, psychological, social, financial, and legal problems of the elderly and their families is essential for success. Keeping up to date on developments in this rapidly changing field is important. Identifying patients who are impaired solely or partially because of depression, substance abuse, or prescription drug intoxication and initiating appropriate treatment can lead to dramatic changes in these individuals. Although the clinician must remain cognizant of the progressive nature of disorders such as Alzheimer's disease and the limited options for treatment, substantial improvements in quality of life for these patients and their families can often be achieved even if the underlying disease process is not reversed.

The energetic clinician who utilizes a variety of treatment modalities, medical and nonmedical colleagues, and available community resources is likely to find that improvements in patient well-being are frequent and provide ample reward for working with this underserved population.

NOTES

P. 163, *In those over eighty:* Skoog, I., Nilsson, L., Palmertz, B., Anderasson, L.-A., & Svanborg, A. (1993). A population-based study of dementia in 85-year olds. *New England Journal of Medicine, 328,* 153–158.

P. 164, *The book by Strub and Black:* Strub, R. L., & Black, F. W. (1985). *Mental status examination in neurology* (2nd ed.). Philadelphia: F. A. Davis.

P. 167, *The most widely used is the Folstein:* Folstein, M. F., Folstein, S. E., & McHugh, P. R. (1975). "Mini-mental state": A practical approach for grading the cognitive state of patients for the clinician. *Journal of Psychiatric Research, 12,* 189–198.

P. 167, *Thus, norms exist:* Crum, R. M., Anthony, J. C., Bassett, S. S., & Folstein, M. F. (1993). Population-based norms for the mini-mental state examination by age and educational level. *Journal of the American Medical Association, 269,* 2386–2391.

P. 168, *Neurobehavioral Cognitive Status Examination:* Kiernan, R. J., Mueller, J., Langston, J. W., & Van Dyke, C. (1987). The neurobehavioral cognitive status examination: A brief but differentiated approach to cognitive assessment. *Annals of Internal Medicine, 107,* 481–485.

P. 168, *the Global Deterioration Scale:* Reisberg, B., Ferris, S. H., DeLeon, M. J., & Crook, T. (1982). The global deterioration scale for the assessment of primary degenerative dementia. *American Journal of Psychiatry, 139,* 1136–1139.

P. 169, *Many other excellent tests:* Spreen, O., & Strauss, E. (1991). *A compendium of neuropsychological tests.* New York: Oxford University Press.

P. 169, *delirium:* Lipowski, Z. J. (1990). *Delirium: Acute confusional states.* New York: Oxford University Press.

P. 171, *25 percent of patients with degenerative dementias:* Burns, A., Jacoby, R., & Levy, R. (1990). Psychiatric phenomena in Alzheimer's disease. III: Disorders of mood. *British Journal of Psychiatry, 157,* 81–86.

P. 173, *Up to 70 percent of elderly persons:* Corey-Bloom, J., Thal, L. J., Galasko, D., Folstein, M., Drachman, D., Raskind, M., & Lanska, D. J. (1995). Diagnosis and evaluation of dementia. *Neurology, 45,* 211–218.

P. 173, *those over eighty-five years of age:* Hebert, L. E., Scherr, P. A., Beckett, L. A., Albert, M. S., Pilgrim, D. M., Chown, M. J., Funkelstein, H. H., & Evans, D. A. (1995). Age-specific incidence of Alzheimer's disease in a community population. *Journal of the American Medical Association, 273,* 1354–1359.

P. 175, *State of California Alzheimer's Disease Centers:* Chui, H. C., Victoroff, J.

I., Margolin, D., Jagust, W., Shankle, R., & Katzman, R. (1992). Criteria for the diagnosis of ischemic vascular dementia proposed by the State of California Alzheimer's Disease Diagnostic and Treatment Centers. *Neurology, 42,* 473–480.

P. 176, *criteria of the National Institute of Neurological and Communicative Disorders and Stroke:* McKhann, G., Drachman, D., Folstein, M., Katzman, R., Price, D., Stadlan, E. M. (1984). Clinical diagnosis of Alzheimer's disease. *Neurology, 34,* 939–944.

P. 181, *Tacrine:* Davis, K. L., & Powchik, P. Tacrine. (1995). *Lancet, 345,* 625.

P. 189, *most states provide a means:* Sprehe, D. J. (1994). Geriatric psychiatry and the law. In R. Rosner (Ed.), *Forensic psychiatry* (pp. 501–507). New York: Chapman and Hall.

P. 192, *there is currently a debate:* Fitten, L. J., Perryman, K. M., Wilkinson, C. J., Little, R. J., Burns, M. M., Pachana, N., Mervis, J. R., Malmgran, R., Siembieda, D. W., & Ganzell, S. (1995). Alzheimer and vascular dementias and driving. *Journal of the American Medical Association, 273,* 1360–1365.

7

PSYCHIATRIC PROBLEMS IN NURSING HOMES

Joel E. Streim

One of the most challenging and rewarding frontiers for managing psychiatric problems of the elderly is in the nursing home setting. The paucity of outcomes research in this area limits what we know about the effectiveness of specific treatment interventions in such settings. Nevertheless, an overwhelming number of elderly residents of nursing homes need psychiatric care and clearly cannot wait for results of definitive clinical trials that will help us establish treatment standards for long-term care.

To this end, clinical practice guidelines, based on what we do know thus far, are currently being developed by several professional organizations. In the meantime, we must do the best we can with the treatment modalities and mental health care delivery models that are currently available. The good news is that many of the problems are treatable; and even for patients with incurable illness, there is much that can be done to manage their symptoms and improve their quality of life.

WHAT'S DIFFERENT ABOUT TREATING PSYCHIATRIC PROBLEMS IN NURSING HOMES?

Nursing homes have unique characteristics that challenge us as clinicians and require adaptations in our approach to mental health care. I believe four key characteristics demand our attention as we shape our approach to managing psychiatric problems in this setting:

1. The very high prevalence of psychiatric disorders
2. Co-morbid psychiatric and medical illness and disability in elderly residents
3. The serious lack of facility design, staff training, programs, and services intrinsic to nursing homes that might be able to meet residents' mental health care needs
4. The federal regulations governing mental health assessment and treatment

The Mismatch of Mental Health Needs and Resources

Perhaps the most striking characteristic is the prevalence of psychiatric disorders in the nursing home population. Epidemiologic studies over the past ten years have consistently demonstrated that 80 percent to 94 percent of nursing home residents have psychiatric disorders diagnosable by *Diagnostic and Statistical Manual* (DSM-III and DSM-III-R) criteria. Approximately two-thirds of these are patients with dementia; 15 percent to 50 percent of patients have clinically significant depression; and the assessment and management of most of these patients is complex, because of co-morbid medical conditions and medication effects and multifaceted disabilities.

Despite the high prevalence of complicated psychiatric disorders, most U.S. nursing homes characteristically have not been designed, staffed, or operated for the management of patients with psychiatric problems. Rather, with few exceptions, nursing homes have been established to care for people with disabling chronic medical illnesses, injuries, and congenital disorders requiring medical, nursing, or rehabilitative—but not mental health—services.

Thus, a serious mismatch exists between mental health needs of the residents and resources of the nursing facilities, and this has historically been a characteristic problem of nursing home care. Mental health practitioners face a serious challenge in attempting to remedy this discrepancy; any attempt must include consultation and training focused on nursing home staff as well as the provision of clinical care directly to patients.

The Misuse of Psychotropic Drugs and Physical Restraints

The mismatch of mental health needs and resources has resulted in a long history of inadequate and inappropriate management of psychiatric problems among elderly nursing home residents. It undoubtedly explains much of the widespread misuse of psychotropic drugs and physical restraints as well as the poor quality of care and even inhumane treatment in nursing homes that became a focus of news media reports in the 1970s. Research has demonstrated that psychotropic drugs are often prescribed without documented assessment of the patient's mental status or without established psychiatric diagnoses. These studies suggest that many patients are treated without clear indications or symptoms that are likely to respond to psychotropic drugs, exposing them to the risk of adverse drug effects without a reasonable likelihood of treatment benefit. In many cases we have seen drugs inappropriately used as "chemical restraints." Clearly, more psychiatric assessment is required to distinguish patients who are inappropriately treated from those who do have appropriate indications and are likely to derive therapeutic benefits from treatment with psychotropic medication.

Studies of physical restraint use reveal a similar story of misuse and abuse. Surveys have shown that physical restraints are used in 25 percent to 85 percent of nursing home residents. Although agitation is a frequent reason for the use of restraints, available evidence indicates that restraints do not effectively decrease behavioral disturbances. Furthermore, physical restraint use is associated with such potential adverse effects as falls and injuries, skin breakdown, physiologic effects of immobilization stress, disorganized behavior and increased agitation, functional decline, and emotional distress. These findings indicate that patients need to be assessed so that the select few who truly require and benefit from restraints can be identified, and the range of effective alternative management strategies can be carefully considered for all patients.

Undertreatment

The problem of inappropriate treatment, however, is not limited to misuse of antipsychotic drugs and physical restraints. For those patients with unrecognized psychiatric symptoms or undiagnosed disorders (such as psychotic symptoms or depressive disorders), undertreatment is a serious problem. Psychiatric symptoms and disorders in nursing home patients can cause subjective distress, complicate co-morbid medical illnesses, lead to excess disability, and interfere with quality of life. It follows, then, that recognition and treatment of potentially reversible symptoms and disorders can alleviate suffering, improve functioning, and enhance quality of life for many nursing home residents. This realization supports the development of mental health services in nursing homes to provide systematic screening and periodic reassessment to ensure identification of treatable psychiatric problems. The challenge to mental health providers is to help integrate such assessment into facilities that are traditionally not equipped for this task, and then to facilitate much needed treatment.

Emergence of Federal Regulation

Concerns about issues of inadequate and inappropriate treatment led to the emergence of consumer advocacy groups, such as the National Citizens' Coalition for Nursing Home Reform and the Alzheimer's Association. Public outrage also was part of the reason that Congress, in 1983, directed the Institute of Medicine to make recommendations for improving the quality of care in nursing homes. The resultant Institute of Medicine report, published in 1986, served as the basis for the Nursing Home Reform Amendments of the Omnibus Budget Reconciliation Act of 1987 (OBRA), passed by Congress. This legislation provided for sweeping reforms through extensive federal regulation of virtually all aspects of nursing home facilities, operation, staffing, and services, including mental health assessment and care.

So we are now in an era in which the shared concerns of consumers, health care researchers, and legislators have led to a federal mandate that includes improving the quality of mental health care in nursing homes. All clinicians providing care to nursing home residents in U.S. facilities that receive Medicare and Medicaid funds now work within the framework set by the federal regulations and the accompanying interpretive guidelines established by the Health Care Financing Administration (HCFA) in 1992. In essence, federal regulation has become an additional characteristic feature of the nursing home setting; mental health professionals must therefore adapt their approach to fit the regulatory characteristics of this health care setting.

The common psychiatric problems and management strategies that are illustrated in the remainder of this chapter are discussed from the perspective of the four characteristics of nursing homes described earlier, that is, prevalence of psychiatric disorders; co-morbidity; lack of facility design, training, and services; and federal regulations.

THE PROBLEM OF DEMENTIA WITH BEHAVIORAL DISTURBANCES

It is fortunate that even in the complex system of the nursing home, some problems have relatively simple solutions.

I was once asked to "help calm down" a seventy-two-year-old man with probable Alzheimer's disease who was restrained in a gerichair (essentially a lounge chair with an attached tray table often used to prevent patients from standing up). The nursing assistants reported that he would frequently bang on the table, yell unintelligible mono-syllables, and try to climb over and under the table. Sometimes he would slide down in the chair and become stuck under the table. His primary care physician had prescribed haloperidol 1 mg. t.i.d., but the staff reported that his restlessness was worsening. The dose was increased to 2 mg. t.i.d., but there was no improvement. His physi-cian and the nursing assistants hoped I could somehow make him sit quietly throughout the day.

Although the manifest problem that prompted the referral for psychiatric consultation was the agitated behaviors, I began by inter-viewing the nursing home staff to better understand the context and nature of the problem and to make sense of the patient's behavioral symptoms. I discovered that when the patient was not restrained in the gerichair, he would wander incessantly up and down the corri-dors, stopping at the doors of other residents along the way, often taking magazines and papers from their rooms. This, of course, upset the other residents, some of whom threatened to retaliate. In response to this problem, the staff had restrained the patient in the gerichair, both to avoid the annoyance to others and to protect the patient from being harmed by residents who were angered by his intrusive behavior.

On reviewing the patient's chart, I learned from the social worker's admission history that the patient had been employed by the postal service for over thirty years. I called his wife. She informed me that he had been a letter carrier with a walking route several miles long in a neighborhood where he had come to know many of the residents, and that he had continued in this role right up to the time of his retirement at age sixty-five. She told me that during her visits with him at the nursing home they would walk up and down the halls together, greeting people along the way; but that when she accompanied him, he never entered the rooms of other residents. She had, however, noticed that he hoarded papers in his own room and was often occupied by handling them and rummaging through them, although he didn't seem to be able to read them or understand what they were for. I also learned from the medication records that the patient had been maintained on cisapride for three episodes of vomiting that had occurred more than one month before this evaluation. Cisapride is a medication that promotes gastric emptying and can relieve nausea and vomiting; but it also has the potential to cause unwanted central nervous system side effects, similar to adverse effects that can occur with the use of antipsychotic drugs like haloperidol.

Continuing the assessment, I examined the patient and found no evidence of delusions or other psychotic symptoms. The neurological exam revealed moderate psychomotor restlessness when he was in the gerichair, but he appeared less anxious and had no significant agitation when he was unrestrained and ambulating with supervision. He had a mild resting tremor in his hands and moderate cogwheel rigidity. My impression was that he had drug-induced Parkinsonian signs, with akathisia, a motor restlessness syndrome that was likely to be exacerbating his agitation. I called the attending physician and recommended that the haloperidol and the cisapride be discontinued, as either could be aggravating the behavioral disturbance.

Next, I shared this information with the staff. They promptly inferred that the patient needed to walk, perhaps throughout most of the day. In addition to the notion that some of the restlessness was related to drug side effects, what they previously regarded as purposeless, annoying "wandering," rummaging, and hoarding behaviors now made sense to them as meaningful activities rather than "problem behaviors." These were, of course, the sorts of activities that had formerly been part of this patient's livelihood. Staff could now entertain various richer and relevant attributions for the behaviors observed in the nursing home: that these had been part of his daily routine, and continuing with activities that were most familiar to him was a way for this patient to find comfort in his new and unfamiliar environment; that these behaviors were really ingrained as "habits" after so many years; that his sense of self and well-being depended on continuing the activity that was his livelihood; that he was accustomed to getting lots of exercise, and that he needed to walk a lot to feel well. Staff also realized that restraining the patient prevented him from meeting these important needs. His agitation and attempts to get out of the gerichair no longer appeared unreasonable but seemed quite logical to them now.

Without my prescription for further intervention, the staff developed an alternative treatment plan of their own. They began to accompany the patient on walks several times a day. They also encouraged him to join them on their "work rounds," and with supervision he helped them collect old newspapers and menus. When he was sitting, they would give him a canvas bag full of papers and magazines that he would handle and shuffle. Attitudes of the nursing home staff toward the patient improved dramatically. With the change in approach by the staff and the discontinuation of haloperidol and cisapride, he spent very little time sitting in the gerichair and was seldom restless or agitated.

The Collaborative Approach

The preceding case illustrates several issues. Although the insights regarding this patient's "problem behaviors" may seem simple and readily accessible, it is not reasonable to expect nursing home staff with little or no training in behavioral science to assess and manage behavioral disturbances without consultative support from mental health professionals. Also, the mental health consultant—whether a psychiatrist, psychologist, therapist, counselor, psychiatric social worker, or geropsychiatric nurse—should not be expected to perform an adequate assessment simply by direct examination of the patient, or single-handedly to implement all the therapeutic interventions he or she recommends.

I have found that it is crucial to establish a working liaison with the front-line staff who provide direct care on a daily basis—nurses and nursing assistants; physical, occupational, speech, and recreation therapists; dietitians; and even house-keeping staff. To achieve the most effective assessment and diagnosis, a reciprocal relationship is needed in which the staff help the consultant by sharing their direct clinical observations, and the consultant helps the staff make sense of the patient's symptoms. Many programs have been described in which nurses and nursing assistants rely on consulting psychiatrists to provide guidance in assessing and understanding patients with psychiatric symptoms and behavioral disturbances. However, it is the nursing home staff who provide daily direct care for residents, including supervision or assistance with activities of daily living. Consequently, they are in the best position to make observations of clinical signs and symptoms; the context in which behavior problems occur; and the patient's involvement in social, recreational, and therapeutic activities.

For purposes of treatment and management, staff depend on mental health consultants to provide direct patient care, but the consultant also relies on the staff to implement therapeutic changes. Staff who provide daily personal care have numerous opportunities for negative as well as positive interactions with patients, and staff-patient contact can either be an important factor in the pathogenesis of psychopathology and behavior problems or a key component in its treatment. Through consultation to staff, the psychiatrist can promote therapeutic staff-patient interactions and can guide staff in reducing maladaptive responses and in supporting adaptive behaviors and independent function in nursing home residents.

In the case illustration of the former postal worker, staff reacted to the patient's wandering and rummaging by restraining him, and this, in turn, caused him to become agitated. When staff altered their approach to the patient, encouraging supervised ambulation, he was able to resume functioning at a higher level. Although my opportunities for ongoing supportive contact with this patient were limited, the therapeutic effect was realized through positive interactions between the nursing home staff and the patient in their daily contacts. This outcome demonstrates that nursing home staff are indispensable as agents who deliver therapy in a system in which psychiatric consulting time is limited or when direct care by the psychiatrist or other mental health professional is not appropriate, practical, or cost effective.

Effects of Drugs and Physical Restraints

In the earlier case illustration, the patient's mental status and neurological exams revealed adverse drug effects that contributed to his agitated behavior. I often see nursing home patients who are continued on drugs that may no longer be required to treat gastrointestinal and other medical conditions and that are causing significant central nervous system side effects. In the illustration, we had to consider the possibility that the effects of cisapride were compounded by the effects of increasing doses of haloperidol. Ironically, when a patient being treated with a neuroleptic such as haloperidol becomes more agitated, nurses and physicians often respond by giving a higher dose of the drug when in fact the increased agitation is due to drug-induced akathisia. The appropriate response in this situation is to treat the motor restlessness by reducing the dose or discontinuing the drug, or adding an anti-parkinsonian agent if continued neuroleptic treatment is required by the patient's clinical condition. In the case cited, restraining the patient likely aggravated his akathisia, further worsening his agitation. Proper management of this patient therefore included discontinuing his medication as well as avoiding the use of physical restraints.

Another aspect of this case that is important for you to keep in mind as a consultant is the federal regulation that restricts the use of physical restraints. The regulations explicitly state that nursing home residents have "the right to be free from any physical restraints imposed for purposes of discipline or convenience and not required to treat the resident's medical symptoms."

According to federal guidelines, restraints may not be used unless there is documentation that efforts were made to identify and correct preventable or treatable factors that cause or contribute to the problem, that prior attempts to use less restrictive measures failed, and that the restraints enable the resident to achieve or maintain the "highest practicable level of function."

Thus, mental health assessment is more than necessary in cases like the one described above; it is essentially mandated by law. Helping to identify and correct factors that caused or contributed to the patient's agitated behavior was an essential goal for me as the psychiatric consultant, and in this case the assessment revealed that avoiding the use of restraints enabled the resident to achieve a higher level of function. Consultants in psychiatry as well as rehabilitation medicine (including physical or occupational therapists) also play an important role in identifying those cases in which restraints are required to ensure physical safety or to enhance body positioning or mobility. In such cases, the consultant must assist nursing home staff with proper documentation of the need for and benefit from restraints.

THE PROBLEM OF SEVERE DEPRESSION WITH MEDICAL CO-MORBIDITY

A ninety-one-year-old woman, widowed for twenty-three years, had been living at the nursing home for the past two years and had become nonambulatory during the last year because of osteoarthritis and congestive heart failure. The social worker observed that she had developed mild depressive symptoms and notified the psychology consultant, who attributed this to a grief reaction in the context of her decline in function and loss of independence. The psychologist met with the patient weekly for individual supportive therapy and also referred her to a movement therapy group. Over a period of ten weeks, her mood improved and she genuinely appeared to enjoy conversation with the other group members. She even began to volunteer in the kitchen, peeling and slicing vegetables while seated in her wheelchair. Despite her disability, she felt useful and looked forward to each day.

However, her participation in individual and group therapy was interrupted by an episode of pneumonia that required five days of hospitalization for intravenous fluids and antibiotics. Although her pneumonia resolved completely within the first week after her return to the nursing home, she had persistent loss of appetite and did not resume her activities and social contact, spending all her time in her room, mostly confined to bed. When staff urged her to come out of her room for meals and activities, she would refuse, saying she was too weak and tired; she complained of pain in her back, shoulders, and hips that was worse when she tried to get out of bed. When they suggested that she might be depressed again, she responded angrily, insisting that she didn't feel sad or lonely, just tired. Staff tried coaxing her out of bed every day but usually ended up in a verbal altercation with the reluctant patient, who began accusing them of being unfair and heartless.

Her family physician examined her and found her to have signs of worsening congestive heart failure, to which he attributed her fatigue and poor appetite. Laboratory evaluation revealed that she also had anemia and mild renal insufficiency (poor kidney function), which can slow the elimination of some medications such as the digoxin used to treat her heart failure. Nevertheless, her serum digoxin level was still within the therapeutic range. She was started on furosemide 20 mg. a day (a diuretic to treat her congestive heart failure) and ferrous sulfate 325 mg. a day (an iron supplement to increase hemoglobin production and correct her anemia), and her ibuprofen dose was increased (a nonsteroidal anti-inflammatory drug for her osteoarthritis).

After four weeks, her weight had dropped eight pounds, so that she now weighed ninety-six pounds (her ideal body weight was calculated to be 122 pounds). I was consulted to address her anorexia and social withdrawal. At this point the patient stated that she was "sick and tired of being sick and tired"; she thought she had nothing left to live for and that she'd be better off dead, though she denied any intentions to starve herself or do anything else that might hasten her own demise. She showed no signs of psychosis or cognitive dysfunction. She appeared gaunt with generalized muscle wasting. Her respirations were unlabored; her lungs were clear, without rales; and her heart rate was regular without a murmur or S3 (a sound indicative of heart failure). She indicated stiffness and pain on passive range of motion at the shoulders, hips, and knees. I rechecked her digoxin level, which had increased to 2.1 (slightly above the upper limit of the therapeutic range for treatment of congestive heart failure). Thyroid functions, serum B_{12}, and folate levels were normal, but her serum albumen was 2.9, indicating significant undernutrition.

The Reciprocal Relationships Between Psychiatric and Medical Problems

My impression was that several factors were now contributing to her symptoms. Although a grief reaction might still be expected and would even seem reasonable as a psychological response to her illness and disability, her current clinical presentation couldn't be explained as a normal grief reaction: she had clearly developed a major depressive episode after her bout of pneumonia. But in this geriatric patient, even a diagnosis of major depression did not explain the entire clinical picture. Her depression was complicated by co-morbid medical problems and physical disability.

Although fatigue and lack of energy are common symptoms of depression, some of these symptoms were also attributable to her anemia and heart failure. Furthermore, geriatric patients who are at bedrest with an acute illness for just a week or two can become seriously deconditioned. Muscle atrophy, weakness, and a marked decline in physical stamina can occur after a relatively short period of reduced mobility. A vicious downhill cycle often ensues, as deconditioning reinforces inactivity, and prolonged inactivity leads to further deconditioning, which thwarts efforts to help the patient recover mobility. This patient also had osteoarthritis, a condition that left her joints increasingly stiff and painful with prolonged inactivity despite increased doses of ibuprofen. Thus, when this patient complained of being too weak and tired to get out of bed, it was not simply the depression talking. Physical illness and disability were contributing to the signs and symptoms of depression.

Similarly, her loss of appetite was explained not only by the depression but was also thought to be aggravated by her congestive heart failure. Ironically, the treatment for her heart failure included digoxin, which can cause or exacerbate diminished appetite and anorexia and has been associated with major depression in geriatric patients, even at serum levels in the "therapeutic" range. Because of her renal insufficiency, clearance of this drug was reduced and serum levels had increased, raising concerns that this side effect might indeed be aggravating her anorexia and malnutrition. Thus, there were several ways that medical illness, medication effects, and disability complicated the presentation and course of this woman's depression.

Conversely, apathy, anergy, and anorexia due to the depression appeared to complicate the course and treatment of her medical illness and disability. These symptoms of depression left her without the initiative to resume essential activities such as eating and ambulating and led to worsening nutrition, arthritic pain, and reduced stamina and mobility. Thus, the reciprocal relationships between her depression, her medical illnesses, and her disability become apparent.

An Interdisciplinary Approach

These complex interactions of medical-psychiatric co-morbidity and disability are common in nursing home residents and create the need for a comprehensive interdisciplinary approach to treatment. In this case, I first contacted the patient's primary care physician to discuss my most immediate concerns: her poor nutrition and mobility. In the absence of definitive treatment, these factors were life threatening.

I recommended hospital admission for electroconvulsive therapy and nutritional support, but the patient refused. I discussed the patient's change in outlook with the psychologist, and together we reminded her that just last month she was feeling and functioning well enough to take pleasure in life, explained that most of her recent symptoms were treatable and potentially reversible, and informed her of the good prognosis for restoring the level of well-being and quality of life that she had enjoyed five weeks ago if she were to receive the appropriate treatment. Although reluctant and unwilling to go to the hospital, she was generally willing to accept whatever treatment could be offered at the nursing home.

We discussed the need to reduce the doses of digoxin and furosemide. Although some of her weight loss was due to diuresis, most of it was from inadequate caloric intake. Her primary care physician therefore prescribed nutritional supplements. Iron supplements were continued. I started her on nortriptyline, an antidepressant medication that was likely to be effective and well tolerated, given her advanced age and multiple medical problems. (There are now several antidepressants on the market that can be used safely in geriatric nursing home patients, though their relative effectiveness has not yet been adequately studied in this setting.) I also ordered physical, occupational, and activities therapies, but the patient initially refused to participate in therapy sessions. The psychologist resumed weekly supportive therapy, and I conducted a series of consultations with nursing home staff to identify and overcome barriers to working with the patient. She ultimately responded well to treatment, with resumption of her usual activities, including her movement therapy group, after approximately five weeks.

As therapeutic effects of the antidepressant drugs are not apparent during the first week or two of treatment—and most drugs take four to ten weeks to exert their antidepressant effects—it was important to plan strategies to help staff manage the patient in the early phase of treatment when her symptoms were not yet in remission and were sufficiently severe to interfere with her participation in treatment. When staff pushed her to do what her untreated symptoms prevented her from doing and criticized her for her lack of initiative and poor performance, she felt unsupported and unfairly treated. Because staff failed to understand that her symptoms, such as anergy and anorexia, were due to illness, and they did not acknowledge that her suffering was "legitimate," the patient became angry and the staff-patient alliance was undermined. In cases like this, there is also a risk that the depressed patient will be made to feel more guilty or worthless, and that staff responses to the patient's complaints and dependency will serve to worsen already compromised self-esteem. Furthermore, staff misses an opportunity to reinforce the notion that the patient's symptoms are treatable, the suffering can be relieved, and quality of life can be expected to improve to the point that life seems once again worth living; but the patient is not expected to accomplish this "all on her own" in the face of unrelenting illness.

I met with nursing, dietary, rehabilitation, and activities staff at the nursing home to discuss the various factors that caused or contributed to the patient's distress, including fatigue and poor appetite, and to coordinate the treatment plan. The psychologist provided guidelines for interpersonal approaches to this withdrawn, inactive patient. It was important to convey the concept that this patient's decline was not a result of characterologic laziness or a long-standing nihilistic attitude toward late life, but that she was unable to function normally because of her illnesses, including the depressive disorder, which were treatable conditions.

Nursing staff needed to know what level of function was reasonable to expect at each stage of the illness with respect to her ability to eat and perform other activities of daily living; and rehabilitative staff needed to know what to expect in terms of her exercise tolerance and ability to participate in therapies. All staff needed to understand that this patient's capacity to respond and participate in treatment would not be restored immediately, and I emphasized the expectation that she would gradually emerge from a position of dependence on staff early in the course of the illness when her symptoms were most severe, toward increasing levels of independence as she began to respond to treatment. This would require continuous adjustment in the way staff related to her.

They began with a nurturing, parental approach, showing patience with her inability to function independently and providing direct support to meet her basic needs for nutrition, hygiene, and mobility. As her anergy and anorexia began to diminish and she was capable of more autonomous function, the staff approach evolved toward requiring her to accept increasing levels of responsibility for her own care, to resume social contact, and then to participate in a wider range of activities as her symptoms remitted.

As described earlier, nursing home staff are not trained to titrate their interpersonal or professional responses to patients with psychiatric co-morbidity. Mental health practitioners play an important role as consultants to staff on how to manage the interactions of psychiatric and medical illness and related physical disability. Inservice programs provide an educational forum to introduce key concepts but are not sufficient to deal with the complexities and nuances of individual cases; such training must be supplemented by ongoing case consultation and liaison by the mental health provider with nursing home staff.

In this case, which involved psychiatric-medical co-morbidity, the primary care provider also needed consultation with me to sort out symptoms with overlapping attributions; that is, symptoms due to the medical illnesses, the psychiatric disorder, and the medication effects. In many nursing home cases, a combination of factors contribute to symptom production; therefore, many patients require concurrent treatment for medical and psychiatric illnesses. Patient care must be orchestrated among physicians as well as psychology, social work, nursing, and rehabilitation staff.

This case also demonstrates factors that commonly lead to underrecognition and undertreatment of depression in nursing home patients, showing how this lack can complicate the course of medical illness and result in excess disability. The patient, who is ninety-one years old, suffers from arthritis and heart failure, is no longer able to ambulate, and lives in a nursing home. It is easy for caregivers to rationalize that anyone in her situation should be expected to be depressed. Caregivers as well as patients often accept the symptoms and signs of depression as an inevitable consequence of old age, chronic illness, disability, and institutionalization, and they presume that there is no remedy. Apathy, which is a common symptom of depressive disorders, renders patients disinterested in their own well-being and often reluctant to try to participate in treatment. When the symptoms can be at least partly attributed to a concurrent medical condition, treatment of the medical illness alone is often erroneously presumed to be sufficient.

For the patient described here, her fatigue and poor appetite were initially ascribed to heart failure and anemia; and for the first month, these were treated without an intervention to help her depression. As a result, her continued poor appetite resulted in further nutritional compromise, she suffered from amplified arthritis pain, her deconditioning and disability worsened, and she felt like giving up, becoming reluctant to accept treatment recommendations. This result illustrates how leaving depression untreated may result not only in persistent distress from the symptoms of depression but in amplified pain and other symptoms of medical illness, poor medical treatment response and compliance, increased medical co-morbidity, and excess disability. Studies of nursing home patients with depression have also shown an associated increase in health care service utilization and mortality.

The Need for Assessment and Coordinated Treatment

Recognizing, diagnosing, and treating depression in nursing home residents is an important goal. To this end, the periodic comprehensive standardized assessment of all nursing home residents required by the federal regulations includes ratings of mood and behavior patterns. However, the Minimum Data Set used by most facilities represents only a first stage screening tool, which then calls for a more in-depth evaluation of those patients who are identified as having a potential problem. Resident Assessment Protocols (RAPs) were developed by HCFA to help nurses initiate an appropriate assessment. For medically ill patients with depression, evaluation by both the primary care provider and a consulting psychiatrist is indicated. Although the regulations mandate mental health services for all nursing home residents with identified problems, they do not guarantee that medical, mental health, nursing, and rehabilitative care will be well coordinated. Case coordination for geriatric patients is often performed by a social worker, nurse practitioner, or the primary care provider; but for many nursing home residents whose primary diagnosis is a psychiatric disorder, the job of case coordination is sometimes assumed by a psychiatrist. For some of these nursing home residents, the psychiatrist, who is familiar with both the medical and psychiatric aspects of patient care, may be best suited to function as the primary care provider.

Nonpharmacologic Therapies for Depression in Nursing Home Residents

The mental health care component of this patient's treatment program included individual supportive therapy and a movement therapy group. The movement therapy appeared to help her maintain mobility in spite of her arthritis and promoted social contact, which in turn encouraged her participation in other activities that bolstered her self-esteem and mood. The individual therapy helped to sustain an alliance with the patient, which was crucial after she became severely depressed and apathetic. A recent review of the literature on psychotherapy interventions in elderly nursing home residents turned up only six randomized, controlled studies that included depression as an outcome measure. Some studies found benefits from groups for exercise, reminiscence, and cognitive therapies, but other studies showed no significant improvement on measures of depression. Unfortunately, there is a stark lack of controlled studies of the effectiveness of individual psychotherapy for depression in nursing home residents.

THE PROBLEM OF DELIRIUM AS A COMPLICATION OF DEMENTIA

The syndrome of delirium has a high incidence in geriatric patients in medical and institutional settings. Diagnosis of delirium poses a special challenge in nursing homes because in this setting, two-thirds of patients already have cognitive impairment due to the syndrome of dementia. Recognizing delirium and distinguishing it from dementia is of critical importance because delirium can exacerbate the cognitive impairment, behavioral disturbances, and functional deficits associated with dementia; and because delirium, unlike most dementias, is usually treatable, and the associated excess disability is usually reversible.

An eighty-one-year-old woman with vascular dementia had moderate cognitive impairment with difficulty recalling recent events and disorientation to time, although she remained aware that she was in a nursing home and remembered the names of her children, whose visits she enjoyed. She ambulated independently, toileted herself without assistance or cues from staff, and was also able to dress herself if the nursing assistants laid out her clothes. Although she did not seek out food or fluids on her own and needed reminders from staff to go to the dining room at mealtime, she did eat and drink when prompted by staff, and her nutrition and hydration were adequately maintained.

Over a period of three days, she failed to get herself dressed and was incontinent of urine on several occasions. At night she had trouble sleeping and would call for help, but when staff approached her she had no specific complaints and could not tell them what she wanted. During most of the day she appeared tired and inattentive to her environment, but when staff told her it was time to eat, she became belligerent and tearful. She did not respond to her own sensation of thirst, and ignored staff cues to drink fluids between meals.

Staff thought she seemed unmotivated and attributed her diminished function to apathy. They enlisted the help of the social worker, who tried to interview the patient to identify what might be bothering her, but the patient began yelling and wouldn't cooperate. After another night of sleeplessness and noisiness, the nurses called the primary care attending physician who prescribed temazepam (a short-acting cousin of Valium) for sedation. The next day she refused to ambulate and was incontinent of both urine and stool. Staff could not tell whether her dementia was progressing or whether she was becoming depressed; they also wondered whether medication had made her condition worse, so they asked me to evaluate her.

During my exam she appeared alternately lethargic and agitated. She was unable to attend to a brief interview. Her affect was irritable. There were no psychotic symptoms, but she was more disoriented than usual and could not recall her daughter's name. My impression was that she had developed a syndrome of delirium, superimposed on her preexisting dementia. This was not a presentation of a depressive disorder, even though she exhibited dysphoria and irritability. Such disturbances of mood and affect are common in delirium.

Although it was possible that the temazepam had exacerbated the delirium by causing disinhibition or paradoxical excitation, this medication effect was clearly not the original cause of the problem. The temazepam was discontinued, but a general medical evaluation was still needed to determine the underlying cause of her delirium. The medical exam revealed a low-grade fever at 100.2 F, abnormal drop in systolic blood pressure when the patient stood up, dry mouth and tongue, and abnormal urinalysis—all consistent with a diagnosis of urinary tract infection and dehydration. An oral antibiotic was prescribed and an attempt was made to get her to take fluids by mouth, but she became verbally abusive when staff tried to administer her medication or encourage her to drink.

Her attending physician asked me to evaluate her competency to refuse medical treatment. My exam confirmed that she was unaware of her illness, did not understand a simple explanation of her problem or the treatment options, was unable to comprehend the potential risks and benefits of treatment, and could not appreciate the possible consequences of a decision to accept or decline treatment. I concluded that she was not capable of making her own decision about treatment and recommended that a surrogate decision maker be identified. The oldest daughter, who had power of attorney for health care matters, gave permission for the physicians and nursing home staff to treat her mother involuntarily. The daughter believed that if her mother could understand the situation, she would choose to accept treatment to relieve her symptoms and restore the level of function and quality of life that she had enjoyed the week prior to this illness.

With the daughter's consent, the staff held the patient down and inserted an intravenous (IV) line through which the first two doses of antibiotics were given and replacement fluids were administered until that night, when the patient pulled out the IV. The following morning, before restarting the IV, the staff requested an order for physical restraints and sedating medication to prevent her from pulling out the next IV. However, I pointed out that this patient's level of arousal waxed and waned (as is characteristic of patients with delirium), and there were frequent periods during which she was naturally less irritable. Also, having already received some antibiotics and fluids, she was somewhat less confused and less agitated on the second day of treatment. We therefore decided to try the oral route again: the nurses would back off during moments when she appeared irritable and reapproach her with the oral antibiotics and fluids when she seemed more receptive. Fortunately, with this approach, she received her antibiotic doses at acceptable intervals; she also took a sufficient quantity of fluids to correct her dehydration so that restraining her to maintain IV access was no longer necessary. Over the next forty-eight hours, the delirium cleared and the patient resumed functioning at the level seen the previous week, consistent with her demented baseline.

Identifying Causes of Cognitive Decline

This case illustrates several phenomena commonly seen by psychiatrists in nursing homes. Remember that although most cases of dementia are incurable, not all the cognitive impairment and functional deficits seen in long-term care settings are irreversible. The syndrome of delirium is common in the frail elderly, especially in medical and institutional settings, and it is usually caused by a medical illness or medication effect that can be remedied.

In the case just described, the delirium was due to a urinary tract infection and associated dehydration; it may also have been aggravated by adverse effects of the sedative-hypnotic medication temazepam. When the cognitive or functional decline is relatively abrupt or occurs over a short period of time, presuming that it is simply the natural progression of the dementing illness is almost always a mistake. Instead, think of delirium—as well as of depression, which the nursing home staff properly considered—in the differential diagnosis of conditions causing cognitive and functional decline.

To assist nursing home staff to recognize delirium and to help them initiate an appropriate assessment, the federal regulations furnish Resident Assessment Protocols (RAPs) on delirium and other problems that may be related to cognitive and functional decline. As a mental health consultant to a nursing facility, it is essential that you be familiar with these protocols. In most cases, the involvement of psychiatrists, as well as other physicians and mental health professionals, is necessary to accomplish a comprehensive assessment as outlined in the RAPs.

Surrogacy and Decision Making

This case also illustrates a principle of health maintenance in cognitively impaired nursing home patients. Caregivers must assume a parental role, much as they would with an infant, when patients do not have the ability to interpret or respond to normal bodily sensations and cues, such as urinary urgency or thirst. In the former case, scheduled toileting is sometimes helpful in averting incontinence. In the latter situation, repeated cues to drink fluids throughout the day may be necessary to avoid dehydration.

Another role for the mental health consultant in this case was the clinical determination of the patient's capacity to make decisions regarding health care matters. Requests for such "competency evaluations" are common in long-term care settings. Although many of the decisions and directives made by cognitively impaired residents are respected and followed without a clinical or legal determination of competence, in some situations a formal determination is appropriate. In the case described here, a legal remedy was not necessary; an argument could be made that even a formal clinical assessment of decision-making capacity by a psychiatrist was not necessary, as the primary care physician could have documented that the patient did not demonstrate adequate comprehension of basic treatment issues concerning her health care. Furthermore, assessing the patient's decision-making capacity might not have been necessary at all if oral medication and hydration had first been attempted during the patient's more receptive moments before resorting to the IV route. This possibility again highlights the importance of translating a knowledge of mental disorders and syndromes into practical strategies for nursing staff.

ᕬ

Thus, we see how the unique characteristics of the nursing home setting and its geriatric resident population pose critical challenges for mental health professionals. The high prevalence of psychiatric disorders demands that there be access to the skills of mental health providers. The high prevalence of medical-psychiatric co-morbidity requires that psychiatric evaluation and treatment be closely coordinated with medical management and well integrated into all other aspects of the care of nursing home patients.

The lack of mental health resources that is too often characteristic of nursing homes must be remedied by psychiatric and other mental health services that continuously address the need for staff-centered consultation. Beyond the obvious need for enhanced mental health care in nursing homes, the federal government has mandated assessment and appropriate treatment, holding nursing facilities responsible for ensuring that patients get what they need. Mental health practitioners therefore have numerous opportunities to engage in a broad range of stimulating and rewarding professional activities and to make substantial contributions toward improving the quality of nursing home care.

NOTES

P. 196, *Epidemiologic studies . . . have . . . demonstrated:* Rovner, B., Kafonek, S., Filipp, L., Lucas, M. J., & Folstein, M. F. (1986). Prevalence of mental illness in a community nursing home. *American Journal of Psychiatry, 143,* 1446–1449; Tariot, P. N., Podgorske, C. A., Blazina, L., & Leivovic, A. (1993). Mental disorders in the nursing home: Another perspective. *American Journal of Psychiatry, 150,* 1063–1069.

P. 197, *a serious mismatch exists:* Streim, J. E., & Katz, I. R. (1994). Federal regulations and the care of patients with dementia in the nursing home. *Medical Clinics of North America, 78,* 895–909.

P. 197, *practitioners face a serious challenge:* Streim, J. E. (1995). OBRA regulations and psychiatric care in the nursing home. *Psychiatric Annals, 25,* 413–418.

P. 197, *prescribed . . . without . . . assessment of . . . mental status:* Avorn, J., Dreyer,

P., Connelly, K., & Soumerai, S. B. (1989). Use of psychoactive medication and the quality of care in rest homes. *New England Journal of Medicine, 320,* 227–232.

P. 197, *without established psychiatric diagnoses:* Burns, B. J., Larson, D. B., Goldstrom, I. D., Johnson, W. E., Taube, C. A., Miller, N. E., & Mathis, E. S. (1988). Mental disorders among nursing home patients: Preliminary findings from the National Nursing Home Survey Pretest. *International Journal of Geriatric Psychiatry, 3,* 27–35.

P. 197, *physical restraints . . . in 25 percent to 85 percent:* Evans, L. K., & Strumpf, N. E. (1989). Tying down the elderly: A review of the literature on physical restraint. *Journal of the American Geriatrics Society, 37,* 65–74.

P. 197, *restraints do not . . . decrease behavioral disturbances:* Werner, P., Cohen-Mansfield, J., Braun, J., & Marx, M. S. (1989). Physical restraint and agitation in nursing home residents. *Journal of the American Geriatric Society, 37,* 1122–1126.

P. 197, *physical restraint . . . associated with . . . adverse effects:* Evans, L. K., & Strumpf, N. E. (1989). Tying down the elderly: A review of the literature on physical restraint. *Journal of the American Geriatrics Society, 37,* 65–74.

P. 199, *Institute of Medicine report:* Institute of Medicine, Committee on Nursing Home Regulation. (1986). *Improving the quality of care in nursing homes.* Washington, DC: National Academy Press.

P. 199, *Nursing Home Reform Amendments . . . of 1987:* Omnibus Budget Reconciliation Act of 1987, Public Law 100–203.

P. 199, *accompanying interpretive guidelines:* Health Care Financing Administration. (1992). *State operations manual: Provider certification.* Transmittal No. 250. Washington, DC: U.S. Government Printing Office.

P. 203, *Many programs have been described:* Colthart, S. M. (1974). A mental health unit in a skilled nursing facility. *Journal of the American Geriatrics Society, 22,* 453–456; Liptzin, B. (1983). The geriatric psychiatrist's role as consultant. *Journal of Geriatric Psychiatry, 16,* 103–112; Loebel, J. P., Borson, S., Hyde, T., Donaldson, D., Van Tuinen, C., Rabbitt, T. M., & Boyke, E. J. (1991). Relationships between requests for psychiatric consultations and psychiatric diagnoses in long-term care facilities. *American Journal of Psychiatry, 148,* 898–903; Sakauye, K. M., & Camp, C. J. (1992). Introducing psychiatric care into nursing homes. *Gerontologist, 32,* 849–852.

P. 203, *best position to make observations:* Streim, J. E., & Katz, I. R. (1995). The psychiatrist in the nursing home, Part II: Consultation, primary care, and leadership. *Psychiatric Services, 46,* 339–341.

P. 203, *consultation to staff:* American Psychiatric Association. (1989). *Nursing homes and the mentally ill elderly.* Task Force Report 28. Washington, DC:

American Psychiatric Press; Moses, J. (1982). New role for hands-on caregivers: Part-time mental health technicians. *Journal of the American Health Care Association, 8,* 19–22.

P. 204, *interactions between the nursing home staff and the patient:* Streim, J. E., & Katz, I. R. (1995). The psychiatrist in the nursing home, Part II: Consultation, primary care, and leadership. *Psychiatric Services, 46,* 340.

P. 204, *"the right to be free from any physical restraints":* Health Care Financing Administration. (1991). Medicare and Medicaid: Requirements for long term care facilities, final regulations. *Federal Register, 56,* 48865–48921.

P. 213, *periodic comprehensive standardized assessment:* Health Care Financing Administration. (1992). Medicare and Medicaid: Resident assessment in long term care facilities. *Federal Register, 57,* 61614–61733.

P. 213, *psychiatrist . . . suited to function as . . . primary care provider:* Streim, J. E., & Katz, I. R. (1995). The psychiatrist in the nursing home, Part II: Consultation, primary care, and leadership. *Psychiatric Services, 46,* 340–341.

P. 214, *controlled studies that included depression as an outcome measure:* Goldwasser, A. N., Auerbach, S. M., & Harkins, S. W. (1987). Cognitive, affective, and behavioral effects of reminiscence group therapy of the demented elderly. (1987). *International Journal of Aging and Human Development, 25,* 209–222; Youssef, F. A. (1990). The impact of group reminiscence counseling on a depressed elderly population. *Nursing Practice, 15,* 32–38; Ames, D. (1990). Depression among elderly residents of local-authority residential homes: Its nature and the efficacy of intervention. *British Journal of Psychiatry, 156,* 667–675; Zerhusen, J. D., Boyle, K., & Wilson, W. (1991). Out of the darkness: Group cognitive therapy for depressed elderly. *Journal of Psychological Nursing, 29,* 16–21; Abraham, I. L., Neundorfer, M. M., & Currie, L. J. (1992). Effects of group interventions on cognition and depression in nursing home residents. *Nursing Research, 41,* 196–202; McMurdo, M.E.T., & Rennie, L. (1993). A controlled trial of exercise by residents of old people's homes. *Age and Aging, 22,* 11–15.

8

THE IMPACT OF MEDICAL ILLNESS ON PSYCHOLOGICAL WELL-BEING

Barbara R. Sommer

As therapists, we attempt to help elderly people to optimize their sense of well-being as they face the loss of friendships and family through death, loss of physical health, and increased dependence on others. But the geriatric therapist must also understand that she is part of a treatment team. The older individual is often also a patient who is being treated by at least one physician and who may be taking at least one medication.

As the therapist, you may see this person more often than any other health care provider; consequently, you may see changes in the patient before anyone else observes them. You may be the first practitioner to notice not only psychological changes as the patient enters a new phase in the life cycle but also mental status changes possibly brought on in part by the patient's medical illness or the medication to treat it.

In this chapter, therefore, I give you an overview of the most common medical problems in geriatrics, along with their medical treatment and their impact on patients' psychological well-being. The goal is to familiarize you with some terms that you may see if you ask the physician for a patient's medical record, and to help you predict when your client could be at risk as a patient for psychological problems compounded by a medical condition.

THE SUBTLETIES OF MEDICAL ILLNESSES
IN THE ELDERLY

Sometimes we meet patients who teach us so much that we remember them for years, and tell our colleagues and students about them.

One such patient for me was a seventy-six-year-old woman whom I met on a psychiatric inpatient ward. She had a long history of severe depression and had even done poorly after a course of electroconvulsive therapy. This was her fifth admission to a psychiatric hospital, and many staff members considered her to be "treatment refractory."

When I evaluated her, she indeed met all the diagnostic criteria for severe depression. But a medical review of her systems revealed the possibility that she was suffering from a subtle case of hypothyroidism (her thyroid gland was not secreting enough thyroid hormone). Her physical exam also was suggestive of this suspicion, and obtaining the most sensitive measure of thyroid function rather than the less expensive screening test corroborated the diagnosis. Although she still needed an antidepressant and psychotherapy, supplementation with thyroid hormone made the real difference in her improvement. One year later, she remained out of the hospital. We were told that she now had a "boyfriend" and had resumed activities that she had not enjoyed for many years.

This case suggests that, particularly in the elderly, medical illnesses such as mild hypothyroidism may either cause psychiatric syndromes or make primary psychiatric disorders almost impossible to treat successfully. The case also emphasizes that the elderly may acquire medical problems that are clinically important and yet do not seem to present as floridly as in the young adult. This mild presentation sometimes fools the treater into thinking that the condition is not significant. In reality, though, almost all medical conditions commonly seen—ranging from those that seem obviously important to brain function (like severe cardiac conditions) to the seemingly noncontributory (like urinary tract infections)—may make the elderly patient seem as though he has a "pure" psychiatric disorder. Neglecting to treat the underlying disorder often diminishes the effectiveness of any psychological or psychiatric treatments.

Thyroid Disease

What is it about disorders such as hypothyroidism that cause the elderly to seem as though they are suffering from primary psychiatric problems? One way to conceptualize the unique difficulties of the elderly in maintaining normal psychological well-being while medically ill is to see the older person as less able to adapt in general to the stress of an illness. The fact is that the older we get, the less able we are to adapt to the physiological changes induced by an illness. For example, with hypothyroidism, a young adult may exhibit signs and symptoms such as coarsening of the hair; dry, scaly skin; weight gain; energy loss; constipation; slowed heart rate; and depressed mood. But the hyperthyroid adult may present in just the opposite way: with oily skin and hair, rapid heart rate, anxiety, weight loss, and diarrhea.

Even in younger adults, a diagnosis is sometimes missed, albeit rarely with the development of sophisticated ways of accurately measuring thyroid function. (A blood test known as Thyroid Stimulating Hormone by RIA [radioimmuno assay] is now used in most laboratories and is highly sensitive.) Hypofunction of the thyroid gland may give rise to the above changes insidiously so that patients at first may seem sluggish, lazy, and unmotivated. The geriatric patient may additionally suffer from memory deficits, resulting in a diagnosis of dementia. As with so many other medical disorders, the changes in brain function are likely because of changes in the heart's ability to pump enough oxygenated blood to the brain. Thus, the brain fails to get enough of the oxygen it needs to maintain well-being.

Whether hypo- or hyperthyroid, the elderly patient may appear in exactly the same way. In fact, the term *apathetic hyperthyroidism* means that the patient may look hypo- and yet be hyperthyroid. This suggests that the ability to adapt to illness changes with age. The impact of this inability may be profound when it comes to brain function, and disorders that may have no or few effects on the brains of young adults can be devastating to the brains of the elderly.

An entire literature exists on the effects of thyroid function on psychological well-being, and suggested readings from these references are cited at the end of the chapter. The unique inability of older patients to compensate for their thyroid dysfunction means that they can seem depressed, manic, demented, or even grossly psychotic just because their thyroid function is awry. Just as the patient cited earlier in the chapter had depression and thyroid disease together, I have also seen thyroid disease cause mania and frank delirium. That the same problem can give rise to any of these diverse psychiatric pictures is intriguing and may be in part a function of the individual patient's genetic predispositions. As we see in this chapter, another way thyroid abnormality causes psychiatric symptoms is by the metabolic changes and changes in use of cerebral glucose that may result. In this chapter, we look at some of the most common medical conditions of the elderly, concentrating on how they may affect the brain's function and how combined treatment of both the medical and psychiatric problems are often necessary for full amelioration of the psychiatric symptoms.

DIABETES

Unfortunately, hypo- and hyperthyroidism are not the only endocrine disorders associated with changes in psychological function. Another endocrine disorder quite common in the elderly is diabetes mellitus. Diabetes results from either a deficiency of insulin production from cells in the pancreas or from a decreased sensitivity of insulin receptors on cell walls. (A receptor is a protein located on a cell membrane that is exquisitely sensitive to a given chemical that binds to it. In this case, insulin is the binder, also called the agonist.)

In either case, the result is that glucose cannot get into the cells of the body. This results in two problems: (1) too much glucose in the circulation, clogging up small blood vessels; and (2) inability of the body's cells to utilize glucose as an energy source. As you can imagine, poorly treated diabetes can give rise to numerous problems in all organs of the body, ranging from the heart and kidneys to the brain.

Whether a patient requires insulin or oral medications to normalize blood glucose, fluctuations of blood glucose may be subtle and may occur during sleep, making the patient unaware of symptoms. As glucose is the only energy source utilized by the brain, even a small decrease in the right amount of blood glucose getting to the brain (hypoglycemia) may result in changes in brain function ranging from subtle to catastrophic. Thus, both too much and too little glucose in the circulation are deleterious.

The effects of years of fluctuations in blood sugars, ranging from hypo- to hyperglycemia, are variable, depending at least in part on the extent to which the individual patient has been in good diabetic control. However, damage to the small arteries that supply organs may give rise to changes in the amount of oxygenated blood ultimately received by the brain. Additionally, neuropathies resulting in pain and tingling from peripheral nervous system damage can cause mental status changes. Please see the section on chronic pain for further discussion of this. The severe destruction to blood vessels often results in strokes, not all of which are classic, with paralysis. Rather, some result only in dementia. As if this were not reason enough to get depressed, small strokes may be accompanied by poststroke depression.

Thus, we have two problems in diabetes: (1) if we control it too well, the patient may at times become hypoglycemic, the brain will be deprived of glucose, and the patient becomes demented; (2) if we do not control it well enough, the patient may suffer from small or large strokes and become demented and depressed. This no-win situation is not as bleak as it sounds at first. When an older patient contracts diabetes, it can often be treated with diet, exercise, and oral hypoglycemics. If an obese patient loses enough weight, the insulin receptors may once again become sensitive to insulin, and the diabetes may "go away." The type of diabetes contracted by the elderly is often this type—not an insulin deficiency but an insulin receptor sensitivity problem.

Cooperation on the part of the patient thus is particularly important in the treatment of diabetes, and its lack can contribute significantly to increased injury to both the brain and to other organs. The diabetic patient who is already suffering from dementia may further aggravate his memory impairment by an inability to be rigorous enough with dietary control and the taking of medications in a coordinated fashion.

Whether young or old, patients with a new diagnosis of diabetes may do well with both individual psychotherapy and support groups. Diabetic patients can no longer eat with abandon the kinds of foods they wish, and they cannot ever forget the illness that often requires daily injections.

Electrolyte Imbalance

In this chapter we cannot completely explore metabolic balance and the impact of imbalances on all mental function. We can, however, look at one example—the electrolyte serum sodium—to see what causes an imbalance in it and how this condition can insidiously give rise to numerous psychiatric problems.

Sodium is an important element that must be present inside and outside cells in exactly the right ratio for the heart to function and for the mind to work. Numerous factors may change this ratio: sodium depletion from heat intolerance, from various conditions of the kidney, and very important, from *medications* prescribed by physicians.

For example, diuretics prescribed for hypertension, tricyclic antidepressants, neuroleptic antipsychotic drugs such as thioridazine (Mellaril, one of the most commonly prescribed sedatives in the nursing home population), and carbamazepine (Tegretol, occasionally prescribed for episodic agitation), all may very slowly over the course of months lower serum sodium concentrations. Often physicians do not routinely order the laboratory test to assess serum sodium once these medications have been initially prescribed, and the depletion may become clinically apparent before it is discovered by the laboratory.

Sodium depletion, called hyponatremia, may appear in the patient as depression, anxiety, and later, lassitude, weakness, and apathy. If these symptoms are not carefully evaluated and instead are treated empirically with antidepressants, the medication may further decrease the serum sodium. If further untreated, patients may then become disoriented from delirium. They may hallucinate and eventually slip into coma.

HYPERTENSION

Disorders of the vascular system are quite common in the elderly, even in those who have never suffered from diabetes. While less common vascular disorders such as systemic lupus, migraine headache, and temporal arteritis are disabling, we discuss here the ubiquitous disorder of the elderly—essential hypertension—and its sequelae.

Hypertension is known as "the silent killer" because people feel no symptoms until their blood pressure becomes high enough to give them "killer headaches." Yet hypertension is among the most common of all medical problems in the United States. It is likely that many people will have hypertension as they age, and by some estimates, 45 percent to 60 percent of people sixty-five to seventy-four have high blood pressure. The experts now feel that even those with mild elevations in blood pressure should be treated lest they suffer from the fallout that we will soon discuss.

Hypertension can have two major outcomes on a patient's mental status: (1) If the condition is not treated, it markedly increases the risk of stroke (hypertension is only one possible cause of stroke; the other common cause is atherosclerotic disease, that is, the development of plaques lining the important arteries that supply the brain). (2) If antihypertensive medications, such as ß-blockers, are necessary, they can have unintended effects on brain function.

Hypertension-Induced Stroke

Also known as cerebrovascular accidents (CVAs), strokes are among the most common causes of death in the Western world, along with heart attacks and cancer. One of the important causes of stroke is hypertension. Rigorous control of diet along with medication has been shown to be effective in decreasing the incidence of stroke. Stroke has been defined as a focal neurological event that results in actual death of areas of brain nerve cells. These events may be diagnosed by special imaging techniques such as CT scans or MRI scans. They result in either subtle brain changes, such as slurred speech; psychiatric disorders, such as depression or dementia; or catastrophic changes, such as paralysis or coma (that is, the patient is "struck down").

There appear to be two linked factors that affect a patient's well-being after a stroke: (1) the location of the lesion and the biochemical changes that occur—giving rise to depression or dementia; and (2) the many powerful psychological changes that take place because of new dependence on others and the grieving that inevitably makes one mourn lost youth and vitality.

The Importance of Location of the Stroke. In the 1980s, new technologies brought tremendous advances in our knowledge about stroke-induced changes in mental function. From writings on MRI and positron emission tomography (PET) to the work on cerebral laterality, the literature in this area has increased markedly. Here we can concentrate on only a few areas as examples, but the interested reader is encouraged to explore the literature cited at the end of the chapter.

Seminal studies conducted by Robinson and colleagues in the 1980s found that the severest depressions for patients who had suffered left hemisphere strokes seemed to occur when the CVA was located in the left *anterior* region of the brain. When the CT scans found the location to be closest to the frontal pole, the severity was increased still further. In the group of patients with right hemisphere strokes, the opposite was found: the more *posterior* the stroke, the more severe the depression. This fascinating group of findings was among the first to suggest that stroke is depressing not just psychologically by its association with mortality and other unpleasant aspects of aging, but that it is also depressing physiologically depending on where in the brain it occurs.

Other literature has suggested that after a CVA the patient may have delusions depending on the location of the lesion and on whether there has been prestroke cerebral atrophy. Furthermore, personality changes may occur after stroke, especially if the patient now has a certain kind of seizure disorder with which to contend. Several authors have corroborated "temporal lobe personality changes" from seizures, and the neurosurgery literature is replete with case reports on personality changes after intracranial war injuries.

Psychological Factors Resulting from Stroke. The findings just cited suggest a medical basis for stroke-induced changes in mental function, but in no way do they tell the whole story. The term *stroke* is apt: the person in apparently good health is struck down, and his or her world may never be the same. Often such people have seen their peers after a stroke and they understand the new dependence that they themselves now have on family and friends. Depending on the size of the CVA, people may have to give up driving, they may become paralyzed or weak on one side, and they may become incontinent. If the patient does not become demented, it may be an even worse situation, as he or she understands the new frailty. The suicide risk is worrisome in such patients. Patients with these difficulties may have to give up their independent living and move in with children or to a nursing home.

These stroke patients and their families would do well with family and individual psychotherapy. There are times when even the whole family needs antidepressant medication along with plans for respite, as the patient continues to have strokes, getting ever weaker. In homes where the children care for the parent, the roles now reversed, children mourn the death of the vital parent they once knew and feel both angry at the situation and guilty because they are mourning someone who has not yet died. Patients who have to go to nursing homes after strokes may have an even worse situation, feeling that they are just putting in time prior to death. Stroke patients embody the geriatric patient in need of a multidisciplinary team of caregivers: psychologist, psychiatrist, social worker, nurse, and family member.

Antihypertensive Drugs

Although modification of lifestyle, including decreasing sodium intake, reducing weight, stopping cigarette smoking, and exercising moderately may in combination obviate the need for antihypertensives, many patients do not have the ability to replace the less rigorous habits they may have had for forty years or more. Thus, they will need pharmacotherapy. As you can see from Table 8.1 (on p. 239), many medications intended for such nonpsychiatric problems as hypertension get into the brain and may subtly or drastically affect mental function.

There are many pharmacological treatment approaches to essential hypertension, ranging from diuretics ("water pills" that can dramatically change serum electrolyte balance and cause delirium, as described above) and ß-blockers, to the newer calcium channel blockers and Angiotensin Converting Enzyme (ACE) inhibitors.

After having fallen into relative disfavor in the 1980s, diuretic therapy is once again considered by many experts to be the first-line treatment for high blood pressure. However, to the patient, this modality is a mixed blessing. Even when taken in the morning, diuretics (such as hydrochlorothiazide, or HCTZ) may impair sleep at night because they cause urination. Furthermore, if the diuretic works too well, patients may urinate so much that they become volume depleted (hypovolemic). This condition may cause the patient to fall if the blood pressure is lowered too quickly. I have seen some patients with mild or moderate memory impairment, responsible for their own medication management, who in their desire to comply with their physician's therapy would take their diuretics more often than prescribed, having forgotten that they had already taken them. Pharmacies usually carry pill boxes with separators to help such patients. The subtle electrolyte imbalances that often occur from diuretics may also cause weakness, lassitude, dysphoria, and an exacerbation of memory problems rather than frank depression. But as Gallagher-Thompson and Coon point out in Chapter One, depression in the elderly may present atypically. Such symptoms from diuretic therapy may be therefore misconstrued as depression.

ß-blockers have also been a mainstay of treatment of hypertension. With diuretics, they are an inexpensive way to lower blood pressure safely. We are not sure whether the drugs in this class (examples include any medication that ends in -olol, such as propranolol [Inderal], and atenolol [Tenormin]) cause major depression matching the criteria in the *Diagnostic and Statistical Manual of Mental Disorders* (DSM-IV) of the American Psychiatric Association. We do know, however, that ß-blockers can cause sedation, lack of energy, and dysphoria. If they are given together with diuretics, they may contribute additively to depressive feelings. They are not to be prescribed to patients with severe emphysema or to diabetic patients.

The most commonly prescribed calcium channel blockers for hypertension in the United States are nifedipine (Procardia), verapamil (Calan), and diltiazem (Cardizem). These agents may be more beneficial to elderly patients than to younger adults, by virtue of their mechanism of action. But because of changes in absorption and binding of these drugs, they usually must be prescribed in lower doses for older than younger patients. The biggest problem with this class of drugs seems not to be psychiatric but gastrointestinal; they tend to cause constipation. As we see in the section on delirium, constipation is not a trivial problem, and when verapamil especially is prescribed, the physician must be careful not to prescribe other constipating medications, such as some antidepressant and antipsychotic drugs.

ACE inhibitors are another class of antihypertensives that have few direct psychiatric effects. Examples include lisinopril (Zestril) and captopril (Capoten). Although the drugs in this class are superb antihypertensives, especially for diabetic patients, two factors may limit their use, especially in high doses, in the elderly: (1) they are excreted in the urine. This means that elderly patients, who often have decreased renal (pertaining to the kidneys) function, may have a hard time excreting the drug, and therefore have an exaggerated response. Lower doses are one way to solve this problem. (2) Nonsteroidal anti-inflammatory drugs, such as indomethicin and aspirin, will impair the effectiveness of ACE inhibitors. Because many of our patients suffer from chronic pain, this may be a drawback in the elderly.

This cursory overview of antihypertensive drugs shows that if an older person seeks antihypertensive pharmacotherapy from an astute geriatric physician, he or she can find a suitable regimen without sacrificing either memory or mood.

CHRONIC PAIN

As we age, we all begin to feel the effects of repetitive use of the joints, muscles, and tendons that have made us mobile. If we have been athletic as young adults, we have degenerative changes localized to the muscles, bones, and joints to look forward to.

And if we have been sedentary, we have osteoarthritis and impaired mobility with age. Therefore, no matter how we live as young adults, we can anticipate either a little or a lot of orthopedic pain as we age.

Chapter One, which deals with depression, describes its multifactorial nature and lists some contributions of physical disorders, including pain, as potential etiologies. Of all the serious medical problems we treat, pain is perhaps the most difficult as it is purely subjective in nature, and we have no way either to quantify it objectively and reliably or to assess its amelioration from therapy. Quite often we see that a patient's subjective sense of illness improvement lags behind our clinical sense of improvement. For example, the elderly patient may still feel ill after the pneumonia has been successfully treated, or still feel depressive symptoms when others have already seen real improvement. Therefore, even if we are successful in treating the origin of a patient's pain, we may nonetheless find that, at least acutely, the patient senses no relief.

Because the elderly in general may experience a lag between a treatment given and its effect, doctors may want to change medications or increase their dose in a faster time frame than is appropriate for this age group. This tendency is particularly common when treating pain as the physician is loath to feel that nothing is being done to make the patient comfortable.

Pain is also a difficult problem because we all have different thresholds for it as individuals and because cultural expectations vary as to how a patient may express pain. I noted this on an obstetrical ward, where some women absolutely would not admit to pain during labor and delivery. Pain medications were prescribed according to how the patients gritted their teeth and by the magnitude of pain the staff assumed they were having. As suboptimal as this method of pain management is, it is still better than that of other circumstances, such as arthritis, when the staff may have no idea of how much pain to expect.

Regardless of the etiology of the pain, be it from degenerative arthritis, quite common in the elderly, or from cancer, with all its frightening connotations to the patient, chronic pain is almost always associated with some depressive feelings. It often disturbs sleep, exacerbating the sleep problems so common in these patients. Some patients with untreated or poorly controlled pain may awaken each morning with pain intensified from not having taken analgesics since the previous night. They may feel that life is no longer worth living, if living means having continued pain to endure. This sense, in the early morning, may be mistaken by the clinician as the diurnal variation of major depression. I have treated many patients who seemed in remission from their depressive symptoms, with the exception of sleep. When give acetaminophen (Tylenol), or long-acting pain killers at night, the sleep would improve dramatically, suggesting that such patients were awakened by pain and were not fully aware that arthritic pain in bed was the problem.

Pain and Dementia

The effects of pain on patients with dementia are not well studied. Animal studies suggest that the pain threshold may actually decrease with age, implying a greater tolerance for pain in older patients. This would make some practical sense, if older age is associated with more pain to endure than younger age. I hypothesize that the patient with dementia may have a further decrease in expressed pain sensation, based on two observations: (1) this patient may have a decreased ability to discuss pain, and (2) there may be an actual change in the way the brain with dementia perceives pain.

I first began to consider these perceptions of pain while I was treating a patient at an outpatient Alzheimer's clinic. He was an eighty-six-year-old man who had a short-term memory deficit, with disorientation and wandering that had begun insidiously over four years prior to his presenting for a multidisciplinary evaluation. After a rigorous evaluation, he was given a diagnosis of probable Alzheimer's disease and was hospitalized for treatment of concomitant hypersexual behavior. Before any medications were begun, the patient fell and fractured his hip. He underwent a hip replacement.

When I visited him on the surgical ward the day after his surgery, he was pleasant and offered no complaints. I asked him if he had pain and he said that he did not. I pressed on his wound site, and the patient did not wince or express any discomfort. I was amazed. Usually, however, if the patient with dementia has an exacerbation of dementia symptoms, pain may be the etiology, with the patient lacking the communicative skills to express the pain.

Treatment of pain may unfortunately result in dementia symptoms, delirium, or depression in the elderly. Even acetaminophen and salicylates may result in such changes in mental status. Likewise, nonsteroidal anti-inflammatory drugs (NSAIDs) such as ibuprofen may cause sedation and dysphoria. Nonetheless, it is recommended that a patient's complaints of pain be taken seriously. If the etiology is found, such as by X-ray, it should be aggressively treated. If no etiology can be found, the patient needs to be evaluated for depression, as complaints of pain in an older patient may actually represent depressive symptoms. Doctors in the United States have been documented as tending to *undertreat* pain. It seems as though even in treating cancer pain, many doctors fear that patients will become addicted to narcotics and thus they may dismiss the magnitude of a patient's pain. In my opinion, this is a grave error. If we believe what our patients tell us and treat the etiology of the pain, then we should also trust that the patient is not trying to obtain narcotics or secondary gain. He or she likely would like pain relief. Many elders are in fact fearful of narcotics and need to be persuaded that they are indicated. Proper treatment of pain, even with the potential psychiatric side effects, may ameliorate mood, sleep, appetite, and quality of life. These factors must be considered as one discusses the amount and type of anti-pain therapy in a patient.

DELIRIUM

The illnesses discussed in this chapter illustrate that one disorder can give rise to a whole range of psychiatric symptoms. Contrarily, one important syndrome that can occur at any age may be caused by a number of medical disorders.

Delirium usually looks similar among patients but it is particularly prevalent in the elderly. Also known in the past as organic brain syndrome, delirium is an example of a "final common pathway"—a constellation of problems that do not represent a disease but rather an organ's response to a disease. Delirium may always look the same, despite the cause, and may result from almost any illness or medication given to an older person. Please see Table 8.1 for a detailed list of such etiologies of delirium.

Delirium is characterized by an acute onset of poor recall, changes in level of consciousness, and often, by anxiety, agitation, and even combativeness, particularly during the hours preceding sunrise. Age and a history of brain injury or brain disease seem to make delirium more florid, and yet these factors make it hard to recognize.

In general, delirium is first seen late at night, when a patient awakens and exhibits disorientation and a change in level of consciousness, either by being hyperalert or by appearing severely sedated and difficult to arouse. He or she may speak as if from a dream and even become assaultive, as in a case where a patient with no prior history of assaultiveness suddenly hits staff members. By early morning, the episode may be finished, with the patient having no recall of the event. Because delirium usually first manifests itself at night, it is often not at first noticed by day shift health care professionals who make most clinical decisions. Even in a nursing home, the night nurse may write a brief note stating that the patient was "confused." The word *confusion* is

Table 8.1
Causes of Delirium

1. Intoxication by Drugs and Poisons
   - Drugs: antibiotics, lithium, aspirin, sedative hypnotics, nonsteroidal anti-inflammatory agents (such as Motrin, Advil), cardiac drugs
   - Alcohol

2. Withdrawal Syndromes
   - Alcohol
   - Sedatives and hypnotics: barbiturates, benzodiazepines (any medicine ending in -epam, such as diazepam [Valium], lorazepam [Ativan]), chloral hydrate, meprobamate (Miltown). While elderly patients do not often abuse "street drugs," abuse of sedatives and hypnotics is quite common. A careful history, corroborated by family, is important.

3. Metabolic Encephalopathies
   - Hypoxia
   - Hypoglycemia
   - Endocrinopathies: diabetes, hyperthyroidism, hypothyroidism
   - Disorders of fluid and electrolyte metabolism (dehydration, water intoxication)

4. Infections, such as Pneumonia

5. Head Trauma: concussion, contusion

6. Epilepsy: during the seizure, after the seizure, and between seizures

7. Vascular Disorders
   - Cerebrovascular
   Transient ischemic attacks ("temporary strokes," lasting less than 24 hours)
   Multi-infarct dementia
   - Cardiovascular
   Myocardial infarction (heart attack, the aftermath of which may include decreases in arterial blood flow to the brain)
   Cardiac arrhythmias

8. Intracranial Space-Occupying Lesions
   - Abscess
   - Tumor
   - Subdural hematoma (blood clot that may result from a fall)

9. Injury from Physical Agents, such as Heat Stroke

Source: Adapted from Lipowski, Z. J. *Delirium: Acute Confusional States.* New York: Oxford University Press, 1990, pp. 133–134. Copyright © 1990 by Oxford University Press, Inc. Reprinted by permission.

nebulous enough that the note may not be recognized as heralding delirium.

If delirium progresses unnoticed, the symptoms and signs are observable during the day. By this time, however, the patient may have been delirious for quite some time, indicating that brain function may likewise have been compromised for a long time. The patient who has been delirious for an extended length of time may not recuperate as completely as he or she would if the delirium had been noticed earlier. The reason delirium connotes a grave outcome may be that it is often not diagnosed early in its course. Some studies have reported that up to one-fourth of elderly hospitalized patients with a diagnosis of delirium die within one month. Geriatricians are encouraged to read Lipowski's authoritative text on delirium referenced at the end of this chapter.

Delirium is to be distinguished from dementia. Delirium is a potentially reversible memory impairment that arises rapidly and is accompanied by the changes in level of arousal and consciousness described earlier. Being hyperalert and assaultive can change to being sedated in the same day. If the underlying disorder that decreased the brain's ability to function properly is reversed, the brain will return to normal, save for whatever permanent damage was done before the syndrome was diagnosed.

Dementia is also characterized by impaired memory, but also lost are other aspects of thinking, reasoning, and perception. The level of consciousness is normally alert, and the underlying pathology changes the brain in such a way as to be irreversible in many cases. The most common cause of irreversible dementia in the United States is Alzheimer's disease, followed by strokes. While there are reversible dementias, they are usually readily diagnosed if the patient sees a fully trained geriatrician. Please see Chapter Six for further discussions on dementia.

In general, any medical disorder resulting in changes in either cerebral metabolism of glucose, the only sugar energy source the brain uses, or cerebral oxygen use may result in either delirium or a variety of other psychiatric syndromes that mimic classic depression, mania, dementia, or psychosis. You may think that as a treater of outpatients, you will never see delirium. If only that were true!

I once directed an outpatient research memory disorders clinic. While there, I met a woman in her eighties who was brought in by her daughter for evaluation of her mild but progressive memory problems. I had seen her over the course of a month when one day she appeared acutely and severely demented—far more so than when I initially had met her. In my office, she became assaultive and tried to disrobe. She startled easily when the phone rang.

I later learned that while she was getting out of the car for a previous appointment to see me, she had bumped her head on the car door and developed normal pressure hydrocephalus. What I had seen was the delirious mental status changes at the beginning of her new problem. If I had interpreted her behavior as the result of the anxiety from dealing with her issues of aging, without thinking of a possible medical concomitant, I would have been mistaken.

This chapter has focused on several medical and medication issues that give rise to changes in mental function in the elderly. The elderly patient is a perfect example of the adage that things are not necessarily as they appear. Even if an older patient does have a psychiatric diagnosis, such as depression, dementia, or psychosis, the symptoms may be worsened by underlying medical problems. Furthermore, attempting to treat the mental symptoms may be quite difficult unless the underlying disorder is also treated.

Getting old and having to face new medical diagnoses, often needing to see more than one physician; having to take medications, frequently up to four times a day, are constant reminders to a previously vibrant individual of her lost health and vitality. As younger adults, we deal with our mortality with denial. This defense mechanism is much harder to use, when you are taking many pills per day for different diagnoses. These powerful reminders are not to be underestimated and may significantly contribute to a patient's loss of well-being and independence. These factors are critical, and the broad-based geriatric care provider must integrate discussion of these losses into any ongoing treatment of the older patient and the family.

FOR FURTHER READING

There are many links between thyroid disease and psychiatric disorder. The following represent just a few of the many review articles:

Heitman, B., & Irizarry, A. (1995). Hypothyroidism: Common complaints, perplexing diagnosis. *Nurse Practitioner, 20*(3), 54–60.

Mintzer, M. J. (1992). Hypothyroidism and hyperthyroidism in the elderly. *Journal of the Florida Medical Association, 79*(4), 231–235.

Whybrow, P. C. (1994). The therapeutic use of triiodothyronine and high dose thyroxine in psychiatric disorder. *Acta Medica Austriaca, 21*(2), 47–52.

The following textbooks will provide detailed descriptions of the major points discussed in this chapter:

Bressler, R., & Katz, M. D. (1993). *Geriatric pharmacology*. New York: McGraw-Hill.

Lipowski, Z. J. (1990). *Delirium: Acute confusional states*. New York: Oxford University Press.

Lishman, W. A. (1987). *Organic psychiatry* (2nd ed.). London: Blackwell.

Winokur, G., & Clayton, P. (1986). *The medical basis of psychiatry*. Philadelphia: Saunders.

For further details on the most recent developments on stroke and psychiatric disorder, the following articles are of interest:

Nelson L. D., Cicchetti, D., Satz, P., Sowa, M., & Mitrusna, M. (1994). Emotional sequelae of stroke: A longitudinal perspective. *Journal of Clinical and Experimental Neuropsychology, 16*(5), 796–806.

Welch, L. W., & Bear, D. (1990, Fall). Organic disorders of personality. *New Directions for Mental Health Services, 47*, 87–101.

About the Authors

David W. Coon, M. Ed., is currently completing his doctoral degree in counseling psychology at Stanford University. He is also a full-time psychology intern at the Veterans Affairs Palo Alto Health Care System in Palo Alto, California, an American Psychology Association–approved internship. Here he is receiving advanced training in geropsychology. Prior to entering the Ph.D. program, he worked for several years in vocational psychology and higher education administration.

Leah Friedman, Ph.D., is a senior research associate in the Department of Psychiatry at Stanford University and has also practiced as a licensed marriage, family, and child counselor. She is on the staff of the Aging Clinical Research Center of Stanford University, where her research on psychological interventions for the treatment of insomnia has been funded by grants from the National Institutes of Health.

Dolores Gallagher-Thompson, Ph.D., is a licensed psychologist with over fifteen years' experience who practices primarily as a geropsychologist doing research, teaching, and clinical care in several different academic and service environments. At present, she is responsible for the development of training programs in geriatrics/gerontology at the Veterans Affairs Palo Alto Health Care System in Palo Alto, California, and is associate director of the Geriatric Research, Education and Clinical Center there. She is also on the faculty of Stanford University School of Medicine in the Department of Psychiatry and Behavioral Sciences. She has been a funded researcher from the NIA and NIMH since 1983, focusing on treatment of late-life depression and the development of interventions to reduce distress in family caregivers.

Robert D. Hill, Ph.D., is a licensed psychologist and associate professor of educational psychology at the University of Utah. Since 1988, Dr. Hill has been involved as a practitioner and a scientist in issues related to the quality of life in older adults. During 1993 and 1994 he was a visiting research scientist at the Karolinska Institute in Stockholm, Sweden, where he studied memory function and quality of life issues in healthy older Swedish adults. He has published numerous articles related to these topics. In his role as a counselor, Dr. Hill treats older individuals facing issues of grief and loss and has directed graduate student research on various topics in geropsychology.

Dale Lund, Ph.D., is director and professor of the University of Utah Gerontology Center. Dr. Lund is well known for his research and publications on spousal bereavement in later life. He has published research articles in numerous professional journals and is the editor of the book *Older Bereaved Spouses*. Dr. Lund is a member of the International Work Group on Death, Dying and Bereavement and founder of the bereavement interest group in the Gerontological Society of America. He is editor of a forthcoming book, *Male Grief Experiences*.

Diane Morrissette, Ph.D., is a marriage, family, and child counselor intern in private practice as well as at the Veterans Affairs Palo Alto Health Care System, both in Palo Alto, California. She specializes in sex and marital therapy and geriatrics. As a postdoctoral fellow at Stanford University School of Medicine, she conducted research in both menopause and chronic illness and their effects on sexual function. She has taught at the University of California, Santa Cruz, and is currently a lecturer at San Jose State University, Department of Psychology.

Greer M. Murphy, Jr., M.D., Ph.D., is assistant professor of psychiatry at Stanford University Medical School and director of the neurobiology component of the Stanford Aging Clinical Research Center. He is board-certified in psychiatry with added qualification in geriatric psychiatry. He treats older patients with a variety of psychiatric disorders on the inpatient geropsychiatry unit at Stanford University Hospital, where he also supervises the training of psychiatry residents and geropsychiatry fellows. His clinical interests focus on behavioral problems in patients with Alzheimer's disease and other neurodegenerative disorders and those with psychiatric disorders and concurrent medical disease. He also heads a laboratory that is investigating the correlation between genetic risk factors for Alzheimer's disease and rate of clinical decline. His laboratory also studies the production of abnormal proteins related to Alzheimer's disease by cultured neural cells.

Ted Packard, Ph.D., is a licensed psychologist, a diplomate in counseling psychology of the American Board of Professional Psychology, and a faculty member in the Department of Educational Psychology at the University of Utah. He currently serves as training director of the counseling psychology program and was formerly director of the Counseling Center at that institution. He is a past president of the Association of State and Provincial Psychology Boards, a former chair of the Ethics Committee of the American Psychological Association, and currently serves as trustee and treasurer of the American Board of Professional Psychology. He has directed graduate student research on various bereavement topics and has also worked with many clients struggling with issues of grief and loss.

Javaid I. Sheikh, M.D., is associate professor of psychiatry at Stanford University School of Medicine and founding director of the Geriatric Psychiatry Program at Stanford Medical Center. He is also the chief of Outpatient Psychiatry and Special Programs at the Veterans Affairs Palo Alto Health Care System in Menlo Park, California. Originally from Pakistan, Dr. Sheikh graduated from the King Edward Medical College in Lahore in 1978. He is board-certified by the American Board of Psychiatry and Neurology with added qualification in geriatric psychiatry.

He is the author of numerous original articles in the areas of anxiety, depression, and cognitive impairment in the elderly. He is a nationally renowned expert in the area of anxiety disorders of late life. His present research focuses on delineating the phenomenology of panic disorder in older patients and identifying psychobiological vulnerabilities in such patients. He is also investigating the effectiveness of various treatment strategies for anxiety disorders in the elderly. Dr. Sheikh is supported in part by a grant from the National Institute of Mental Health.

Barbara R. Sommer, M.D., is a board-certified psychiatrist with added qualification in geriatric psychiatry. After her residency training at Tufts University and Harvard Medical School's McLean Hospital, she held positions in the psychiatry departments of the University of California, San Francisco, and the State University of New York at Stony Brook. Formerly, she was with the Mount Sinai School of Medicine in New York, where she was assistant professor in psychiatry and research psychiatrist at Pilgrim Psychiatric Center. Presently at the Veterans Affairs Health Care System in Palo Alto, California, she is coordinating a new teaching and research geropsychiatry inpatient program.

Joel E. Streim, M.D., is a graduate of the University of Rochester School of Medicine. After completing a residency in internal medicine at the University of Rochester and a residency in psychiatry at the University of Wisconsin, he did a fellowship in geriatric psychiatry at the Veterans Affairs Medical Center in Madison, Wisconsin. He is currently assistant professor of psychiatry in the Section of Geriatric Psychiatry, Department of Psychiatry, at the University of Pennsylvania and the Philadelphia Veterans Affairs Medical Center. In his role as director of the Geriatric Psychiatry Fellowship Training Program at Penn, he has worked extensively in long-term care settings, teaching fellows and nursing home staff and developing consultation models. His research, teaching, and clinical efforts reflect his long-time career focus on the problems of elderly patients with co-morbid medical and psychiatric illness.

Antonette M. Zeiss, Ph.D., is a graduate of the doctoral program in clinical psychology at the University of Oregon. She began training as a sex therapist in her first year of graduate school and now has twenty-three years of experience in assessment and treatment of sexual dysfunction. She is a licensed psychologist and works at the Veterans Affairs Palo Alto Health Care System as the Director of the Interdisciplinary Team Training Program. She is also co-director of the Andrology Clinic, an interdisciplinary program for assessment and treatment of sexual dysfunction, with special emphasis on treatment of geriatric male veterans and their partners. Dr. Zeiss is also a clinical lecturer at the Stanford University School of Medicine. She is co-author, with her husband Robert Zeiss, Ph.D., of *Prolong Your Pleasure* and also co-author of *Control Your Depression*. She has authored over fifty journal articles and book chapters on sexual dysfunction, depression, training in geropsychology, and interdisciplinary team function. She was recently elected president of the Association for Advancement of Behavior Therapy.

Robert A. Zeiss, Ph.D., a graduate of the doctoral program in psychology at the University of Oregon, is a clinical psychologist with more than twenty years of experience in the treatment of sexual dysfunction. He is a licensed psychologist at the Veterans Affairs Palo Alto Health Care System where he is co-director of the Andrology Clinic and program director of the Psychiatric Intensive Care Unit. Dr. Zeiss is also clinical assistant professor in the Department of Psychiatry and Behavioral Sciences of the Stanford University Medical School. He is co-author of *Prolong Your Pleasure*, a treatment guide for rapid ejaculation, and he has authored many journal articles and book chapters on various aspects of the treatment of sexual dysfunction.

INDEX

A

Abstraction function, 166

Abuse: of elders by family, 27–28, 191; in family history, 27

Acetaminophen, 237

"Active senior" movement, 10–11

Activities: on early waking, 125–126; evening, 118–119; late night, 121

Activity level: and bereavement adjustment, 55; sexual, 134–135

Adjustment Disorder with Depressed Mood, 20

Adult children, stress and conflict with, 27–28. *See also* Family

Age difference, therapist-patient, 12–13

Ageism, *xv–xvi*, 16–17; about sexuality of the elderly, 131, 132, 138–139; about substance abuse among elderly, 28–29. *See also* Stereotypes

Aging: biology of, and medication action, 31–32, 99; body image changes in, 139; hormonal changes with, 132–134, 146; myths about, *xv–xvi*, 16–17, 28–29, 131, 132, 136, 138–139; sexual changes with, 131–136

Agitation: caused by medication, 197, 204–205; management of, 181–186; management of, in nursing homes, 199–205; nocturnal, 186

Agoraphobia, 78, 79–80, 95, 96

AIDS, 175

Alcohol, and insomnia, 116–117

Alcohol abuse: and anxiety, 87; as cause of dementia, 172, 177; and sexual function, 151–152. *See also* Substance abuse

Alcoholic dementia, 172

Alpha-blockers, 150

Alzheimer's disease (AD), 170; agitation in, 181–186; and anxiety, 172; and chronic pain, 236–237; and depression, 171; diagnosis-by-exclusion of, 173–176; diagnostic criteria for, 176; and driving, 191–192; end-stage of, 188–189; genetic predictors of, 180–181; hostile and uncooperative behavior in, 181–186; medication for, 181; prevalence of, among dementia patients, 173; prognosis for, 178. *See also* Cognitive impairment; Dementia

Alzheimer's Disease Assessment Scale, 169

American Psychiatric Association, 2, 49–50, 77–78

Amitriptyline (Elavil), 32

Amnesia, 172

Andrology Clinic, Veterans Affairs Palo Alto Health Care System, 131–132

Angiotensin Converting Enzyme (ACE) inhibitors, 150, 232, 234

Anticonvulsants, 100, 151

Antidepressants: for anxiety, 100; for depression, 31–33, 209–210; and sexual dysfunction, 149–150

Antipsychotics, 100, 150; for dementia, 184–186, 201, 204

Anxiety: associated with dementia, 100, 172; in bereavement, 53; clinically significant, 76–77; co-morbidity of, 87–89; defined, 76, 77; depression associated with, 32, 81, 82–84, 88–89; differentiation of, from depression, 88–89; management of, 90–100; medical problems and, 84, 87; medication as cause of, 84; prevalence of, in the elderly, 75;

and sexual functioning, 139; and substance abuse, 87; underdiagnosis of, in the elderly, 75, 101
Anxiety and Its Disorders (Barlow), 91
Anxiety disorders: assessment of, 84–86; behavioral symptoms of, 77, 78; clinical course of, 89; clinical evaluation of, 85; cognitive symptoms of, 77, 79–80; cognitive-behavioral therapy for, 92–99; defined, 77; described, 79–84; diagnostic categories of, 77–78; management of, basic principles of, 90; medications for, 99–100; physiological symptoms of, 77, 79, 82, 84; premorbid personality of, 89; prevalence of, in the elderly, 75; psychometric assessment of, 85–86; psychotherapy combined with medication for, 83, 101; and sexual functioning, 140; symptoms of, 77, 89; treatment of, 90–100; treatment of, versus depression, 89; types of, 76–77; underdiagnosis of, in the elderly, 75, 100. *See also* Agoraphobia; Generalized Anxiety Disorder; Panic attacks; Panic Disorder
Anxiety Disorders and Phobias (Beck), 91
Anxiolytics, 99–100, 149–150, 186
Apathetic hyperthyroidism, 226
Apolipoprotein E (Apo E), 180–181
Arthritis: and chronic pain, 234, 236; and sexual function, 147–148, 154
Assessment: of anxiety disorders, 84–86; of cognitive impairment, 164–176; of delirium, in nursing homes, 215–218; of depression, 14–20, 41, 111; of depression, in nursing homes, 213; of family dynamics, 60–61, 180; of sexual problems, 141–152; of sleep disorders, 109–113; of substance abuse, 28. *See also* Neuropsychological assessment; Observer-rated scales; Self-report scales

Atenolol, 233
Attention ability, 165
Autonomic hyperactivity, 82, 87; cognitive therapy view of, 92; relaxation of, 97
Avoidance behaviors, panic-associated, 77, 80, 96; behavioral techniques for, 97–98
Azapirone, 100

B
Barlow, D. H. 91
Beck, A. T., 63, 91
Beck Anxiety Inventory (BAI), 86
Beck Depression Inventory (BDI), 15
Bed: getting out of, 120–121; use of, 124
Bedtime: routine for, 122–123; schedule for, 119–120; as sleep stimulus, 123
Behavior therapy: for bereavement adjustment, 63–64; combined with medication therapy, 33; for depression, 36. *See also* Cognitive-behavioral therapy; Sleep hygiene treatment
Behavioral interventions: for bereavement adjustment, 63–64; for depression, 35–36; for insomnia, 113–126; for Panic Disorder, 92, 95, 97–99. *See also* Desensitization techniques; Exposure techniques; Sleep hygiene treatment
Belief systems: about bereavement, redefining of, 61–63; about religion and spirituality, 66–67. *See also* Cognitive-behavioral therapy; Cultural differences
Benign prostatic hypertrophy, 147
Benzodiazepines, 99, 100, 186
Benztropine, 185
Bereavement: anxiety in, 53; complicated, 45; cultural/individual differences in, 24–25, 51–52; depression in, 20, 24–26, 63; effects of, on family, 59–60; ego integrity and,

67–68; gender differences in, 25, 54; generalizations about, 52–55; grief in, complicated/abnormal, 25–26, 49–50; grief process in, normal, 24–25, 48–50; losses of, 46–47; mourning process in, 48, 50–52; normal process of, 24–25; psychological impact of, 47–52; reading material about, 72–74. *See also* Grief

Bereavement: Reactions, Consequences, and Care (Osterweis, Solomon, Green), 58

Bereavement adjustment: coping strategies in, 54–56; effects of maladaptive assumptions on, 62–63; and health, 48, 53; individual characteristics and, 53–54; intervention strategies for, 36, 56–68; religion and spirituality in, 66–67; variables in, 24–26, 52–55

Beta blockers, 100, 186, 230, 232, 233

Biological factors, in depression, 7, 21–24, 30, 31. *See also* Medical problems

Bipolar disorder, 31, 150

Black, F. W., 164, 167

Blazer, D., 19

Blessed-Roth Dementia Scale, 169

Blood pressure: and antipsychotic medications, 185; medications for, 150–151

Body image, 139, 159

Boston Naming Test, 169

Brain imaging, 174–175

Brain trauma, 175, 241

Breast pain, 151

Breathing, diaphragmatic, 92, 97

Burns, D., 36

Buspirone, 100, 186

C

Caffeine, and insomnia, 116

Calcium channel blockers, 150, 232, 233–234

Calculation ability, 166

Cancer: and anxiety, 87; and bereavement, 53; and body image, prostrate, and sexual problems, 146; skin, and light exposure, 117

Captopril (Capoten), 234

Carbamazepine (Tegretol), 186, 229

Cardiovascular disease: and anxiety, 84, 87; and bereavement, 53; and depression, 205–207; and insomnia, 109; and sexual dysfunction, 144–145. *See also* Hypertension

Caregivers, elderly: for dementia patients, 183, 184, 186–188; depression in, 26–27; stress management for, 186–188; support services for, 26–27, 187–188; and sexuality, 139–140, 159–169; treatment for, 36

Caregiving, for dementia patients, 182–183; stress management for, 186–188

Cerebrovascular accidents (CVAs). *See* Strokes

Change, older adults' capacity to, *xv–xvi*

Chemotherapy, 159

Chronic depression, 19–20. *See also* Depression

Chronic pain: and aging, 234–235; and dementia, 236–238; and depression, 235, 236; medication for, psychological effects of, 237

Cicero, *xiii, xv*

Cisapride, 201, 204

Clitoral stimulation, 133

Clocks, 124

Cocoon, 131, 132, 136

Cognex (Tacrine), 181

Cognition: abstraction dimension of, 166; attention dimension of, 165; calculation dimension of, 166; constructional dimension of, 166–167; dimensions of, 164–165; ideomotor praxis dimension of, 166; language dimension of, 165–166; level-of-consciousness dimension of, 165;

memory dimension of, 165; orientation dimension of, 165
Cognitions: negative, 62; panic-associated, 96
Cognitive-behavioral (CB) therapy: for anxiety disorders, 91–99; for bereavement adjustment, 36, 61–63; combined with psychodynamic psychotherapy, in case example, 95–99; for depression, 35–36, 63; principles and premises of, 35, 91; procedures in, 91–92; reading material about, 36, 43–44; ten-session outline of, 93–94. *See also* Behavioral interventions; Cognitive interventions; Psychoeducation; Relaxation training
Cognitive distortions, and complicated grief, 25
Cognitive impairment: assessment of, 164–169; causes of, 169–176; chronic versus acute, 169–171; versus dementia, 164; differential diagnosis of, 169–176, 217–218; and driving, 191–192; due to alcohol abuse, 172; due to Alzheimer's disease, 173–175; due to depression, 171–172; due to medication use, 173; due to vascular dementia, 174–175; irreversible causes of, 175–176, 177; management of, 176–192; management of, financial aspects of, 189; management of, legal aspects of, 189–191, 218; management of, team approach to, 163, 202–204; minimizing disability in, 178–179; prevalence of, 163; reversible causes of, 176; safe environments for, 179. *See also* Alzheimer's disease; Dementia; Delirium
Cognitive interventions: for bereavement adjustment, 61–63; for depression, 35; for Panic Disorder, 92, 93–94, 96–97; specific techniques of, 97

Cognitive restructuring: for bereavement, 55, 61–63; for Panic Disorder, 92, 96–97
Communication, of elderly patients, *xvi–xvii*; regarding depression, 1–2, 13
Community living environments, and attitudes towards depression, 10–11
Co-morbidity: of anxiety with dementia, 100; of anxiety with depression, 32, 81, 82–84, 88–89; of anxiety with medical problems, 84, 87; of anxiety with sleep disturbances, 87–88; of anxiety with substance abuse, 86, 87; of dementia with depression, 23–24, 36, 171–172; of depression with medical disorders, 21–23, 205–214, 224–226, 235; of insomnia with psychological disorders, 111; management of, in nursing homes, 205–214; of medical disorders with depression, 21–23, 205–214; of medical with psychological disorders, *xvi*, 223–242; of substance abuse with psychological disorders, 28–29, 86, 87. *See also* Medical problems
Competency evaluation, 189–191, 218
Compliance/noncompliance: causes of, in elderly, 12–13, 101; with medication, 33; and misdiagnosis, 101; with sleep hygiene treatment, 127
Computerized tomography (CT), 174, 230
Congestive heart failure, and depression, 205–208
Consciousness, level of, 165
Constructional ability, 166–167
Cooking, and cognitive impairment, 179
Coon, D. W., *xvi–xvii*, 1–44
Couples therapy, 154
Cue-controlled relaxation, 92, 97
Cultural differences: in attitudes towards depression, 11–12; in

bereavement process, 24–25, 51–52; in mourning, 51–52

D

Day of the Dead (*el día de los muertos*), 51
Death, loss by, 45, 46–47. *See also* Bereavement; Losses
Delirium: causes of, 170, 237–239; defined, 169; differential diagnosis of, and dementia, 169–171, 214, 240; management of, in nursing homes, 214–218; medical conditions underlying, 170–171, 238–241; mortality of, 240; nighttime onset of, 238, 240; symptoms and signs of, 238, 240. *See also* Cognitive impairment; Dementia
Delusions: in dementia, 183–184; at night, 186; and strokes, 231. *See also* Psychosis
Dementia: agitation in, management of, 181–186, 199–205; alcoholic, 172; anxiety associated with, 100; behavior therapy for, 36; causes of, 169–176, 240; chronic pain and, 236–238; versus cognitive impairment, 164; versus delirium, 169–171, 214, 240; delirium superimposed on, 214–218; depression associated with, 23–24, 36, 171–172, 177; differential diagnosis of, 169–176; driving and, 191–192; due to Alzheimer's disease, 173–175; due to medication use, 173, 204–205; due to vascular dementia, 174–175; end-stage of, 188–189; HIV-induced, 175; hostile and uncooperative behavior in, 181–184; irreversible causes of, 175–176, 240; management of, 176–192; management of, financial aspects of, 189; management of, legal aspects of, 189–191, 218; management of, team approach to, 163, 202–204; medications for, 100,

181; minimizing disability in, 178–179; in nursing homes, 188–189, 190, 191, 199–205; prognosis for, 178; psychotic symptoms in, 183–186; respite care for, 187–188; reversible causes of, 176; safe environments for, 179; sexuality and, 159–160; telling patients about, 177–178; tube-feeding in, 188–189. *See also* Alzheimer's disease; Cognitive impairment; Delirium; Vascular dementia
Demographics, *xiii*
Depression: anxiety associated with, 32, 81, 82–84, 88–89; assessment of, 14–20, 41, 111; assessment of, in nursing homes, 213; in bereavement, 20, 24–26, 53, 63; biological substrate in, 7, 30, 31–32; caused by medical problems, 21–23, 205–214, 224–226, 235; caused by medications, 18, 208, 233; and chronic pain, 235–236; clinical course of, 89; with co-morbid medical problems, in nursing homes, 205–214; dementia associated with, 23–24, 171–172, 177; diagnosis of, importance of, 1–2; diagnostic categories of, 19–20, 31; differentiation of, from anxiety, 88–89; differentiation of, from delirium, 215; differentiation of, from dementia, 171–172; in elderly caregivers, 26–27; elderly patients' language of, 1–2, 3–5; and family conflict, 27–28; gender and, 9; insomnia associated with, 111; medications for, 31–33; in nursing homes, 205–214; premorbid personality of, 89; psychosocial context of, 5–13, 22, 30; and sexual functioning, 140, 149; signs and symptoms of, 1–5, 89; situations that trigger, 21–29; sociocultural context of, 5–13, 40–41; and strokes, 231; and substance abuse, 28–29; subsyndromal, 6, 20; treatment

interventions for, versus anxiety, 89; treatment interventions for, nonmedical, in nursing homes, 213–214; treatment interventions for, selection of, 29–31; treatment interventions for, specific, 31–40, 63; treatment settings for, 41–42

Depression in Late Life (Blazer), 19

Depressive episode with psychotic features, 31

Desensitization techniques, for bereavement intervention, 63–64. *See also* Behavior therapy; Behavioral interventions; Exposure techniques

Desipramine (Norpramin), 32

Diabetes: and psychological functioning, 226–228; and sexual dysfunction, 145–146

Diagnostic and Statistical Manual of Mental Disorders (DSM-IV), 2, 19, 49–50, 77–78

Diagnostic categories: of anxiety disorders, 77–78; of depression, 19–20, 31

Diagnostic Interview Schedule (DIS), 16

Diet: and medication metabolism, 31–32; and sleep, 116

Digestive problems: and insomnia, 109; medication for, side effects of, 201

Digoxin, 151, 208, 209

Diltiazem (Cardiazem), 233–234

Disability, minimizing, 178–179

Disopyramide, 151

Diuretics: and electrolyte imbalance, 229; and insomnia, 117, 233; and psychological functioning, 232, 233; and sexual functioning, 150

Doxepin (Sinequan), 32

Driving, 191–192

Drug half-life, 32

Dyspareunia (painful intercourse), 133, 137; fear of, 139; medical

problems associated with, 146, 147; medical treatment of, 156

Dysthymia, 19–20. *See also* Depression

E

Early waking, 106; techniques for managing, 125–126. *See also* Insomnia; Sleep hygiene treatment

Educational level, and bereavement adjustment, 54

Ego integrity, 67–68

Ejaculation: changes in, due to aging, 134; effects of medication on, 150; retrograde, 145, 147

Elavil (amitriptyline), 32, 149

Elderly persons: attitudes of, towards emotional problems, *xvi–xvii*, 4–5, 14; biology of, and medication action, 31–32, 99; common mental health problems of, *xiv–xv;* language of, for emotional disorders, *xvi–xvii*, 1–2, 13; medical versus psychiatric illness in, subtleties of, 224–226; normal sexual changes of, 131–136; normal sleep patterns of, 87–88, 118–119; respect for, 16–17, 106; substance abuse among, 28–29

Electroconvulsive therapy (ECT), 33–34

Electrolyte imbalance, 228–229, 233

Emptiness, sense of, 3–4

Endocrine disorders: and anxiety, 84, 87; and depression, 224–225; differential diagnosis of, from psychiatric disorders, 224–228

ErecAid pump, 157, 158

Erectile dysfunction: and alcohol, 151; and anxiety, 139; and cardiovascular disease, 145; and cultural stereotypes, 138–139; and effects of aging, 133–134; medical treatment of, 157–158; and medication, 149, 150–151; prevalence of, 137; after prostate surgery, 147; and tobacco

use, 151–152; in widower's syndrome, 139
Estrogen reduction, 133
Evaluation. *See* Assessment
Evening activities, to prevent early sleep, 118–119
Exercise: and medication metabolism, 31–32; and sleep, 118
Exposure techniques: for Panic Disorder, 92, 93–94, 95, 97–98; self-administered, 97–98; in vivo versus in vito, 92, 95
Extrapyramidal reactions, 185

F
Family: abuse of elders by, 27–28, 191; attitudes of, towards emotional problems, 9–10; attitudes of, towards physical illness, 22; conflict with, and depression, 27–28; dynamics of, assessment of, 60–61, 180; effects of bereavement on, 59–60; and elderly caregivers, 27; role of, in depression assessment, 18–19
Family history: of anxiety, 85; of depression, 31
Family involvement: in bereavement adjustment, 54–55; in cognitive impairment management, 179–181, 191; power versus nurturance issues in, 38–39
Family therapy: in abusive situations, 27–28; in bereavement adjustment, 59–61; and cognitive impairment management, 180; in depression treatment, 27–28, 37–39; for stroke patients, 232
Faulty logic analysis, 97
Feedback loops, 64
Feeling Good: The New Mood Therapy (Burns), 36
Feeling Good Handbook, The: Using the New Mood Therapy in Everyday Life (Burns), 36

Fluid intake, and insomnia, 117
Fluoxetine (Prozac), 32, 149
Folstein, M. F., 167–168
Freud, S., *xv*
Friedman, L., 105–129
Fuld Object Memory Test, 169
Functional impairment, in bereavement, 50

G
Gallagher-Thompson, D., *xvi–xvii*, 1–44
Gender differences: in attitudes towards emotional problems, 9; in bereavement process and adjustment, 25, 54, 65; in life skills training, 65. *See also* Men; Women
Generalized Anxiety Disorder, 78, 81–84; in case example, 82–84; symptoms of, 81–82
Genetic tests, for Alzheimer's disease, 180–181
Geriatric Depression Scale (GDS), 15–16, 111
Global Deterioration Scale (GDS), 168
Grief: communication of, 49; complicated/abnormal, 25–26, 49–50, 62–64; feelings of, 48; guidelines for dealing with, 50; interventions for, 26, 62–64, 66–67; noncommunication of, 49; normal process of, 24, 26, 48–49; physical signs and symptoms in, 48. *See also* Bereavement; Bereavement adjustment; Widowhood
Grief work, 24. *See also* Bereavement
Group interventions, for depression, 39–40. *See also* Self-help groups; Support groups
Guilt, in bereavement, 50

H
Haldol, 150
Hallucinations: in bereavement, 50; in

dementia, 183–184, 186; at night,
186. *See also* Psychosis
Haloperidol, 185, 201, 204
Hamilton Anxiety Rating Scale
(HARS), 85–86
Hamilton Rating Scale for Depres-
sion (HRSD), 16, 111
Hauri, P., 113, 127
Health Care Financing Administra-
tion (HCFA) nursing home guide-
lines, 199, 213
Health status, and bereavement
adjustment, 54. *See also* Medical
problems
Hearing disability, 178
Helplessness, 3
Heterocyclic antidepressants (HCAs),
32
Home health aides, 187–188
Hopelessness, 3
Hormonal changes, 132–134, 146
Hormone replacement therapy
(HRT), 133, 156
Horowitz, M., 63
Hospitalization, of demented patients,
190–191
Human immunodeficiency virus
(HIV) encephalitis, 175
Huntington's disease, 175
Hyperarousal, 82, 87; cognitive ther-
apy view of, 92; relaxation of, 97
Hypertension, 87, 229; impact of, on
psychological functioning,
229–234; medication for, and psy-
chological functioning, 230,
232–234; medication for, and sexual
functioning, 150–151
Hyperthyroidism, 87, 226
Hypogonadism, 146
Hypothyroidism, 224–226

I
Ibuprofen, 237
Identity, sense of: and bereavement
adjustment, 54; and ego identity,
67–68

Ideomotor praxis, 166
Imipramine (Tofranil), 32
Immune system functioning, and
bereavement, 53
Impotence, 137. *See also* Erectile dysfunction
In-home care, 187–188
Inflammatory conditions, 176
Insomnia: age of onset of, 107–108; in
anxiety disorders, 82–84, 87–88;
assessment of, 109–113; consequences of, 105, 106; and chronic
pain, 236; depression associated
with, 111; early-waking type of,
106, 125–126; effects of daytime
activities on, 113, 116–118; effects
of sleep environment on, 123–124;
food/drink consumption and,
116–117; etiology of, 108; exercise
and, 118; in highly conscientious
and busy persons, 107; in inactive
persons, 107; information-collecting on patient's, 112–115; light
exposure and, 117; medical problems associated with, 109–110,
111–112, 127; medications and,
110, 111, 117; napping and, 122;
personal characteristics affecting,
107; prevalence of, in the elderly,
105; psychological disorders associated with, 111; reading material
about, 129; sleep scheduling and,
118–123; treatment of, using sleep
hygiene techniques, 108, 113–126;
types of, in older versus younger
people, 106; worrying and, 125.
See also Sleep hygiene treatment
Institute of Medicine, 199
Intercourse: difficult, for men, 134;
painful, in women, 133, 137, 146,
147, 156
International Work Group on
Death, Dying and Bereavement,
66–67
Interviews: conduct of, 16–17,
142–144; for depression assess-

ment, 16–17; for sexual problems, 142–144
Isolation, 3; and bereavement, 53; and physical illness, 22

K

Kaplan, H. S., 159
Klosko, J., 36
Knight, B., 60–61
Korsakoff's disease, 172

L

Laboratory tests, in anxiety assessment, 86. *See also* Medical evaluation
Language: ability, 165–166; of elderly patients for emotional problems, *xvi–xvii*, 1–2, 13
Learning theory, and sleep stimuli, 123, 124
Leg movements, during sleep, 112
Legal issues, in management of cognitive impairment, 189–191, 218. *See also* Regulations
Life review interventions: basic elements of, 68; for bereavement adjustment, 67–68; for depression, 40. *See also* Personal story approach
Life roles: and bereavement adjustment, 54, 64–66; and sexuality, 139–140; skills training for, 64–66
Life satisfaction, and bereavement adjustment, 54
Light exposure, and sleep cycles, 117
Lipowski, Z. J., 240
Lisinopril (Zestril), 234
Listening, 106, 182
Lithium, 149, 150, 186
Loneliness, and bereavement, 53
Lorazepam, 100
Losses: bereavement, 46–47; cognitive restructuring of, 55; cumulative, among elderly, 46; depression as response to, 6; and personal growth, 46–47; and personal mortality, 241–242. *See also* Bereave-

ment; Bereavement adjustment; Grief
Lovemaking, and sleep regulation, 123, 124. *See also* Sexuality

M

Magnetic resonance imaging (MRI), 174–175, 230
Major depression, 19–20. *See also* Depression
Managed care, 42
Marks, I., 64
Mastectomy, and sexual functioning, 158–159
Maxide, 150
Meal scheduling, and sleep, 116
Medicaid, 189, 199
Medical evaluation: in anxiety assessment, 81, 85, 86; in cognitive impairment assessment, 174–175; in depression assessment, 17–18, 23; in insomnia assessment, 109; neurologic, 174–175
Medical problems: associated with anxiety, 84, 87; associated with depression, 17, 20, 205–214; associated with insomnia, 109–110, 111–112, 127; as cause of cognitive impairment, 170–171; as cause of delirium, 170–171, 238–241; caused by grief, 53; with chronic pain, 234–238; cognitive-behavioral therapy and, 36; with co-morbid depression, in nursing homes, 205–214; co-morbidity with, *xvi*; differential diagnosis of, from psychiatric disorders, 224–226; impact of, on psychological well-being, 223–242; impact of, on sexual functioning, 139, 144–148; screening for, 17–18, 84, 109–110, 174–175; subtleties of, 224–226; as trigger to depression, 21–23. *See also* Physical symptoms. *See also specific listings*
Medicare, 199
Medications: abuse of, 28–29; for anx-

iety associated with dementia, 100; for anxiety associated with depression, 32; for anxiety disorders, 99–100; biological processing of, in aging bodies, 31–32; as cause of anxiety symptoms, 84; as cause of cognitive impairment, 173; as cause of depression symptoms, 18, 208, 233; as cause of psychosis, 184; as cause of sexual dysfunction, 149–151, 155–156, 159; for chronic pain, 237; for dementia management, 181; for depression, 31–33, 209–210; and electrolyte imbalance, 228–229; for erectile dysfunction, 156–157; for hypertension, 150–151, 232–234; and insomnia, 110, 111, 117; misuse of, in nursing homes, 197, 204–205. *See also* Compliance; Side effects

Mellaril, 150, 229

Memory disturbance: assessment of, 165; from electroconvulsive therapy, 33–34

Men: sexuality of, effects of hormonal and physical changes on, 133–134, 146; sexuality of, effects of widowhood on, 135–136, 139; sexuality of, stereotypes of, 138–139. *See also* Erectile dysfunction; Gender differences; Sexuality

Menopause, 109; effects of, on sexuality, 133, 147

Mental disorders: associated with insomnia, 111; caused by bereavement, 53; differential diagnosis of, from medical disorders, 224–226; effects of, on sexuality, 140–141; of elderly persons, *xiv–xv*; prevalence of, in nursing homes, 196. *See also* Anxiety disorders; Cognitive impairment; Depression; Insomnia; Sexual dysfunction

Mental health professionals: ageist attitudes among, *xv–xvi*, 16–17; and pastoral/spiritual grief counseling, 66; preparation of, for elderly population, *xii–xiv*; and professional role boundaries, 41; role of, in sexuality counseling, 141–142

Mental status examination: in anxiety assessment, 85; for cognitive impairment assessment, 164–167; complicating factors in, 167; dimensions of, 164–167; quantifying, 167–168

Metabolic disorders: cognitive impairment due to, 176, 240; and electrolyte imbalance, 228–229; and insomnia, 109

Mexican-American mourning traditions, 51

Mini Mental Status Examination, 167–168, 169

Minority elders: and attitudes towards depression, 11–12; as caregivers, 27; and self-report measures, 15–16

Mobility problems: and depression, 207–208; minimizing, in cognitively impaired patients, 178–179; and sexual functioning, 147–148, 154

Monoamine oxidase (MAO) inhibitors, 32, 149

Mood Disorder Due to a General Medical Condition, 20

Morrissette, D., 131–162

Motor tension, 82

Mourning, 50–52. *See also* Bereavement; Grief

Movement therapy, 213

Murphy, G. M., Jr., 163–194

Musculoskeletal disorders, and insomnia, 109

N

Napping, 121–122

Nardil, 149

National Institute of Neurological and Communicative Disorders and Stroke (NINCDS), 176

Negative affect, 64

Neurobehavioral Cognitive Status Examination (NCSE), 168
Neurodegenerative diseases, 175. *See also* Alzheimer's disease
Neuroleptics, 100, 150, 184–186, 201, 204
Neurological illnesses: and anxiety, 84; and insomnia, 109. *See also* Dementia
Neuropsychological assessment: for cognitive impairment evaluation, 168–169; in depression evaluation, 23–24
Neurosyphilis, 176
Nifedipine (Procardia), 233–234
Nighttime activities, 121
Nocturnal agitation, 186
Nonsteroidal anti-inflammatory drugs (NSAIDs), 237
Nonverbal communication, *xvi–xvii*
Norpramin (desipramine), 32
Nortriptyline (Pamelor), 32, 209–210
Nursing Home Reform Amendments, Omnibus Budget Reconciliation Act of 1987, 199
Nursing homes: characteristics of, 195–199; collaborative approach with, 202–204; consumer advocacy and, 198–199; delirium diagnosis and management in, 214–218; dementia management in, 188–189, 190, 191, 199–205; depression with medical co-morbidity in, management of, 205–214; diagnosing cognitive decline in, 217–218; federal regulation of, 198–199, 204–205, 213, 217–218; financial aspects of, 189; interdisciplinary approach in, 208–212, 213; legal aspects of, 190, 191; managing psychiatric problems in, 195–219; mental health needs versus resources in, 196–197, 219; misuse of physical restraints in, 197–198, 204–205; misuse of psychotropic drugs in, 197, 204–205; nonpharmacologic therapies in,

213–214; prevalence of psychiatric problems in, 196, 219; Resident Assessment Protocols (RAPs) for, 213, 217–218; stroke patients in, 232; undertreatment in, 198
Nutritional deficiencies, and cognitive impairment, 176–177

O
Observer-rated scales, for anxiety, 85–86
Obstructive pulmonary disease (COPD), 87
Omnibus Budget Reconciliation Act of 1987, Nursing Home Reform Amendments, 199
Oral sex, 135
Orgasm, 134, 149
Orientation ability, 165
Osbon ErecAid System, 157, 158
Oxazepam, 100

P
Pain: and aging, 234–235; and dementia, 236–238; and depression, 235, 236; medication for, psychological effects of, 237
Pamelor (nortriptyline), 32, 209–210
Panic attacks, 77, 78, 79–81; cognitive-behavioral therapy for, 92–99
Panic Disorder, 78, 79–81; and cardiovascular disease, 87; in case examples, 80–81, 95–99; cognitive-behavioral therapy for, 92–99; early-onset (EOPD), 80; and insomnia, 111; late-onset (LOPD), 80–81; symptoms of, 79–80
Parkinson's disease, 175
Parkinsonian symptoms, 185, 201, 204
Parnate, 149
Paroxetine (Paxil), 32, 149
Past behavior, and bereavement adjustment, 55–56
Pastoral grief counseling, 66–67
Paxil (paroxetine), 32, 149

Personal growth, and bereavement losses, 46–47

Personal story approach: and bereavement intervention, 68; and depression treatment, 34, 40–41. *See also* Life review interventions

Pharmacology. *See* Medications

Physical illness. *See* Medical problems

Physical restraints, 197–198, 204–205

Physical symptoms: of anxiety, 77, 79, 82, 84; of depression, 4; of grief, 48, 50; of Panic Disorder, 92, 96. *See also* Medical problems

Physicians: collaboration with, in anxiety treatment, 81, 84, 99; collaboration with, in dementia management, 178; collaboration with, in sleep disorder treatment, 109–110; as referral source, *xvi*, 4, 5, 14

Pick's disease, 175

PLISSIT model of sex therapy, 152–155; Intensive Therapy stage of, 154–155; Limited Information stage of, 153; Permission stage of, 152–153; Specific Suggestions stage of, 153

Population, elderly, *xiii*

Positron emission tomography (PET), 230

Powers, L., 62

Praxis ability, 166

Prazosin, 150

Priapism, 149, 150, 157

Prolixin, 150

Propranolol, 186, 233

Prostaglandin-E injections, 156–157

Prostate disorders, 147

Prozac (fluoxetine), 32, 149

Pseudodementia, 23, 171

Psychoanalysis, 37

Psychodynamic psychotherapy: for anxiety disorders, 91, 98–99; for depression, 36–37; developmental oriented, 37; psychoanalysis-oriented, 37; self-psychology oriented, 37

Psychoeducation: for anxiety, 92; for cognitive impairment, 180; for depression, 36, 39; in groups, 39

Psychometric instruments. *See* Mental Status Examination; Mini Mental Status Examination; Neuropsychological assessment; Observer-rated scales; Self-report scales

Psychosis: in dementia, 183–184; in depression, 31; due to medication, 184; evaluation of, 183–184; medications for, 184–186

Psychosocial context: of anxiety disorders, 83; of depression, 5–13, 22, 30. *See also* Sociocultural context

Psychotherapy: for anxiety disorders, 83–84, 90–99; combined with medication, 83, 84; for depression treatment, 34–40, 213–214; for elderly patients, special considerations of, 34–35, 37, 41–42; in nursing homes, 213–214; for stroke patients, 232; termination issues in, 37; transference in, 37. *See also* Behavior therapy; Cognitive-behavioral therapy; Family therapy; Group interventions; Pastoral counseling; PLISSIT model of sex therapy; Psychodynamic psychotherapy; Sleep hygiene treatment

Psychotherapy with Older Adults (Knight), 60–61

Pulmonary disorders, and anxiety, 84, 87

R

Referral sources: of anxious patients, 79; of depressed patients, 4, 5, 14; of elderly patients, *xvi*; for group interventions 40; for medication prescription, 31; for neuropsychological assessment, 23; for sleep disorders, 109, 112, 127

Refocusing, 97
Refractory period, 134
Reframing, 97
Regulations, for nursing homes, 198–199, 204–205, 213, 217–218
Reinventing Your Life (Young, Klosko), 36
Relaxation training, for Panic Disorder, 92, 93–94, 97
Religion: and bereavement intervention, 66–67; and sexuality, 143
Reminiscence interventions, 67–68. *See also* Life review interventions
Resident Assessment Protocols (RAPs), 213, 217–218
Respect, showing of, 16–17, 106, 108; to dementia patients, 182–183
Respiratory disease: and insomnia, 109; and psychosis in dementia, 183–184; and sexual function, 148
Respite care, for demented patients, 187–188
Restless legs syndrome, 112
Risperidone, 185
Robinson, 231

S

Safety: and cognitive impairment, 179, 191–192; and driving, 191–192; and sleep disturbances, 124
Salicylates, 237
Schizophrenia, and insomnia, 111
Screening. *See* Assessment
Selective serotonin reuptake inhibitors (SSRIs), 32, 100, 149, 156
Self-esteem: and bereavement adjustment, 50, 56, 65; and skills training, 65
Self-expression, and bereavement adjustment, 55, 56
Self-help groups: for bereavement adjustment, 56, 57–59; for depression, 39–40. *See also* Support groups
Self psychology, 37

Self-report scales: for anxiety, 85, 86; for depression, 15–16; validity of, for minority elders, 15–16
Self-statements, changing of, 97
Sertaline (Zoloft), 32, 149
Sex therapy. *See* PLISSIT model of sex therapy
Sexual desire disorders, 137; associated with medical disorders, 145, 146, 159; medical treatment for, 156, 158; and medication, 151; psychological treatment for, 154
Sexual dysfunction: assessment of, 141–144; assessment of medical problems associated with, 144–148; causes of, multifactorial, 138, 141, 160; communication about, 141–142, 143, 154–155; couple's goals and, 144; effects of medication on, 149–151, 155–156, 159; effects of substance abuse on, 151–152; psychological issues in, 138–141, 154–155; semistructured interview for, 142–144; treatment of, and mastectomy, 158–159; treatment of, medical, 156; treatment of, PLISSIT model of, 152–155; types of, 136–137. *See also* Erectile dysfunction
Sexuality of the elderly: behavioral changes of, 135–136; and body image, 139; common patterns of, 135–136; effects of hormonal and physical changes on, 132–134, 146; effects of physical illness on, 139; effects of sexual activity on, 134–135; stereotypes of, 131, 132, 136, 138
Sheikh, J. I., *xiii–xxi*, 15, 75–103
Side effects: agitation, 201; of Alzheimer's medication, 181; of antidepressants, 32; of antipsychotics, 184–186; in elderly patients, 99; of electroconvulsive therapy, 33–34; psychotic, 184
Significant others, and attitudes

towards depression, 9–10. *See also* Family

Silverman, P., 58

Sinequan (doxepin), 32

Skills training, 64–66

Sleep apnea, 111–112, 127

Sleep clinics, 109, 127

Sleep disorders: anxiety associated with, 82–84, 87–88; assessment of, 109–113; consequences of, 105, 106; prevalence of, in the elderly, 105; types of, in the elderly, 111–112. *See also* Insomnia

Sleep environment, 123–124

Sleep hygiene treatment: daytime behavior aspect of, 113, 116–118; duration of, 127; early-waking management in, 125–126; effectiveness of, 108, 113; elements of, 113, 116, 119–120, 126; individualization of, 126–127; routine scheduling in, importance of, 116, 119–120; session frequency in, 127; sleep scheduling aspect of, 118–123. *See also* Insomnia

Sleep logs, daily: sample, 114–115; use of, for assessing insomnia, 112–115

Sleep medications, 110

Sleep patterns: information-collecting on patient's, 112–115; normal, of the elderly, 87–88, 105, 118–119

Sleep requirements, of the elderly, 105

Sleep scheduling, 118–123

Social activities, and sleep scheduling, 119

Social support systems: and bereavement adjustment, 54–55, 57; for elderly caregivers, 26–27; of minority groups, 27. *See also* Family; Support groups

Sociocultural context, of depression, 7–13, 40–41. *See also* Psychosocial context

Socioeconomic level, and bereavement adjustment, 54

Sodium imbalance, 228–229

Sommer, B. R., 223–242

Spiritual Care Work Group, International Work Group on Death, Dying and Bereavement, 66–67

Spiritual grief counseling, 66–67

Stanford Alzheimer's Center, 169

State of California Alzheimer's Disease Centers, 175

State-Trait Anxiety Inventory (STAI), 86

Stereotypes, xv–xvi, 16–17; about sexuality of the elderly, 131, 132, 136, 138–139; about substance abuse among elderly, 28–29

Steroids, 151

Stigma: of emotional problems, xvi–xvii, 4–5; of physical illness, 22

Streim, J. E., 195–221

Strokes: defined, 230; hypertension-induced, 230–232; impact of, on psychological functioning, 230–232; location of, 230–231; psychological treatment of, 232. *See also* Vascular dementia

Strub, R. L., 164, 167

Structured Clinical Interview for Diagnosis (SCID), 16

Structured/semistructured interviews: for depression, 16; for sexual problems, 142–144. *See also* Personal interviews

Substance abuse: and anxiety, 86, 87; and bereavement adjustment, 64; and depression, 18, 28–29; effects of, on sexual dysfunction, 151–152; laboratory tests for assessing, 86; signs and symptoms of, 28. *See also* Alcohol abuse

Subsyndromal depression, 6, 20

Suicidality, and depression, 38

Suicide prevention, family therapy for, 38

Suicide rates: among men versus women, 9; ratio of attempted to completed, *xvii*
Sundowning, 186
Support groups: for bereavement adjustment, 56, 57–59; for caregivers of demented patients, 187; for depression, 39–40
Surgery: breast, 158–159; for erectile dysfunction, 156; prostate, 147
Surrogacy, 189–191, 218
Symptom Checklist (90-Item)-Revised (SCL-90-R), 86

T
Tacrine (Cognex), 181
Tagamet, 151
Tardive dyskinesia, 185–186
Tegretol (carbamazepine), 186, 229
Television watching, and sleep, 119, 126
Temperature, and sleep, 124
Terazosin, 150
Testosterone deficiency, 146, 156, 158, 159
Testosterone replacement, 156, 158, 159
Therapeutic relationship: in anxiety disorder treatment, 83–84; in depression treatment, 12–13
Thorazine, 150, 229
Thought patterns. *See* Cognitions; Cognitive-behavioral therapy; Cognitive restructuring
Thought-stopping, 97
Thyroid disease, 224–226
Tofranil (imipramine), 32
Trail Making Test, 169
Transference, 37
Transurethral resection of the prostrate, 147
Trazadone, 100, 149
Treatment. *See* Behavior therapy; Cognitive-behavioral therapy; Family therapy; Group interven-

tions; Life review interventions; Medications; Pastoral counseling; PLISSIT model of sex therapy; Psychodynamic psychotherapy; Sleep hygiene treatment; Support groups
Tricyclic antidepressants (TCAs), 32, 149, 229
Tube feeding, 188–189

U
Urinary infection, and dementia, 183–184
Urination, frequent nighttime, 117, 233

V
Vacuum constriction device, 157
Vagina, changes in, 134, 135
Vaginal lubrication: artificial, 133, 134, 156; maintenance of, through sexual activity, 134–135; and medical disorders, 145–146; medical treatment of, 156; and medication, 151; and tobacco use, 151–152
Vascular dementia, 170; diagnosis of, 174–175; with delirium, in nursing home, 214–217; end-stage of, 188–189; medication for, 181; prognosis for, 178. *See also* Strokes
Verapamil (Calan), 233 234
Veterans Affairs Palo Alto Health Care System, Andrology Clinic, 131–132

W
WAIS-R, 169
Wake-up schedule, 120
Wampold, B., 62
West, J., 51
Widow-to-widow programs, 58
Widowhood: effects of, on sexual behavior, 135–136, 139; prevalence of, 46. *See also* Bereavement
WMS-R, 169

Women: sexual dysfunction in, 137;
sexuality of, effects of hormonal
and physical changes on, 133, 146;
sexuality of, effects of widowhood
on, 135–136. *See also* Dyspareunia;
Gender differences; Sexuality;
Vaginal lubrication
Worrying, and sleep, 125

Y

Yesavage, J., 15
Young, J., 36

Z

Zantac, 151, 156
Zeiss, A., 131–162
Zeiss, R. A., 131–162
Zoloft (sertaline), 32, 149